Braja-Vrindavan and Manipur

About the Editors

Shukhdeba Sharma Hanjabam (MSW, PhD) is currently holding the position of Director, College Development Council, Manipur University and served as a Professor at the Department of Social Work at Indira Gandhi National Tribal University, Amarkantak, Madhya Pradesh. He completed his PhD from the School of Social Work, Tata Institute of Social Sciences, Mumbai, and his post-doctoral from the University of Florida, Florida, USA (2014-15) as a Fogarty International Centre Fellow. He can be contacted at <hanjabam@gmail.com>.

Kakchingtabam Ruhinikumar Sharma (MA, PhD) is Head and Assistant Professor, Department of History, Ideal Girls College (Government of Manipur), Akampat, Imphal East–795001, Manipur, India. He is the Life Member of North-East India History Association, Shillong and Manipur Historical Society, Imphal. He can be contacted at <kruhinikumar@gmail.com>.

Braja-Vrindavan and Manipur
A Journey for Cultural Oneness

Edited by
Shukhdeba Sharma Hanjabam
Kakchingtabam Ruhinikumar Sharma

Intellectual Forum for North East—Manipur
College Development Council, Manipur University

CONCEPT PUBLISHING COMPANY PVT. LTD.
NEW DELHI - 110 059

ISBN: 978-93-6344-015-9

First Published 2026

Published and Printed by

Concept
Since 1974

Concept Publishing Company Pvt. Ltd.
A/15-16, Commercial Block, Mohan Garden
New Delhi-110059 (India)
T: +91-11-41101460
E: publishing@conceptpub.com, *W*: www.conceptpub.com

Cataloging in Publication--Courtesy: D.K. Agencies (P) Ltd. <docinfo@dkagencies.com>

Braja-Vrindavan and Manipur : a journey for cultural oneness / edited by Shukhdeba Sharma Hanjabam, Kakchingtabam Ruhinikumar Sharma.

pages cm

"Intellectual Forum for North-East - Manipur, College Development Council, Manipur University."

Includes bibliographical references and index.

ISBN 9789363440159

1. Meithei (South Asian people)--India--Vrindāvan--Religion. 2. Meithei (South Asian people)--India--Rādha Kund--Religion. 3. Radha (Hindu deity)--Cult--India--Vrindāvan. 4. Radha (Hindu deity)--Cult--India--Rādha Kund. 5. Chaitanya (Sect)--India--Vrindāvan. 6. Chaitanya (Sect)--India--Rādha Kund. 7. Hindu pilgrims and pilgrimages-India--Vrindāvan. 8. Hindu pilgrims and pilgrimages--India--Rādha Kund. 9. Manipur (India)--Relations--India--Mathura (District) 10. Mathura (India : District)--Relations--India--Manipur. I. Hanjabam, Shukhdeba Sharma, 1983- editor. II. Sharma, Kakchingtabam Ruhinikumar, editor. III. Sharma, Kakchingtabam Ruhinikumar, editor. IV. Intellectual Forum of North East (Manipur, India)

LCC BL1239.36.V75B73 2026 | DDC 294.53609542 23

Dedicated in Honouring
The Legacy of Our Forefathers
Who Created a Lasting Influence
For a Indic Culture in Manipur

Preface

This book is an attempt at documenting the historical, cultural, and religious linkage between Manipur, once an Asiatic sovereign kingdom and Indic civilization which have a lasting imprint on shaping the world view of the former. Various schools of Hinduism have permeated in the kingdom of Manipur which was emerging as a regional power to reckon with in the first half of the eighteenth century. Rāmānadī, Nīmandī, Kṛṣṇa cult and Gauḍīya Vàiṣṇavism have found a place in Manipur and its assimilation with the belief system and practices of the natives led to the development of a synthesized Hinduism in Manipur. This was made possible as successive rulers of the land, viz., Garibniwaz, Rājarṣi Bhāyachandra (Jai Singh/Chingthangkhomba), Gambhīr Singh, Nar Singh and Chandrakīrti, etc., played pivotal roles in patronizing the religion by introducing a number of religio-cultural rituals and festivals like Rath-Yātrā, Janmāṣṭamī, Jhulon and Yaoshang to mention a few.

Along with these religio-cultural rituals and festivals, the narrative art form of Wari-Leeba which had been conducted in the local *maṇḍapa*s since the later part of the eighteenth finds a place in the heart and minds of the Manipuri Hindus. Tales from epics of *Mahābhārata* and *Rāmāyaṇa* were circulated at regular interval in the native *maṇḍapa*s have gone a long way in popularizing the ideology and philosophy of the new faith.

Thus, it is no wonder that places like Nabadwīp, Vrindavana and Purī where presiding deities of Hinduism reigned became sacred places for the Hinduized Manipuris since the beginning of the nineteenth century. Hence, visiting these places once in their lifetime have become a wish for the Manipuri Hindus as there was a strong belief that a dip in the River Ganges will wash off the sins one committed in this mortal life. And these beliefs had goaded many a Manipuri Hindus to undertake arduous journey to those sacred places of Hinduism. Not contented with visiting those sacred sites, many Manipuri Hindus including the rulers established temples at Nabadwīp and Vrindavana dedicated to a number of deities. In this way, many sacred sites of Hinduism have developed not only as centres of Hinduism but also formed inalienable heritage sites of the Manipuri Hindus. It is a desideratum that prodded the editors to make an attempt at documenting the accounts of the pilgrimage that the Manipuri Hindus undertook since the last two and quarter centuries.

This book is in gestation for a long time owing to various reasons. However, with the active cooperation of the devotees and scholars we are able to make a humble beginning with the publication of this small volume. Constructive criticism and comments are solicited from the learned readers to make this venture more meaningful. If this publication helps to throw light on some of the objectives we set, it will have been well worth the trouble of compiling it.

Shukhdeba Sharma Hanjabam
Kakchingtabam Ruhinikumar Sharma

Acknowledgements

We begin by thanking all the chapter contributors and translators, who have kept their faith in us and helped us complete the book on time.

We are grateful to Shri Rajkumar Dusarigopal Singh for helping us to get permission from the family members particularly Dr. Rajkumar Imotomba Singh son of renowned scholar Shri Rajkumar Jhalajit Singh to reproduce the chapter, "Chingthnagkhomba Maharajah Ganga Chatpa (Mahārājā Chingthang Khomba's Going to the Gaṅgā)" by Rajkumar Jhalajit Singh, which is reproduced from the book, *A History of Manipuri Literature*, Volume I (1976 and 1987), Volume II (1998). Publisher: Rajkumar Jhalajit Singh, Imphal.

We thank the family members of the renowned poet, Shri Ashangbam Minaketan Singh, for the permission to reproduce the chapter "Vrinam Chatpa" (Pilgrimage to Brinam) from the book *Punsi Saktam* (Larol Anee, 1983) by Ashangbam Minaketan Singh, Publisher: Ashangbam Minaketan Singh, Uripok, Imphal.

We thank the family members of the late senior journalist Shri Akoijam Sanaton for their permission to reproduce the chapter "Vrindavan Gee Lamdamda" (The Land of Vrindavana), which is taken from the book, *Laifam Yaona Bharat Ki Lamdamsingda Khongdaruba Lamkoi Wari* (2012), by Akoijam Sanaton, Publisher: Akoijam Ongbi Roma Devi, Imphal (2012).

We thank the renowned writer, Dr Ch Jamini Devi, for her permission to reproduce the chapter "Radhakunda: Govardhan Parikrama" from the book *Gangagi Matambakta: A Memoir* (2005) by Dr Ch Jamini Devi, Publisher: Raipraveena Brothers, Imphal.

We appreciate the encouragement of Shri S. Premananda Sharma, OSD, Delhi, Government of Manipur, and colleagues of the Intellectual Forum of North East for their constant encouragement in compiling the book.

Shukhdeba Sharma Hanjabam
Kakchingtabam Ruhinikumar Sharma

Contents

SECTION II
Literature (Manuscript)

SECTION III
Pilgrimage (Yātrā)

Contributors Profile

A.K. Sanaton (1948-2019) during his lifetime, has been a very vocal journalist and has served as the editor of *Ehou Daily* and president of All Manipur Working Journalist. He was instrumental in pushing through the journalist pension scheme, which every working journalist is entitled to today. Apart from being a respected journalist, he was politically and socially active, serving as the General Secretary of the Manipur Peoples Party and president of the SEYO Club. He had been a constant advisor to many journalists. He was 71 years old when he passed away and is survived by his wife, two sons and one daughter.

Ashangbam Minaketan Singh (1906-1995) is a name to reckon with among the pioneer poets of Manipuri literature. He belonged to the generation that had grown up and saw the difficult times of Manipur in terms of socio-economic conditions under the monarchic system of the government shaped by the colonial rule of the British Empire. But at the same time, the early part of the twentieth century was a glorious year, a transcendental period that we call the Renaissance period of Manipuri literature. Minaketan was born at Wangkhei in the Ashangbam family but was brought up in the family of Royal descendants of Mahārāja Nara Singh by Sanajaobi Devi, the granddaughter of Mahārāja Nara Singh at Moirangkhom Sougaijam Leirak. He graduated from University of Calcutta in 1930, and by that time, he had mastered English, Bengali, Hindi, Sanskrit, and the old Manipuri languages with utmost fluency. Minaketan left his footprints on every field of literature and touched every aspect of literary products: poetry, prose, essays, translations, mythology, biography, autobiography, and criticism. His published works numbered more than twenty-five books on these different branches of literature. He was honoured and decorated with many titles and awards during his lifetime. He was awarded Sahitya Ratna (1971), Sahitya Akademi Award (1976), Kavi Samrat (1980), the most eminent citizen of Manipur (1985), Padmashri (1985), Swarna Jayanti Sanman Award (1986), Jamini Sundar Guha Gold Medal (1988), Thoibi Award (1988), Lalit Memorial Gold Medal (1990) and many, many more prestigious awards. He had associated himself with many state advisory committees. The list is endless, and it is beyond the purview of this column to write everything. In short, Minaketan himself was an institution, a school of a variety of thoughts. Minaketan had lived a fruitful long 89 years encompassing the whole of the twentieth century. He was rightly the representative of Manipuri literature for the whole twentieth century.

Chongtham Jamini Devi (Dr) was born on 1 March 1936 as the second child of thirteen children of Chongtham Benudhor Singh, who taught at Bengali High School, and R.K. Sanatombi, a housewife at Keishamthong Top Leirak. In 1956, she took her matric exams at Gauhati University from Tamphasana Girls High School. She passed in the 1st Division—a feat which was highly commendable given the fact that not many people could manage 1st Class marks at that time. After passing her Intermediate from Gauhati University in 1957, she went on to obtain her certificate in Physical Education from Patna University in 1958. In the same year, she joined as a teacher of Physical Education and Sports DM College, Imphal—a post which she served till 1964. In 1962, she married Dr P. Raikumar Singh, who was a well-known educationist in the state. However, a job and marriage was no deterrent for a knowledge seeker like Jamini. In 1961-63, she obtained her BA and BT degrees from Gauhati University and a Master's in Education from Allahabad University in 1964. She also has a diploma in Journalism from the British Institute, Bombay, in 1980. She completed her PhD in 1980 from Gauhati University specializing in Physical Education and Guidance Services on the topic "Physical Education and its influence in the adjustment of adolescent girls in the Secondary School of Manipur". In 1965, she joined as a lecturer in Education at GP College, where she taught for over three decades before leaving in 1996 as a Reader. She served as the Principal of DM College of Commerce in 1997-98 before retiring from active service. She also served as the Chairperson of the Manipur State Women Commission. Dr Jamini is associated with many academic, sociocultural, and religious organizations. A prolific writer, Dr Jamini is a regular columnist for the local daily *Poknapham* and has written around thirty books on varied topics. These include the children's textbooks on *Physical Education* (for Class I, III, IV, V, VIII, IX, and X), *Anganggi Vigyan: Bhugol Anouba* (1968), *Anganggi Leikol* (1983) and the award-winning children's book *Khangningbashingdo*. A regular broadcaster, scriptwriter, and commentator for the AIR and DDK Imphal, Dr Jamini has participated in seminars all over the country and abroad. She is the founder and Director of the Dr Jamini Devi Ashram (Centre for Women and Children's Development) at Changangei Uchekon on Airport Road, Imphal.

Kakchingtabam Ruhinikumar Sharma (Dr) is an Assistant Professor and Head of the Department of History at Ideal Girls' College (Government of Manipur), Akampat, Imphal-East, Manipur.
Email: kruhinikumar@gmail.com

Laimayum Bishwanath Sharma (Professor) is a Professor and Head of the Department of Philosophy at Manipur University. He is also a member of the Council of Indian Council of Philosophical Research (2024-27), New Delhi.
Email: laibishwanath@yahoo.com

Manindra Konsam is a senior journalist and editor of *Sanathong* (a popular weekly magazine) based in Imphal, Manipur.
Email: manindraningthouja@gmail.com

Mayanglambam Sadananda (Dr) is an Assistant Professor at the Department of Manipuri, Dhanamanjuri University, Imphal.
Email: sadafolk@gmail.com

Pandit Kakchingtabam Brajamani Sharma is a renowned Sanskrit scholar. He is a renowned Vedic scholar of Manipur, known for wisdom in *Bhagavadgītā* and Vedas. He was a Librarian in a Degree College at Kakching Khunou. He has contributed many scholarly works on Hindu philosophy, particularly in rituals and practices.

Pebam Nganthoiba Mangang (Dr) is a Social Development Specialist with the Department of MAHUD, Government of Manipur. He earned his Doctoral degree from the School of Social Work, Tata Institute of Social Sciences, Mumbai.
Email: pebamng@gmail.com

Potsangbam Milan Khangamcha (Dr), Department of Philosophy, Manipur University. He was a member of the Council of Indian Council of Philosophical Research, New Delhi.
Email: pmilanmuni@yahoo.com

Rajkumar Jhalajit Singh (1924-2021) was a historian, teacher, poet, litterateur, and, above all, a social and political activist, a firm believer in the Gandhian philosophy of simple living and high thinking. Respected in academic circles for his frank opinion and observations, yet derided by critics for his political views for sailing against the currents of his time. Born on 14 September 1924 at Yaiskul Hiruhanba Leikai,

Imphal, to late Maipak Sana and Ningthemchaongbi Rajani Devi, Oja Jhalajit has been honoured with many coveted awards including the Padmashri in 1999. Started his early education at Yaiskul Nupimacha School, Pettigrew L.P. School, Moirangkhom Upper Primary School, Johnstone High School till 10th standard. He studied at Gauhati Cotton College for graduation and completed his Master's in Economics and LLB from University of Calcutta. He was deeply engrossed with the idea of Manipur. This very idea prompted him to explore and discover Manipur as reflected in *A Short History of Manipur* (1965), *Manipur* (1975), *A History of Manipuri Literature,* Vol. I (1976 and 1987), Vol. II (1998), *Bharatki Swaraj* (a translation of Gandhi's *Hind Swaraj*, 1995) and in addition innumerable essays including a serialized autobiography and a book of poems *Kavita Nikunja* (1997). He also laid his hand in journalism as editor of *Anouba Matam*, a Manipuri daily newspaper for some time.

Sanasam Amal Singh (Dr) is an Assistant Professor at the Department of Sociology, Mayai Lambi College, Government of Manipur.
Email: amalsanasam17@gmail.com

Sonia Wahengbam (Dr) is an Assistant Professor at the Department of Mass Communication at Manipur University.
Email: soniawahm@gmail.com

Shukhdeba Sharma Hanjabam (Professor) is a Professor and Head of the Department of Social Work at Indira Gandhi National Tribal University, Amarkantak, Madhya Pradesh, India. He completed his PhD from the School of Social Work, Tata Institute of Social Sciences, Mumbai, and his post-doctoral from the University of Florida, Florida, USA.
Email: hanjabam@gmail.com

Sukadeva Das, a resident of Bishnupur district, Manipur, is a pious devotee of ISKCON. He presently offers service at the ISKCON, Radha-Kunda, Mathura district, Uttar Pradesh.

Tīrtha Yātrā (Pilgrimage)

An Overview

Kakchingtabam Ruhinikumar Sharma,
Shukhdeba Sharma Hanjabam, and *Kadam Ibotombi Singh*

I

The roots of pilgrimage as an institution can be linked to the initial stages of human cultural practices, and its practice is a time-honoured aspect of human history. It began to take shape as an established custom with the emergence of major religions such as Christianity, Hinduism, Buddhism, Islam, and Judaism. The word pilgrimage originates from the Latin term, *peregrinatio*, which means "wandering around" or "being an outsider", leaving one's homeland and wandering for the love of God. Multiple elements contribute to the concept of pilgrimage, as well as motivations that elevate an experience to the threshold of pilgrimage.

Simply put, pilgrimage denotes a journey undertaken by a pilgrim toward a hallowed site with the hope and anticipation of having a significant encounter with the divine. Turner and Turner, the leading scholars in the study of pilgrimage, described it as a "liminoid" or "quasi-liminal" experience. They argue that pilgrimage occurs within a liminal state, implying a situation where usual social hierarchies are temporarily set aside, permitting pilgrims to shed the concerns and structures of their daily lives and distance themselves from "occasions of sin", while embarking on a quest for the divine, salvation, and a renewal of faith. Along the way, they form connections with other pilgrims, resulting in a *communitas* whichrefers to a heightened sense of social togetherness, equality, and solidarity that often arises during liminal periods, particularly in rituals or ceremonies characterized by the dissolution of regular social inequalities. Nevertheless, since pilgrimage is an act of choice rather than an obligatory rite marking a transition in an individual's normal life, the Turners categorize pilgrimage as a liminoid phenomenon.[1]

A key characteristic of pilgrimage is mobility. A pilgrim moves from one place to another as part of the pilgrimage experience. Does this suggest that all trips to sacred sites, regardless of their short duration, can be considered as pilgrimages? Can regular visits to a church, temple, or mosque each week be categorized as a pilgrimage?

In this context, Turner and Turner have suggested that pilgrimage involves the movement of an individual away from their immediate environment. They argued that a pilgrimage signifies a journey directed towards a sacred site or holy place that lies a distance away from the pilgrim's residence and daily routine.[2] Thus, rather than asserting that a pilgrimage must surpass a certain distance, it can be defined as a movement that is "greater than local". Consequently, a pilgrimage is described as "an event consisting of longer than local journeys by numerous persons to a sacred place as an act of religious devotion."[3] A pilgrimage embodies a journey toward a designated destination that the pilgrim embarks upon for various reasons, seeking a divine encounter or spiritual awakening. Thus,

> "Pilgrimages operate in a tension between the movement of unsure feet and the promise of arrival, at a place where certainty abounds. People journey from far and wide to stand in defined

> and delineated places that offer the promise of a meaningful encounter."[4]

A pilgrimage requires the tangible movement of the pilgrim to a specific destination. Therefore, a pilgrimage cannot take place without a pilgrim who undertakes the journey and a destination, which is a sacred site.

As travel becomes more attainable, pilgrimage sites attract people from diverse faiths and various parts of the world. For example, a traveller may opt to visit a sacred location while abroad. During their stay, this individual might engage in local rituals or experience a moment of spiritual awakening. Given that they have travelled to a holy site, can they be classified as pilgrims? Alternatively, a pilgrim might also visit palaces or historical landmarks en route to a sacred destination. So, who can genuinely be regarded as a pilgrim? Diana Eck of the Harvard Divinity School differentiates a tourist from a pilgrim by describing a tourist as someone who comes mainly to "see the sights", while a pilgrim aims for a *darśana* (the act of seeing or witnessing) of a sacred site or image. Furthermore, she argues that pilgrims on their journeys are not simply casual tourists, but rather "sacred sightseers" who concentrate not just on the aesthetic appeal of a location, but on the spiritual importance of the site where salvationcan be attained.[5] A pilgrimage begins when a pilgrim commits to embark on a journey as an act of devotion to God, with a clear intent. Thus, it is the purpose of the traveller at the start of their journey that delineates both a pilgrim and a pilgrimage. A pilgrim is someone who departs from the confines of everyday life and the usual practice of their faith to embark on a journey to engage with the elements and symbols of their beliefs in their most sacred forms. Once a pilgrim undertakes a pilgrimage, it is widely believed that they have achieved a spiritual progression.[6]

The primary aim of pilgrimage is to access God and seek divine assistance. Within this broad objective, there are several reasons and goals for going on a pilgrimage. Generally, pilgrims undertake pilgrimages:

(1) To request a blessing, such as the birth of a child, protection from sickness, or financial welfare.
(2) To express gratitude for blessings received, like a safe birth or general well-being.
(3) To honour a promise made in thankfulness for previous favours sought.
(4) To pursue forgiveness, endure hardship as an act of worship, or make a sacrifice for atonement.
(5) To fulfil an obligation, such as a religious duty to participate in pilgrimage-related practices, like the Hajj.
(6) To gain merit and achieve salvation.[7]

Sacred geography: Imagined Landscape

A pilgrimage requires a destination, and for a journey to qualify as a pilgrimage, its destination must be regarded as sacred. What defines a location as sacred? Various factors contribute to a place or site being deemed sacred in a particular religion. Locations referred in the stories and sacred texts of a faith are viewed as sacred. Some of the most ancient pilgrimage centres worldwide are those mentioned in a religion's sacred narratives as the sites of the birth, death, and mission of its central spiritual figure. Such locations gain sacred status as they create a connection to the spiritual authority of the religion, and pilgrims visiting these sites seek to emulate or unite with the founder spiritually. These places also act as powerful reminders of the founder's teachings and messages and are commonly believed to enhance one's spiritual awareness. Additionally, sites linked to the disciples, saints, and martyrs of the faith may also attain sacred status.[8]

Such places become sacred due to their association with the founder preceptor of the faith after their passing. For example, Hindu pilgrimages to Mathurā and Vrindavana have become sacred because of their links to significant events in Śrī Kṛṣṇa's life. Likewise, Navadwip in Bengal has become a sacred place for the Manipuris since the latter half of the eighteenth century, as an idol of Lord Govindajī known as Anuprabhu was installed and worshipped by the then king of Manipur Bhāgyacandra, popularly known as Jai Singh. Consequently, not just the locations themselves, but also the relics associated with the central spiritual figure, are revered as sacred. Moreover, not only the sites but also the relics of the central spiritual figure and objects tied to crucial events in the religious history of a particular faith can attain sacredness.

Locations linked to a holy individual or events from their life may evolve into important pilgrimage destinations. Sites related to the remains of a holy person or their relics can become revered, even if they were not considered sacred during their lifetime. Such sacred locales are created by associating the charismatic influence of a holy individual or event with a specific space.[9]

Certain locations where the founder had visions, or where sightings of the founder, disciples, and saints occurred, or places believed to have been the embodiment of divine power, may also become pilgrimage shrines. Pilgrimage sites are thought to be locations where "miracles once happened, still happen, and may happen again."[10]

Sacred sites can be interconnected, forming sacred geographies. For example, the *cāra dhāma* (four dwelling) pilgrimage guides a Hindu pilgrim in a circumambulation of India, including Badrināth in the north, Purī in the east, Rameshvaram in the far south, and Dvārakā in the far west. For Manipuri Hindus, Navadwip (Bengal), Jagannāth Kṣetra (Odisha), Rādhā- Kuṇḍa (Uttar Pradesh), and Shree Shree Govindajee of Manipur have emerged as holy sites for pilgrimage.

When a pilgrim embarks on a pilgrimage, they typically return with an item (such as holy oil, images, water, or soil) that serves as a memento of the journey, symbolizing their identity as a pilgrim and providing a physical link to their sacred experience, thus infusing their everyday life with a sense of the sacred. These keepsakes may also be integrated into local rituals at home, serving to connect a network of sacred locations; for example, the waters from the Ganges are spread across other pilgrimage sites throughout India.

The practice of pilgrimage differs across various religions. It has unique historical developments and shapes the identities of practitioners in distinctive ways. Since the book deals with Manipuri Hindus, it will reflect on selected places of pilgrimage associated with Hinduism. In Hinduism, a pilgrimage is known as a *yātrā*, and individuals embark on *yātrā*s to visit *tīrtha*s (crossings or fords). "A *tīrtha* acts as a site for spiritual crossing, where the presence of deities is felt intimately and worship brings numerous benefits."[11] Ancient Hindu scriptures, such as the Vedas, Upaniṣads, and *Mahābhārata*, made references to the *tīrtha*s. The Vedas regarded the fire altar as a site for spiritual crossing, while the Purāṇas characterized *tīrtha*s as spiritual fords that pilgrims strive to reach. In the first millennium CE, *tīrtha yātrās*—pilgrim journeys became increasingly important in religious practices and literary works. It is believed that *tīrtha yātrā*s can absolve individuals of their sins and sorrows, acting as a means of spiritual purification.

A Hindu may undertake a *yātrā* to a certain *tīrtha* for various motivations or needs. For example, one might travel to Tirupati in Andhra Pradesh for family welfare or go to Kāśī, Gayā, or Prayāga for ceremonies related to the deceased. Kāśī, known as the city of lights, is viewed as a place for spiritual liberation, and death in Kāśī is thought to lead to liberation.

Benares, or Varanasi, is recognized as one of the most revered sites for Hindu pilgrims. However, Hindu pilgrimage destinations in India are not limited to one location, with Benares being part of a vast network of pilgrimage sites throughout the country, creating a sacred landscape interconnected through local, regional, and trans-regional pilgrimage practices.

Bhardwaj[12] suggested that Hindu pilgrimage locations might be understood as "a system of nodes at varying levels":

1. Pan-Hindu—Badrināth
2. Supraregional—Hardwar, Ujjain
3. Regional—Kaṅgṛā, Jwālājī, Cintpūrṇī
4. (a) Subregional (high)—Nainā Devī
   (b) Subregional (low)—Mansā Devī, Rewalsar
5. Local—Baijnāth, Bhagsunag, Śiva Bāṛī

According to his findings, high-level sacred sites are visited for general purification, while lower-level shrines, such as regional and sub-regional ones, serve specific purposes for pilgrims. At the pan level, the linguistic and regional variance among pilgrims is at its peak, gradually diminishing at the lower levels. The high-level sites highlight aspects of Hinduism upheld by diverse cultural regions of India, while the lower nodes showcase the diversity within Hinduism and local integration foundations.[13] The choices made by pilgrims regarding their destinations and the character of their pilgrimages are sometimes influenced by political conditions. Pilgrimage sites often become areas of contention, but they can also be used to validate the authority of rulers through appeals for divine intervention. Many noteworthy places hold sacred importance for various denominations or faiths, resulting in competition and conflict, as well as cooperation. As pilgrims travel between countries, crossing various cultural and geographic barriers across different eras, they are both impacted by and help shape political, cultural, and trade dynamics. Pilgrimages are not only shaped by local and regional histories but are also influenced by national and global events. At times, they have been linked to popular nationalism, peasant uprisings, and anti-colonial movements, among others.[14]

Turner and Turner further proposed that during pilgrimages, individuals establish a *communitas* with fellow pilgrims, a perception that is based on equality and mutual support, contrasting with conventional societal hierarchies.

They viewed pilgrimage as a transformative experience that enables participants to diminish social stratification and inequality, while also allowing them to escape the routine challenges and significances of their lives. This phenomenon is identified as anti-structure. They concluded that this perspective sheds light on the resurgence of pilgrimage.[15] Scholars have noted that pilgrimage can unite individuals from various ethnic and cultural backgrounds, promoting a sense of belonging and unity as they come together to worship. It is believed that pilgrimage strengthens a pilgrim's identity within their faith, enhancing their connection to their religious community and deepening their beliefs. For Hindus, the vast network of interlinked pilgrimage sites enhances a sense of Indian "nationhood", creating a shared living landscape that reflects its intricacies and diversities.[16] Academics have differing opinions on whether pilgrimages help in forming communities. Bhardwaj contends that visits to sacred sites may offer some social advantages to certain castes, like the Scheduled Castes, since higher castes, such as brāhmaṇas, cannot avoid interaction with lower castes amidst the crowds of pilgrims. Moreover, *prasādam* (food given to the deity and later shared among pilgrims) is something that everyone must accept, even if it has been touched by the Scheduled Castes. Therefore, he argues that pilgrimage provides the Scheduled Castes a semblance of equality, at least within the sacred areas of a temple.[17] Nevertheless, Coleman and Elsner assert that pilgrimage practices often uphold many of the discriminatory customs concerning caste at various Hindu shrines, where the fear of "polluting" contact with lower castes prevents individuals identified as "untouchables" from accessing certain shrines. When "untouchables" were granted entry into the Golden Temple of Viśvanāth at Benares in 1954, a second Viśvanāth temple was constructed in protest against their admission.[18]

Pilgrimage writers have recorded their journeys, conveying their insights, feelings, and experiences, which later inspired various legends, myths, literature, and folklore. Numerous key pilgrimage locations have generated devotional literature that provides insights into cultural variances and transformations in practices, trends, and beliefs. Often, the movement of pilgrims across different regions, both internationally and domestically, enabled the sharing of knowledge and cultural interactions.

A notable work of the early nineteenth-century Manipur is *Chingthangkhomba Maharaj Ganga Chatpa* (Marāhāja Chingthangkhomba's Sojourn to Gaṅgā), a combined effort of three writers—Nabachandra Wangkhei, Hari Charan Thaunapaton, and Wahengbam Madhavram, during the reign of King Labanayachandra (1798-1800 CE). The three scholars took up the episodes relating to King Bhāgyacandra's abdication of the throne of Manipur, his journey on pilgrimage to Navadwip, and his death at Murshidabad during the course of the journey. (Sanahal, 1964). The three writers compiled the work with the help of their students, viz. Haricharan Khangenba, Biramani Louremba, Khagendra Yimnaba, and Khongchon Aheibafall within this genre. In this work, the writers clearly described the exploits of King Chingthangkhomba (Bhāgyacandra or Jai Singh), his virtues, intelligence, generosity and devotion to Lord Kṛṣṇa, etc. According to Cheitharol Kumbaba, the royal chronicle of Manipur, the journey of King Chingthangkhomba on pilgrimage to Navadwip took place on Monday, 20th of Phairen, 1798.[19] The diction was archaic, but the writers used a mixture of Indo-Aryan words. In this book, the writers clearly mentioned the politico-administrative systems and religious practices then prevalent in Manipur.

Given the intrinsic nature of pilgrims traversing various local and international boundaries, pilgrimage encourages and nurtures market and economic growth along its routes and at pilgrimage destinations. As transportation technology progressed and pilgrimage became more organized and predictable, pilgrims began to arrive in structured groups on specific days or according to a carefully coordinated schedule. Furthermore, a market emerged for religious items such as rosaries, devotional statues and images, inspirational literature, and sacred artefacts for pilgrims to purchase and take home (Turner and Turner, 1978: 25). Pilgrimage has consistently featured a substantial economic element and offers entrepreneurs chances to generate profits. Pilgrimage sites foster a socio-economic atmosphere and significantly contribute to urban development, road construction, and market expansion, among other aspects.[20]

Thus, pilgrimage remains a significant activity and a meaningful expression for the faithful. As an essential aspect of religious practice, pilgrimage offers a fascinating view of faith where individual and group identities are shaped and sometimes challenged. Over time, pilgrimage as an institution and practice has evolved, influenced by and influencing changes in the secular world.

II

This book consists of twelve chapters broadly divided into three sections, viz., (i) dhārmic connection, (ii) literary accounts, and (iii) pilgrimage to Braja-Vrindavana and other holy places and shrines connected with Hinduism.

In the first chapter of the book titled "Manipuri Mandirs at Rādhā-Kuṇḍa" by Shukhdeba Sharma Hanjabam, the author endeavours to portray an account of the *mandira*s established at Rādhā-Kuṇḍa and Vrindavana by Manipuri royal families and devotees. Mention may be made of the Śrī Śrī Rāsabihārījī Mandira, the first *mandira* of Manipur, constructed at Rādhā-Kuṇḍa by Jubaraj Chourajit (Later Mahārājā of Manipur) in 1799 in memory of Rājarṣi Bhāgyacandra. Mahārājā Labanyachandra (1798-1800) financially supported the development of the temple. The temple complex is known as Purāṇa-kuñja.

The successive Mahārājās of Manipur deputed officials to oversee the construction of *mandira*s and *akhāḍā*s (*akhāṛā*) at

Rādhā-Kuṇḍa. Mahārājā Gambhīr Singh deputed his officials to construct the Śrī Gokulananda Mandira.

Another temple dedicated to Shri Thakur Radha Govind Devjee Maharaj was also constructed under his aegis. The footsteps of Gambhīr Singh were followed by his brother Nara Singh, the noble prince, by constructing Shri Naol Gobinda *mandira*, known as Jubarāj-Kuñja or Naol-Kuñja. By the closing decades of the twentieth century, there were around 30 *mandira*s at Rādhā-Kuṇḍa and four *mandira*s in Vrindavana built by the Mahārājās and Vaiṣṇavas of Manipur. The Rajarshi Bhagyachandra Cultural Foundation Manipur, has played a leading role in conducting the pilgrimage to Rādhā-Kuṇḍa for the last 40 years. But there is an urgency on the part of the state as well as philanthropists for the upkeep and maintenance of these *mandira*s which are an inseparable part of the Vaiṣṇavite heritage and tradition of Manipur.

The second chapter titled "Manipuri Vaishnava and Sri Radha Kunda" by Kakchingtabam Brajamani Sharma, asserts that the Manipuri Vaiṣṇavas follow the Rāgānuga Bhakti system of Lord Caitanya Mahāprabhu, who introduced the philosophy called "Acintya Vedaveda Vāda", in which the *jīva* (individual soul) is different and also not different from *brahmān* (the universal soul), which cannot be perceived by human intellect. In this paper the author has explained the importance attached to three places which are considered sacred to the Manipuri Vaiṣṇavas namely, Navadwip in West Bengal, Purī in Odissa, and Vrindavana, as centres of pilgrimage and other places become secondary choices for them.

The third chapter titled "On the Way to Braja-Vrindavana: A Reflection on Khangembam Gulapi's Manaḥ Śikṣā" by Kakchingtabam Ruhinikumar Sharma attempts to highlight how the Manipuris worshipped God through dance and music in their traditional religion and situate the role played by Guru Khanembam Gulapi Singh in the through his beautiful lyrics of *Manaḥ Śikṣā* enthralled the listeners and in propagating the idea of salvation through Bhakti.

In "The Rādhā-Kuṇḍa of the 'Bhūloka-Braja-Vrindavana': The Tīrthasthāna of Manipuri Gauḍīya Vaiṣṇavas" which forms the fourth chapter of the book by P. Milan Khangamcha and L. Bishwanath Sharma strongly argue that Hinduism in Manipur is a synthesis of local and incoming elements of an indigenously revisualised GauḍīyaVaiṣṇava religious philosophy of Bengal which was not imposed from outside, but it was so ingeniously adapted by the eighteenth-century monarch of Manipur—Rājarṣi Bhāgyacandra (Meidingu Chingthangkhomba 1763-1798 CE) which had become a highly ethnicized, self-sufficient version of the Devotional Religion (that is, the traditional path of *bhakti* is its own end and not *mokṣa*) of the then kingdom of Manipur. Nevertheless, it is based on the totally aestheticized Bengal Vaiṣṇavism. Yet, the Meitei Hindus earnest longing for the national consciousness to give a respectable highlight to this religio-historical fact and to include it in the re-imagined idea of Bhārata has met with little success. The unwillingness of the mainstream scholars to recognize the fact that Manipur is the last and easternmost cultural and religious frontier of the pan-Indian devotional religion of Monotheistic Vedānta is what has been missing in the pan-Indian collective spiritual and cultural consciousness. This has serious political implications in the matters of National Integration and the very idea of Bhāratavarṣa, which, as a matter of principle, is supposed to be inclusive. If this historic phase of the then Manipur which is still a living spiritual and socio-cultural tradition is reflected in the finale blue print of the problematic task of accomplishing the still pending task of the national integration would go a long way in making it as the source of internal strength of the country the authors convincingly argued in this thought-provoking write-up.

"Glories of Rādhā-Kuṇḍa and the Permanent Residents of Manipuri Vaiṣṇavas" by Sukadeva Das explain the meaning and purpose of *deva-darśana* which can be understood as *deva* means "God", and *darśanaḥ* means "seeing" or "an audience with a great personality" that reveals something of the richness of the *Śrīmad-Bhāgavatam*'s language. The author apart from drawing a panoramic sketch of the temples established by the Manipuris in and around Rādhā-Kuṇḍa and Vrindavana also provided an account of the little Manipuri Vaiṣṇavas who almost led an ascetic live for attainment salvation at the lotus feet of Rādhā and Kṛṣṇa.

"Chingthang Khomba Maharajah Ganga Chatpa" rendered into English as a summarized account by renowned historian Rajkumar Jhalajit Singh is a travelogue describing Mahārājā Jai (popularly known as Rājarṣi Bhāgyacandra) Singh's pilgrimage to Vrindavana. On 5 February 1798, i.e., 20 Phairen 1719, Śakābda. The book which was prepared at the initiative of Mahārājā Labanyachandra (1798 to 1801 CE) is the joint work of three writers, Navachand, Haricharan, and Madhav Ram Wahengba, and is considered the first full-length travelogue in Manipuri literature. In his journey, Mahārājā Jai Singh was accompanied by his queens, five sons, three daughters, and a large number of pilgrims. The pilgrims, including the king, queens, princes, princesses, and nobles, numbered about 200, and their porters about 300. The king took with him arms, ammunition, and the royal insignia in this journey.

The seventh chapter of the book titled "Mahārājā Gambhīr Singh and Śrī Vrindavana" by Manindra Konsam attempts to portray an account of one of the most heroic rulers of Manipur, Gambhīr Singh (1825-34 CE) and his spiritual attachment with Śrī Vrindavana where he desires to spend his last days in the service of Śrī Rādhā-Kuṇḍa; as such, the king confided his yearning to his confidant brother-in-law Langmaithem Kirti Nongthonba and deputed him with a big amount of money for acquiring a convenient place inside Vrindavana to construct a temple and also a separate building for dwelling. The task of acquiring land and constructing a temple and dwelling house was completed, for which material evidence still exists in the form of a temple complex at Rādhā-Kuṇḍa near Vrindavana as a living testimony of the great king's service to the cause of Vaiṣṇavism.

"Pilgrimage to Brinam (Brinam Chatpa)" by the scholar poet Ashangbam Minaketan Singh and translated from Manipuri to English by Mayanglambam Sadananda is taken from the memoir-cum-autobiographical account of the writer. In this piece, the writer portrays his lived experiences of the journey he undertook with his maternal grandfather in the beginning of the early twentieth century to have *darśana* and pay obeisance to Vrindavana, where the pantheon of Hindu deities resides. This account is filled with a lot of adventure and thrills as recollected vividly by the writer. This is one of the finest pieces of writing from the pen of the scholar-poet.

In the paper titled "Tongjei-Maril Road: The Ancient Route of Manipur for Indic Pilgrimage" by Sanasam Amal Singh, himself a sociologist by profession makes a humble attempt at reconstructing the historical importance of Tongjei-Maril Road which served as the western frontier gateway of Manipur and vice versa with the Indic world for Manipur's political and economic intercourse with her neighbours especially with the Cacharis, Ahoms, and Tripuris and with Bengal. Later, this road also served as the route through which the Manipuris were able to establish their spiritual connection with holy shrines of Navadwip in Bengal, Purī in Odisha, and Braja-Vrindavana in present Uttar Pradesh.

"Rādhā-Kuṇḍa: Govardhana Parikramā" by Chongtham Jamini Devi and translated from Manipuri by Sonia Wahengbam, which constitutes the tenth chapter of the book, is an account of the transformative journey that the author experienced as a sacred pilgrimage from Delhi to Vrindavana and Mathurā. Rādhā-Kuṇḍa, at a distance of 4 km north of Govardhana and 22 km west of Vrindavana, holds sacred significance for Vaiṣṇavas. In the Vedas, Rādhā-Kuṇḍa and Śyāma-Kuṇḍa are extolled with the utmost reverence. The perspective of witnessing Rādhā-Kuṇḍa, Śyāma-Kuṇḍa, and Vrindavana together is purportedly beyond human reach. Legendary tales recount Rādhā-Kuṇḍa's genesis from the tears shed by Rādhikā upon parting with Śrī Kṛṣṇa, while Śyāma-Kuṇḍa emerged from Śrī Kṛṣṇa's tears when separated from Rādhikā. The author feels that not everyone is fortunate enough to experience a life filled with happiness and contentment, especially where familial support in old age is concerned. In places like Vrindavana, Mathurā, and Purī, the presence of numerous beggars may serve as a poignant testament to how divine providence sustains them. While witnessing this reality, she sought solace by telling herself that this might be the kārmic result of actions in her past life.

The eleventh chapter of the book titled "The Land of Vrindavana" by Akoijam Sanaton, a well-known journalist, and translated from Manipuri by Pebam Nganthoiba Mangang, is a fascinating account of the land of Vrindavana, considered a unique place, enthralled by its natural divine ecstasy by the devotees of Lord Kṛṣṇa. The landscape covering the Vrindavana extending from Rādhā-Kuṇḍa to Śyāma-Kuṇḍa, including religious places like Mathurā, is known as Chaurāsī Kosa. Though the author was born and brought up in a Vaiṣṇavite Hindu Meitei family, he tried his best to look at Vrindavana from a common man's perspective. One important piece of information the author had outlined in the paper is the importance attached by the devotees to the Jugol Parikramā, which refers to the circumambulation or *parikramā* of a sacred place, often associated with the deities Rādhā and Kṛṣṇa, specifically within the context of Braja-Vrindavana and Govardhana. It's a practice of showing respect and devotion by walking around a holy site. The term "Jugol" signifies the divine couple, Rādhā and Kṛṣṇa, highlighting the devotional aspect of the *parikramā*. However, in today's busy lifestyle, as one needs to spare 14 to 16 days to visit the place and participate, hardly people can attend such festivals, and people have started forgetting such festivals,the author posed with amusement.

"Pilgrimage to Rādhā-Kuṇḍa by Shukhdeba Sharma Hanjabam, which constituted the twelfth and concluding chapter of the book, portrays how Rādhā-Kuṇḍa, from the beginning of the nineteenth century, has become a prominent pilgrimage site of Manipuri Vaiṣṇava of India (mainly from Manipur, Assam, and Tripura), Bangladesh, and Myanmar, apart from Navadwip in Bengal. However, the opportunity to go on a Pilgrimage to Rādhā-Kuṇḍa was mainly confined to the members of the royal families and people under state patronage. The common people used to seek blessings from those who had visited Rādhā-Kuṇḍa, assuming that it was like offering a prayer or visiting Rādhā-Kuṇḍa. The author contends that it was only at the beginning of the twentieth century that the commoners, who were close to the royal families, started visiting Rādhā-Kuṇḍa and dedicating the *mandira* in Rādhā-Kuṇḍa. For instance, the *mandira* dedicated by Gurumayum Madhav Sharma and his wife Bidhumukhi Devi (1932), Irengbam Anganghal (1943), and Koijam Akhiljit Singh (1945) were some of the pioneer *mandira*s beyond the royal families. The commoners, on a limited scale, have since been going on Pilgrimage to Rādhā-Kuṇḍa.

According to the author, the Manipuri Vaiṣṇava goes to Rādhā-Kuṇḍa on four occasions that fall on the four seasons of Manipur. The pilgrimage is to coincide with the religious occasion (Prabaddin) of the Śrī Śrī Govindajī. They are (i) Wakching (December/January)—Mahā Snān; (ii) Meera (October/November)—Jugol Parikramā/Rādhā Aṣṭamī; (iii) Lamta/(February/March)—Holī; and (iv) Thawan (August/September)—Badra Parikramā.

Last but not least, it may be said that this book, which is a collection of articles, is a humble attempt at portraying a connected account of Manipuri Viṣṇavas' spiritual connect with Braja-Vrindavana and other sacred sites connected with Hindu Dharma, which remain almost a neglected domain for researchers and academics connected with Hindu Dharma. It might not be an exaggeration to say that Hindu Dharma as observed in Manipur, has a unique characteristic that complements what is seen or experienced in other regions of India. Some articles may present information that feels repetitive, which is not something within the control of the editors, and we seek indulgence of the learned readers.

NOTES

1. V.W. Turner, & E.L.B. Turner (1978). *Image and Ppilgrimage in Christian Culture: Anthropological Perspectives.* Columbia University Press, pp. 253-54.
2. *Ibid.*, p. 4.
3. Robert H. Stoddard (1997). *Defining and Classifying Pilgrimages*, Geography Faculty Publications. University of Nebraska, Lincoln, DigitalCommons@University of Nebraska, Lincoln, Geography Programme (SNR), pp. 45-49.
4. Brent S. Plate (2009). "The Varieties of Contemporary Pilgrimage", *Cross Currents*, *59*(3): 264.
5. Diana L, Eck (1998). *Darśan, Seeing the Divine Image in India*, Columbia University Press, p. 5.
6. Turner and Turner (1978). *Op. cit.*, pp. 13-15.
7. Robert H. Stoddard (1997). *Op. cit.*, p. 56.
8. Turner and Turner (1978). *Op. cit.*, pp. 33-34.
9. Simon Coleman and John Elsner (1995). *Pilgrimage: Past and Present in the World Religions,* Cambridge: Harvard University Press, p. 134.
10. Turner and Turner (1978). *Op. cit.*, p. 6.
11. Diana L. Eck (1998). *Op. cit.*, p. 7.
12. Surinder Mohan Bhardwaj (1973). *Hindu Places of Pilgrimage in India: A Study in Cultural Geography*, California: University of California Press, p. 146.
13. *Ibid.*, pp. 145-62.
14. Turner and Turner (1978). *Op. cit.*, p. 32.
15. *Ibid.*, p. 38.
16. Diana L. Eck (1978). *Op. cit.*, p. 15.
17. Bhardwaj (1983). *Op. cit.*, pp. 151-52.
18. Coleman and Elsner (1995). *Op. cit.*, p. 154.
19. L. Iboongohak Singh and N. Khelchandra Singh (ed.) (1989). *Cheitharol Kumbaba (The Royal Chronicle of Manipur),* Manipuri Sahitya Parishad, Imphal, 2nd edition, p. 172.
20. Anton M. Pazos, (ed.) (2012). "Introduction", In *Pilgrims and Politics: Rediscovering the Power of the Pilgrimage*, Surrey, Ashgate Publishing Limited, pp. 1-8.

Section I
Dhārmic Connection

1

Manipuri Mandiras at Rādhā-Kuṇḍa

Shukhdeba Sharma Hanjabam

Introduction

Manipur's introduction to Hindu Dharma came from the east particularly from the Shan kingdom of Pong in upper Burma in the second half of the fifteenth century. However, successive Manipur kings adopted the Hindu Dharma that originated from the West, particularly the Rāma cult, Kṛṣṇa cult, and Caitanya school of Vaiṣṇavism, influenced the indigenous cultural way of life during the eighteenth century, of which Caitanya school had the greatest impact. Mahārāja Charairongba (1697-1709 CE), Mahārājā Garibniwāz (1709-48 CE), and Rājarṣi Bhāgyacandra (1759-61 & 1763-98 CE) initiated, promoted, and popularized the growth and development of the synthesized Hindu Dharma with the indigenous cultural way of life. Thus, religious places like Navadwip, Purī, Vrindavana, Kāśi, Mathura, Dvārakā, and Ayodhyā have found a prominent place in the religious discourse of the Hinduized Manipuris.

In this connection, we have the authority of Rājarṣi Bhāgyacandra's desire to visit Vrindavana in his last days, as recorded in a text called *Chinthangkhomba Maharaja Ganga Chatpa* (A Pilgrimage Account of Chingthangkhomba Mahārāja Going to Gaṅgā) which was jointly composed at royal order by three scholars, Nabachandra Wangkhei, Hari Charan Thounapaton and Wahengba Madhabram at the later part of the eighteenth century. But his wishes could not be materialized as Rājarṣi Bhāgyacandra died on the way near Murshidabad in 1798 (October). However, his son, Jubaraj Chourajit, continued the pilgrimage to fulfil the last wishes of his beloved father and reached Rādhā-Kuṇḍa in early January 1799 with a portion of his father's remains to perform the *śrāddha* ceremony and bury the bone-relics (*asthi*/ashes in the courtyard of Śrī Ghara. Jubaraj Chourjit[1] was followed by nine officials namely:

1. Angom Biramani, Sellungba (Financial Officer),
2. Naorem Dhaani (Captain of Malom Battalion),
3. Brāhmaṇa Valabha,
4. Brāhmaṇa Harikṛṣṇa,
5. Hikhambam Madan,
6. Huirom Madananda,
7. Sapam Valabhava,
8. Nameirakpam Vrindavana, and
9. Lourembam Poornanda.

Similarly, the book *Gambhir Singh Nonggaba* (Demise of Gambhīr Singh), composed by the two *paṇḍita*s, namely Dayārām Louremba and Nabaśyāma Ningthoujamba, reflects the devotion of Mahārāja Gambhīr Singh, to Śrī Rādhā-Kṛṣṇa and his love for Śrī Vrindavana can be clearly seen. The present *akhāṛā* built by Mahārāja Gambhīr Singh still exists at the Rādhā-Kuṇḍa near Śrī Vrindavana, though now fallen in the hands of outsiders due to mismanagement from the side of descendants, will remain ever as an epitome of Mahārāja Gambhīr Singh and his love of Śrī Vrindavana.

Development of Manipuri Mandira in Rādhā-Kuṇḍa and Vrindavana

The first *mandira* of Manipur (Śrī Śrī Rāsabihārījī Mandira) was constructed at Rādhā-Kuṇḍa by Jubaraj Chourajit (Later Mahārājā of Manipur) in 1799 in memory of Rājarṣī Bhāgyacandra. Mahārājā Lābaṇya Candra (1798-1800) financially supported the development of the temple. The temple complex is known as Pūraṇa-Kuñja[2]. The temple is presently managed by the descendant of Jubaraj Chourjit under the banner of Śrī Śrī Rāsabihārījī Mandira Seva Trust, having its head office at Pūraṇa-Kuñja, Rādhā-Kuṇḍa, Mathura district, Uttar Pradesh and branch office at Keishamthong Top Leirak, Imphal, Manipur.

Rājarṣi Bhāgyacandra, besides his administrative, warfare, and diplomatic skills, was known for his cultural creativity and has immensely contributed to the sociocultural domain of Manipur. Śrī Śrī Govindajī, the source and epicentre of Manipur Vaiṣṇavism, traced its roots to Rājarṣi Bhāgyacandra. In the present context, two of his cultural contributions have been recognized as an important cultural heritage of India: (i) Rāsa Līlā of Manipur, which is now one of the classical dance of India, and (ii) Saṅkīrtana of Manipur, which is among the fourteen elements inscribed on the Representative List of the UNESCO Intangible Cultural Heritage of Humanity.

The successive Mahārājās of Manipur deputed officials to oversee the construction of *mandira*s and *akhāḍā*s (*akhāṛā*) at Rādhā-Kuṇḍa. Mahārājā Gambhīr Singh deputed[3] Nongmaithem Kīrti Singh to construct the Śrī Gokulānanda Mandira. The *mandira* is located near Gopālagṛha, along the east side of Śrī Śyāma-Kuṇḍa, which is known as Borkuñja. Mahārājā Gambhīr Singh bought the land from the British Empire in 1830 on payment of Rs. 13,000 (thirteen thousand) to develop it into a pilgrimage site by constructing the temple of Śrī Ṭhākur Rādhā Govinda Devajī Mahārājā[4]. Mahārājā Gambhīr Singh could not see even a glimpse of the *mandira* of his dream. He tried to go on a pilgrimage to Rādhā-Kuṇḍa after giving up his throne. But because of his health, he breathed his last in 1834 in Manipur.

Mahārājā Gambhīr Singh's last wish to go on a pilgrimage to Rādhā-Kuṇḍa was reflected in the Manipuri text *Gambhir Singh Nonggaba* (The Heavenward Journey of Gambhīr Singh), which was jointly composed at royal order by Dayaram Louremba and Nabashyam Ningthoujamba. The text, *Gambhir Singh Nonggaba*, mentioned that Mahārājā Gambhīr Singh, a great fighter and a devout Vaiṣṇava, having sat on the throne for about eight years, made up his mind to make a pilgrimage to Vrindavana after entrusting the state and his little son to Nara Singh. One can reflect the yearning that throbbed in every Manipuri Vaiṣṇava's heart when he says to the brāhmaṇa *paṇḍita*s:[5]

> "Leaving aside the mundane pleasure and other human jealousies, I have decided to seek peace of mind in Vrindavana in the westerly direction where the ever bountiful *kalpavṛkṣa* grows, where six season in a year make their invigorating visits, where the Rasarāja Kṛṣṇa took his birth, where Rādhā and Kṛṣṇa the very manifestations of *Brahman* were both present, where the fountain of love springs and where the soul after death finds its resting place."

The development of Rādhā-Kuṇḍa continued with Jubaraj Nara Singh (later Mahārājā of Manipur) constructing Śrī Naol Govinda Mandira during his times as Regency (1834-44) of Manipur. The place is known as Jubaraj Kuñja or Naol Kuñja.[6]

Manipuri Mandira in Rādhā-Kuṇḍa

There has been 30[7] Manipuri *mandira*s at Rādhā-Kuṇḍa and four *mandira*s in Vrindavana were built mainly by pious Vaiṣṇavas of Manipur since the 1930s. Mahārājās of Manipur built four *mandira*s out of the thirty in Rādhā-Kuṇḍa. The *mandira*s are:

(i) Śrī Rāsabihārījī Mandira, Pūraṇa-Kuñja (built by Jubaraj Chourjit),
(ii) Śrī Rādhā-Govindajī Mandira, Boro-Kuñja (built by Mahārājā Gambhīr),
(iii) Śrī Naol Govindajī Mandira, Yubarāj Kuṇḍa (Yubarāj Nara Singh), and Śrī Gopālajī Mandira (built by Mahārājā Churachand).

Manipuri temple/*mandira* in Rādhā-Kuṇḍa—an association formed in 2017 that aims to promote and preserve the Manipuri *mandira*s in Rādhā-Kuṇḍa stated that presently, there are 23 *mandira*s in Rādhā-Kuṇḍa and two *mandira*s in Vrindavana (Seva Mandira and Yubaraj Mandira). Shri Takhellambam Irabot,[8] Spokesperson of the Rajarshi Bhagyachandra Cultural Foundation Manipur, who has been leading the pilgrimage to Rādhā-Kuṇḍa for the last 40 years, has stated that there are only sixteen *mandira*s that can be counted as Manipuri *mandira*s as of now. Only about half are actively performing the *aṣṭakāla* (daily rituals), including *prasādam* and Prabadin (yearly rituals), while the rest are performing on a low scale. Shri R.K. Dusarigopal[9], and Shri Takhellambam Irabot[10] stated that some of the *mandira* seems to have sold off. One new temple (Maṇipureśvara Mandira) was also developed in 2022 (October), Shri Takhellambam Irabot. The total list of *mandira*s in Rādhā-Kuṇḍa listed with Manipuri temples/ *mandira*s in Rādhā-Kuṇḍa is as follows:

1. Śrī Rāsabihārījī Mandira
2. Rādhā-Govindajī Mandira
3. Śrī Naol Govindajī Mandira
4. Śrī Gopālajī Mandira
5. Śrī Rādhābinoda Mandira
6. Śrī Giridhārī Mandira
7. Śrī Ācārya Mandira
8. Śrī Nabīnkiśore Mandira
9. Śrī Gopīnātha Mandira
10. Śrī Giridhārī Mandira

11. Śrī Mahāprabhu Mandira
12. Śrī Rādhābrajanātha Mandira
13. Śrī Biśambara Mandira
14. Śrī Rādhārājabihārī Mandira
15. Śrī Sītānātha Mandira
16. Śrī Rādhā Mandira
17. Śrī Brajanātha Mandira
18. Śrī Girirāja Mandira
19. Śrī Gopīnātha Mandira
20. Śrī Bhāgavata Mandira
21. Śrī Kamom Kuñja Mandira
22. Chapak Kuñja Gopālajī Mandira
23. Maṇipureśvara Mandira

Note: The association does not have updated data on the details of the sold-out Manipur *mandira*s.

Rādhā-Kuṇḍa and Martial History of Manipur

Rādhā-Kuṇḍa was also associated with the martial history of Manipur. Two significant instances are:

(i) The Kālāpānī exiled Anglo-Manipur War (1891) Heroes led by Mahārājā Kulacandra were denied entry to Manipur even after their release from Kālāpānī. So, they chose to breathe their last at Rādhā-Kuṇḍa, considering the dhārmic connection of Manipur, and ending their life at Rādhā is like surmounting to visiting or meeting the God;

(ii) Legendary Warrior of Manipur, Paona Brajabashi left Manipur in 1850 and performed the last rites of his father Tulsiram at Vrindavana. Paona Brajabashi stays at Vrindavana for seven years and learns about advanced warfare techniques.[11] He returned to Manipur in 1856. The name "Paona Brajabashi" was given to him by Mahārājā Candrakīrti for his association with Vrindavana, particularly Rādhā-Kuṇḍa. His birth name was Paonam Naol Singh. Under state patronage, Paona Brajabashi was deputed to Vrindavana to acquire advanced knowledge of various martial traditions.[12]

Issues of Manipuri Mandiras at Rādhā-Kuṇḍa

The Manipuri *mandiras* at Rādhā-Kuṇḍa were initially established only by the *mahārājās* and their families. The tradition of dedicating *mandiras* at Rādhā-Kuṇḍa became very popular among the influential Manipuri in the early 1930s. Thus, the influential Vaiṣṇavas of Manipur started dedicated/building *mandiras* in Rādhā-Kuṇḍa and Vrindavana. Of the 30 *mandiras* (now only 23) at Rādhā-Kuṇḍa, only four were built by *mahārājās* and their families. The increasing number of Manipuri *mandiras* and the growing number of pilgrims to Rādhā-Kuṇḍa and Vrindavana is mainly because of the dedication to the Vaiṣṇava tradition by the people of Manipur.

The tradition of dedicating *mandira* seems to have slowly faded by the end of the twentieth century. The main reason mainly concerns the families who had dedicated the *mandiras*. The dedicated families or their descendants of some of the *mandiras* no longer support and maintain the *mandiras*. The situation is mainly because of the economic conditions, the declining spiritual tradition of the new generations, a difference of descendants' opinions on the property, and the changes in belief system, under whose hands the *mandira* is now being handed over. In such a situation, they rarely visit the *mandira*. They mostly try to maintain the *mandira* through the local people (Brajavāsīs) by sending the monthly expenditures with little supervision.

Considering the expenditure in maintaining the *mandira*, some tend to see the *mandira* as a "white elephant". The cost/expenditure of sustaining the *mandira* can explain the situation. Śrī Dusāri Gopāl,[13] who is the descendant of Mahārājā Chourjit, who built the first *mandira* (Śrī Śrī Rāsabihārījī Mandira), explained to us that, at the minimum, the expenditure of the *mandira* is around Rs. 10,000-15,000 and on average, the expenditure ranges from Rs. 20,000-30,000 for a month to perform the daily and yearly religious activities of the *mandira*. So, if we calculate for a year, it ranges from 1,50,000 to 3,50,000. The *mandira* does not generate any income it does not equips to generate income like well furnish guest house, and is dependent on source of the dedicated families. Besides the monthly expenditure, there is a need for renovation and other activities that require additional expenditures. In this condition, if any families stop sending the expenditure of the *mandira*, the *mandira* will automatically stop the religious activities and likely to decline. This situation has reduced the Manipuri *mandira* from thirty to only sixteen *mandira*s in Rādhā-Kuṇḍa. The *pujārī*s used to start begging to survive themselves and the *mandira*.

Unlike the *sevāyata*s from other states of India, most of the *sevāyata*s of Manipur could not be registered with the local administration. They thus could not get the ration card, which can help them in terms of government supply of PDs items. The main reason, as stated, was that the *sevāyata*s from Manipur could not stay for a continuous period and thus could not get the benefits of the government facilities. Takhellambam Irabot shared that if the *sevāyata*s/*pujārī*s could get the ration card and PDs items, they could have easily survived themselves and maintained the Manipuri *mandira*s, even if the dedicated families failed to support them.

In some cases, the local *sevāyata*s mortgage the *mandira* to continue the religious activities. But when the dedicated families fail to send the money continuously, it gets occupied by others. Mahārājā Gambhīr Singh's *mandira* complex is an example. The selling of a few Manipur *mandira*s at Rādhā-Kuṇḍa and Vrindavana could also be examined from this perspective. So, to sustain the *mandira*, the dedicated families/descendants need to create a dedicated source of funds flow, which may not be able to be disturbed/diverted in any case, even by the families. Despite the situation, the tradition of dedicating the *mandira* continues at Rādhā-Kuṇḍa with the inauguration of a new Manipuri *mandira* in 2021-22.

Mahārājā Gambhīr Singh Mandira, Boro-Kuñja, Rādhā-Kuṇḍa

The Mahārājā Gambhīr Singh's *mandira* complex at Boro-Kuñja is now embroiled in a legal battle between the descendants and *sevāyata*s. Attempt to restore/buy the *mandira* by the people of Manipur failed as the dedicating/descendants fought over the properties and started leasing them out to local Brajavāśīs in exchange for certain monetary benefits. It is not sure how much the unofficial transaction is. The financial involvement in leasing out the *mandira* came to light when the Bari Kunja Revival Committee of Manipur started negotiating with the descendants and *sevāyata*s from Manipur and also simultaneously mobilizing resources to rejuvenate the *mandira* and the complex at Boro Kuñja (Baṛī Kuñja). In the letter to the Shri Adityanath Jī, hon'ble chief minister of Uttar Pradesh,[14] the Chairman of the Bari Kunja Revival Committee, Mahārājā Leishemba Sanajaoba (presently Member of Parliament, Rajya Sabha from Manipur), stated that they are in the process of negotiating for an amount of Rs. 1 crore (nearly).

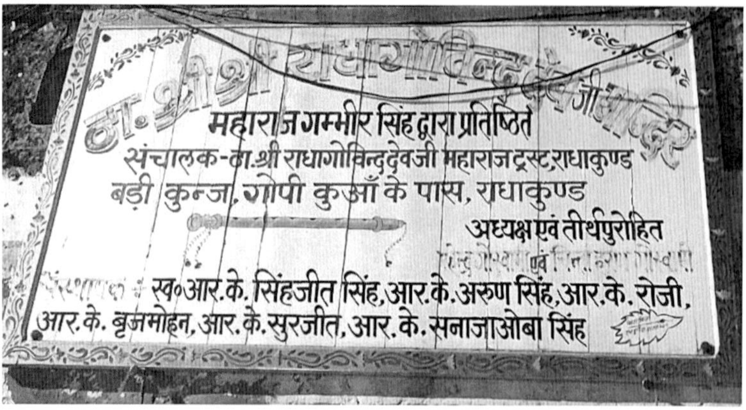

The descendants and *sevāyata*s of the *mandira* (first party), namely R.K. Singhajit Singh, R.K. Gopinatha Singh, R.K. Brijmohon Singh, Arunkumar Singh, R.K. Surjit Singh, R.K. Sanajaoba Singh, have a lease[15] out the *mandira* and its premise for thirty (30) years for a premium amount of Rs. 11,000 and a yearly rent of Rs. 1,200 to (second party) Shrimati Radhika Bhatia, Shrimati Babita Govil and Kumari Dimple Barsneya from Mathura, Uttar Pradesh in 9 September 2004. The English translation of the lease states that,

> "That the abovesaid temple, having stood for the last about 200 years, became by this time eroded and broken; due to the price hike in the essential commodities, there is no person who can extend charity to protect the temple from further deterioration, while funds are badly in need to ensure minimum ritual service of the Lord like offering of Bhog and observing the temple routine.
>
> Now, all the *sevāyata*s unanimously came to the resolution that properties described hereunder, which are not used in the daily services of the Lord, be entrusted in lease so that the rent accrued from that place may be utilized to meet the day-to-day services of the Lord.

> Hence, all the *sevāyata*s hereby create the lease of the said land as demised property, in favour of the second party, for a period of 30 years on realization of a premium of Rs. 11,000 which both parties voluntarily appreciated with full knowledge that it is the consideration for creation of the lease."

However, the issue of property of the Boro (Baṛī) Kuñja, rather than maintaining the day-to-day rituals of the *mandira*, is clearly reflected in the *sevatanāmā* of the lease. The *sevatanāmā*[16] stated that,

> "Whereas the first party for the smooth running and for control and for lookafter the said Ṭhākurajī Śrī Govinda Deva Jī Mahārāja installed in *mandira* Baḍī Kuñja, Rādhā-Kuṇḍa Tahasil district Mathurā for Bhorag, *sevā-pūjā* and for the maintenance and control of the property and for the smooth running of all affairs as done earlier appoint the second party for controlling by us. The second party in place of the first party from this day are only *sevāyata* and controller of the said Ṭhākurajī in place of the first party.
>
> All the rights for transfer, ownership and, *sevāyatī* etc. and, gives effect and for performing the *pūjā*s and for transferring the name of the first party to the second party before the authorities in government documents/papers and the "second party has the right to do anything over the said property as they desire". "Now, rights of any kind remain over the said property by the first party or their successors in interest for any rights or shares over the said property in the future or at any time. "Now, the second party becomes the absolute controller of the *mandira* and Ṭhākurajī property as a single *sevāyata* and controller and shall remain the owner. They have the right to do

> anything in the interest of the said *mandira* and Ṭhākurajī property". The first party and their LR's successors have no objection in this regard. Any person/s successors in the interest of the first party or any person/s of the first party claims or quarrels or creates disputing shall be not enforceable in the eye of the law. This deed executed by the first party in their sound minds without having liqueurs or any influence and after gone through its contents in full knowledge are executing this deed. This *sevatanāmā* executed shall first party to second party favour for evidence and for effect in time."

Considering the gravity of the situation, some of the concerned *sevāyata*s/*sevāhita*s of Manipur have requested the hon'ble chief minister to restore the temple/estate and to develop it as the heritage site of Manipur in particular and the nation at large.

In a memorandum[17] to the chief minister, Manipur, on 1 December 2017, the *sevāyata*s/*sevāhit*s Shri R.K. Dorendra Singh, Smt. R.K. (Ongbi) Ranjana Devi, Shri Moirangthem Ashok Singh, Secretary of Rajarshi Bhagyachandra Cultural Foundation Manipur and twenty other signatories (Manipuri Vaiṣṇavas), stated that,

> "The temple complex has been occupied forcibly by some local people of Rādhā-Kuṇḍa, and the original *sevāhita*s and pilgrims of our state are barred from entering the temple complex by the said occupants."

In response to the situation of the Mahārājā Gambhīr Singh *mandira* and its complex at Boro-Kuñja, the hon'ble chief minister of Manipur[18] has appraised the hon'ble chief minister of Uttar Pradesh, Shri Yogi Adityanath Jī, on 14 August 2018. The letter (D.O No. 2/2/2018-CM) stated that

> "It has been brought to my notice that the temple has been transferred to some local persons. I am also appraised that pilgrim from Manipur are not allowed to enter the temple complex. The matter is sensitive to the people of my state and it is desired that the temple is restored to the Manipuri Hindus."

Shri Leishemba Sanajaoba,[19] Mahārājā of Manipur, presently hon'ble MP, Rajya Sabha, representing Manipur, have also written to the Shri Yogi Adityanath Jī, hon'ble chief minister of Uttar Pradesh, dated 19 September 2018 that,

> "That unfortunately, around 15/20 years back, the *sevāyata*s (descendants) had transferred the temple in a very miserable amount illegally to some local person which is against the will and the sentiment of the Manipuri people (particularly the Manipuri Hindu Vaiṣṇavites). This is illegal because any *sevāyata*(s) has no rights to transfer or sell any movable property(ies) because they are not the real owner of the property. The real owner of the said temple is the Mahārājā of Manipur and the people of Manipur. The only duty of the *sevāyata*(s) is to look after the temple, not to sell or transfer or gift, etc., etc."

The attempt to restore and rejuvenate Mahārājā Gambhīr Singh's *mandira* and its complex has not been successful, as some descendants/*sevāyata*s in Manipur have not been cooperating. The reason for not cooperating by the descendants could be because of the financial benefits (nearly crores). Besides the amount, the prestige (ego) and decline in the religious life, even to the extent of discarding their forefathers by the descendants (*sevāyata*s), could also be the issue in restoring the *mandira*.

Way Forward

The sacredness of Rādhā-Kuṇḍa is even more sacred with the existence of the Manipuri *mandira*s, the *samādhi* of Mahārājā Kulacandra and Bhaktisvarūpa Dāmodara Swāmī (a native of Manipur)—the leader of Gauḍīya Vaiṣṇava of the International Society for Krishna Consciousness (ISKCON). The contribution of Dāmodara Swāmī in sustaining the Manipuri *mandira*s at Rādhā-Kuṇḍa and Vrindavana is immense. The ISKCON temple maintains the *mandira* of Mahārājā Churachand Singh and the Śrī Ācārya *mandira*. Damodara Swāmī, through ISKCON, has tried its best to sustain the Manipuri *mandira*, and in some cases (if someone sold out), they tried their best to buy it so that the *mandira* remains with Manipur Vaiṣṇavas. It remains successful in some cases and fails in others as the families see the *mandira* as real estate and try to sell to the highest buyers.

To conclude, the dhārmic connection (particularly by constructing *mandira*s) of Manipur and Rādhā-Kuṇḍa will commemorate the 225th (by 2024) years. The first *mandira* of Manipur (Śrī Śrī Rāsabihārījī Mandira) was constructed at Rādhā-Kuṇḍa in 1799 in memory of Rājarṣi Bhāgyacandra. Besides the *mahārājā*s, Rādhā-Kuṇḍa has become a prominent pilgrimage site for the Manipuri Hindus of India, Bangladesh, and Myanmar. They have chosen to spend the rest of their lives dedicated since the beginning of the nineteenth century. There have been more than twenty-four Manipuri temples at Rādhā-Kuṇḍa since the eighteenth century, but presently, there are only twenty temples in Rādhā-Kuṇḍa and three in Vrindavana. It is high time that the connection between Manipur and Rādhā-Kuṇḍa is rejuvenated as it is not only a pilgrimage site for Manipuris but also linked to Manipur's War of Independence.

NOTES

1. Dusari Gopala (2023). *Śrī Śrī Rāsabihārījī*, Śrī Śrī Rāsabihārījī Mandira Seva Trust, Mathurā, UP & Imphal, Manipur, pp. 4-5.
2. *Ibid.*, pp. 6-7.
3. N. Shyamkanhai (2012). *Paona Brajabashi and 1891*, Research Forum, Manipur (REFORM), Imphal, p. 113.
4. A Memorandum submitted to the hon'ble chief minister Manipur (Shri Nongthonbam Biren Singh) on Restoring Possession of "Baṛī Kuñja' (Boro Kuñja) at Rādhā-Kuṇḍa, Mathurā district, UP, India, and Renovation of the Site, etc. by Shri R.K. Dorendra Singh, Smt R.K. (Ongbi) Ranjana Devi and Shri Moirangthem Ashok Singh, dated 1 December 2017, p. 1.
5. Ch Manihar Singh (1st Edn. 1996, 2003). *A History of Manipuri Literature*. Sahitya Academi, New Delhi, pp. 160-61.
6. N. Shyamkanhai (2012). *Paona Brajabashi and 1891*, Research Forum, Manipur (REFORM), Imphal, p. 113.
7. A.K. Sanaton (2012). *Laifam Yaona Bharati Lamdamsingda Khongtharuba* (Manipuri), Akoijam Ongbi Roma Devi (Publisher), Imphal, p. 111.
8. Interview with Shri Takhellambam Irabot by the authors on 22 October 2023.
9. Interview with R.K. Dusari Gopala (President of the Śrī Rāsabihārījī Mandir) on 12 October 2023.
10. Interview with Shri Takhellambam Irabot (Secretary of Rajarshi Bhagyachandra Cultural Foundation Manipur) by the authors on 22 October 2023.
11. N. Shyamkanhai (2012). *Paona Brajabashi and 1891*, Research Forum, Manipur (REFORM), Imphal, p. 101.
12. *Ibid.*, p. 113.
13. Interview with Shri Gopala Sharma with the author on 12 October 2023.
14. Memorandum: Bari Kunja Revival Committee Manipur, to the Honourable Chief Minister, Uttar Pradesh State, India; Subject: Submitting a Memorandum regarding the Restoration of a Manipur Temple "Baṛī Kuñja" at Parikramā Mārga, Rādhā-Kuṇḍa, UP State by Mahārājā Sanajaoba Leishemba, Chairman, Bari Kuja Revival Committee, dated 19 September 2018.
15. Lease Document, dated 24 September 2004, Mathurā (English translation), Original Text in Hindi.
16. *Sevatnāmā*, dated 24 September 2004, Mathurā (English translation), Original Text in Hindi.

17. A Memorandum submitted to the hon'ble chief minister Manipur (Shri Nongthonbam Biren Singh) on Restoring Possession of "Baṛī Kuñja' (Boro Kuñja) at Rādhā-Kuṇḍa, Mathurā district, UP, India, and Renovation of the Site, etc. by Shri R.K. Dorendra Singh, Smt. R.K. (Ongbi) Ranjana Devi and Shri Moirangthem Ashok Singh, dated 1 December 2017, p. 2.
18. Shri Yogi Adityanath, hon'ble chief minister of Uttar Pradesh, Lal Bahadur Shastri Bhawan, Lucknow, from Shri N. Biren Singh, hon'ble chief minister Manipur, D.O 2/2/2018/CM, dated 14 August 2018.
19. Memorandum: Bari Kunja Revival Committee Manipur, to the hon'ble chief minister, Uttar Pradesh State, India; Subject: Submitting a Memorandum regarding the Restoration of a Manipur Temple "Baṛī Kuñja" at Parikramā Mārga, Rādhā-Kuṇḍa, UP State by Mahārājā Sanajaoba Leishemba, Chairman, Bari Kunja Revival Committee, dated 19 September 2018.

2

Manipuri Vaiṣṇava and Śrī Rādhā-Kuṇḍa

K. Brajamani Sharma

Vaiṣṇavism is one of the sects of Hinduism, which believes Viṣṇu and His incarnations as the supreme. In this sect, morality, ethical codes, and other human activities are based on non-violence, purity, neatness, and cleanliness. Sacrifices of living beings are not allowed in temples and other places. There are different sects like Śaiva, Śākta, Gāṇapatya, and others in Hinduism.

Manipuri Vaiṣṇavas follow the Rāgānuga Bhakti system of Lord Caitanya Mahāprabhu, who introduced the philosophy called Acintya Vedaveda Vāda, in which the *jīva* (individual soul) is different and also not different from *Brahman* (the universal soul), which cannot be perceived by human intellect, is explained. He regarded Śrī Kṛṣṇa as the Absolute and Rādhāraṇī as His power. The relationship between Śrī Kṛṣṇa and Rādhāraṇī differs from that of Nārāyaṇa and Lakṣmī. It is not a husband-wife relation and is described in *Caitanya Caritāmṛta* of Kṛṣṇadās, such as—

pahilahi rāga nayana bhaṅga bhelo, anudina baralo abadhi na gelo.
na so ramana na hamo ramani .... (Madhya Līlā, Rāmānanda Sāṅgā).

Rādhārānī is described as Śrī Kṛṣṇa's power of happiness, joy, enjoyment, rejoicing, gladness, delight, and excitement (*hlādinī śakti*).

Caitanya Prabhu picked up three factors in human behaviour for using as easy means to have union with God, Śrī Kṛṣṇa. They are *saundarya* (absolute beauty), *prema* (maximum affection), and *ānanda* (absolute happiness). Beauty is a thing of attraction where the mind and body are attached to it. If it is an absolute beauty, without any defect, the practitioner or the one who is attracted by the beauty personified will certainly absorb that. That is Śrī Kṛṣṇa, who is all beauty, and thus, the practitioner has to achieve what a *yogī* would get in deep meditation (*samādhi*). There is no practice of *āsana*s and *prāṇāyāma*s, there is no hard and fast rule for worshipping and observing fasts and festivals, etc. There will also be no *brahma vicāra* (Studies of the Upaniṣads and other scholarly criticisms on Vedas), and there will also be no sacrifices and other forms of self-control and scriptural decree to follow. However, the degree of concentration on the physical form of Śrī Kṛṣṇa will be the maximum when He is an absolute beauty.

The next one is *prema* or love. It is termed as *praṇaya* which may be translated as manifestation of one's affection in both body and soul without any reserve for the beloved. This is absorption in love. It is love for loves sake. There are many forms of love—love between neighbours, between friends, between master and servant, between mother and child, and between hero and heroine. The last one is the greatest form because whatever the lover has can be offered to the loved one without a little reserve. There are three properties of any person; they are body, mind, and possessed things. These three things can be offered by those in the fifth category and not by those in the other forms of love. Śrī Caitanya Prabhu wanted the form of love, which in normal life is not regarded as respectable and is one of the disgraceful acts, that Śrī Kṛṣṇa be loved as if a married woman thinks of another person, though she lives, serves, and does everything in her husband's house. The simile was selected because human behaviours, particularly mental activities, are generally more powerful when they are not expressed to others and the intensity of love has ever increased. It is kept untold, unexpressed, and unfulfilled. This is the system of amour, love, and intrigue. This is like venom for healing purposes, a very difficult practice to practice with proper guidance; otherwise, it may turn to mockery.

The third one, bliss, is the fruit of the above two processes. Where there is bliss, there is contentment, passion-free, mental peace, and harmony with everything and everybody. We know that a pauper likes money, but when he gets money in abundance, he experiences another form of suffering; that is, a man without wealth suffers, and also a man with wealth suffers. The first suffering is for want of, and the second is for protection of wealth. It remains the same when it is a child to the parents, a degree to a scholar, a prominent chair in administration, a reputation to a hard-working fellow in any field, and so on. Suffering means no happiness. If there happens a sense of happiness when the person suffers much, it is called delight with excitement. Such a condition can be had only when there is devotion and dedication in the right way by the person for the one who is loved. A mother rejoices when her child eats her share of food, but such a dedication retard to zero when the child marries and enjoys family life. In the right way of devotion and dedication will mean everlasting process. There are devotees and disciples but dedication with devotion is very-very rare.

Now, the theory gives us a glimpse of the achievement that may be arrived at by those who follow the *rāgānuga bhakti* or devotion with great attachment. But who would be the competent *guru* or teacher, by following whose nature anyone can have the desired destination? Is that the problem? We have got Satī, who, with vigorous austerities, had Śiva as her Lord, Sāvitrī, who could save the husband from the hands of Lord Yama, and so on. But, is there anyone who, without having united formally and even without meeting for more than a century of years, never forgets the Lord? It was Śrī Rādhārānī of the Vrindavana. She played with Śrī Kṛṣṇa at a tender age, from about six years of age to about eleven years, only for five years, and separated till the end of their lives in the mortal world, for more than 100 years. The beloved Lord, though, had more than 16,000 and more ladies as life partners in Dwārkā; Śrī Rādhārānī never withdrew Her love for Him and still lived happily as if living together.

The question arises, how, without having physical contact, can you enjoy the object? Can we be satisfied by remembering the delicious food, cherishing the sweet notes, and so on? No. There is little satisfaction in remembering those things, but it kindles for physical enjoyment and thereby creates anxiety and then despair. Such a condition is described in ten stages; they are *lālasā* (keen desire), *udyoga* (exertion), *jāgarya* (waking), *tanaba* (thinness), *jarima* (insensibility), *veiyagra* (distraction), *vyādhi* (sickness), *unmāda* (insanity), *moha* (perplexed) and *mṛtyu* (death) which are all explained in the book *Ujjvalanīlamaṇi*, a supplement to *Bhaktirasāmṛta Sindhu*. Thus, the practitioner has to meet death and destruction. But, the death that is used here is the stage in which the sense of the body is totally abandoned, and the astral body alone works. In the *yoga* system, ten stages are also described, which are concerned with different sounds being listened to. They are *laladighoṣa* (the sound produced when blowing with lolling tongue), *chanināda* (the sound of a cow having excretion), *mṛdaṅganāda* (the sound of a tom-tom), *ghaṇṭānāda* (the sound of bell), *kalanāda* (the sound of ankles), *kiṅkinīnāda* (the sound of the ornaments in the waist), *veṇunāda* (the note of the flute), *bhramaranāda* (the humming sound of bees), and *praṇavanāda* (the sound of *auṁkāra*), which are all explained in *Amṛta Gītā* of Swāmī Śivānanda Saraswatī. When the two are compared, the *gopī*s of Vrindavana could have listened to the eighth stage, that is, *veṇunāda*, the note of the flute, as is described in *Śrīmad Bhāgavata Mahāpurāṇa*, X Canto, 29th chapter. This shows that *rāgānuga bhakti* also takes a Yogic approach towards the Supreme. It is designed to foster human behaviours without trying to annihilate them as described in the stages of Patañjali Yoga or *ṣaḍ sampat* in *jñana-yoga*, but to use them towards the Lord. That is why, it is said, following the way of passion.

The question is, who practically showed the world that the way is infallible? Janaka, Sūryadeva, and others have proved that *karma-yoga* doctrines are true. Similarly, Jñānadeva, Śaṅkarācārya, and many others have proved that *jñāna-yoga* is the true way to be adopted for liberation. Similarly, innumerable *yogī*s, *bhakta*s, and other followers of several ways to the Lord had already proved the true ways they are. For this reason, the best example is Rādhārānī, who, without having physical relations for more than 100 and more years, could retain pure love for Śrī Kṛṣṇa regardless of the conduct of the Lord during that long time. It is said that, Rādhārānī was married to someone called Ayan (or Rayan) and left him with a blessing for Her stay in the groves of Vrindavana, just from the period Śrī Kṛṣṇa left Vrindavana for Mathurā. Thus, the foremost figure, Jagadguru of this way to God, is necessarily Śrī Rādhārānī. Hence, Rādhā-Kuṇḍa becomes the centre for the Manipuri Vaiṣṇavas.

Śrī Kṛṣṇa Caitanya is the next personality who proved Himself to be a Jagadguru of this way to God. He dropped all sāṁsāric relations and became a *saṁnyāsī* who found out the places related to Śrī Kṛṣṇa and Rādhārānī, assisted by His devotees like Sanātana, Jīva, Rūpa, Raghunātha, and other Goswāmīs (saints), the forgotten Rādhā-Kuṇḍa, Śyāma-Kuṇḍa and several other important places in Vrindavana by His Divine power. Thus, Navadwip in West Bengal becomes the centre for the Manipuri Vaiṣṇavas. The last days of Caitanya Mahāprabhu were in Purī, Odisha. Therefore, a Manipuri Vaiṣṇava had to visit Navadwip, Purī, and Vrindavana, and other places become secondary choices for them.

History tells us that the presentation of a Viṣṇu Cakra by the king of Pong, Choufa Khekhomba, to the king of Manipur/Meitei, Kiyamba (1467-1508 CE) may be regarded as the entrance of Hinduism in this state. But, the actual date for the introduction of *rāgānuga bhakti*, as is now following, may be the time of Rājarṣi Bhāgyacandra Mahārāja (1759-98 CE). Manipuris followed the Rāmānandī sect during the time of Garībniwāj Mahārāja (1709-48 CE).

It is a well-known fact that Rājarṣi Bhāgyacandra, introduced by Rāsa Līlā, the Naṭa Saṅkīrtana, and a host of others, is regarded as an unparalleled gift of the Rājarṣi to the people. The son Chourajit Mahārāja carried out the father's wish by bringing the king's ashes to Vrindavana, Rādhā-Kuṇḍa. Thereby, it was embedded in the soil. Chourajit Mahārāja established the Rāsabihārī Mandira there in 1799 CE, and hence many others from Manipur were established there in later days.

3

On the Way to Braja-Vrindavana

A Reflection on Khangembam Gulapi's *Manaḥ Śikṣā*

Kakchingtabam Ruhinikumar Sharma

Introduction

Hinduism began to establish its presence in the hilly kingdom of Manipur during the latter half of the fifteenth century CE. However, it was not until the eighteenth century that it achieved dominance over other religious beliefs and practices, largely due to the active support and patronage from the rulers of this kingdom. Consequently, various sects of Hinduism, including Rāmānandī, Nīmānandī, and Gauḍīya Vaiṣṇavism, have continued to thrive in the region. The rise and expansion of these sects also coincided with the introduction of diverse art forms such as *kīrtana, saṅkīrtana, nāṭa saṅkīrtana,* and *rāsa-līlā,* alongside numerous religious rituals and celebrations. Additionally, Manipur's interactions with Bengal, the birthplace of Caitanya Mahāprabhu, contributed to the development of a distinctive form of Manipuri Vaiṣṇavism rooted in the Gauḍīya Sampradāya, which facilitated the incorporation of works like *Gīta Govinda* by Jayadeva, Caṇḍīdās, and Vidyāpati into the cultural fabric of Manipur's *maṇḍapa*s.

In this regard, the esteemed historian Gangmumei Kabui remarked,

> "The Manipuris worshipped God through dance and music in their traditional religion. When the spirit of Vaiṣṇavism pervaded the whole Hindu community of the kingdom specially the king, it was revealed in his dream, the composition of the *Rāsa-Līlā*" (Gangmumei Kabui, 1991: 276).

Thus, devotional and mystic poems and songs that were recited and sung became an inseparable part of the Manipuri Hindu way of life. Till the beginning of the twentieth century, the lyrics of *kīrtana*s and *nāṭa saṅkīrtana*s were rendered through Bengali and Sanskrit language as there was a ban on any attempt at translation or original composition in Manipuri (E. Nilakanta Singh, 1993: 95).

Since the third decade of the twentieth century, Manipuri literature has progressively emerged from the influence of Bengali language and literature, a transition that scholars have identified as the beginning of a renaissance in Manipur. This period saw an increasing desire for devotional and mystical songs to be performed in the Manipuri language. The first recorded instance of a Bāsak performance in the native language took place at a *maṇḍapa* in the Singjamei locality, as documented in *Cheitharol Kumbaba*, the royal chronicle of Manipur (L. Iboongohal Singh & N. Khelchandra Singh, 1989: 611). This significant development was facilitated by the patronage of Mahārājā Churachand Singh, who reigned from 1891 to 1941 CE.

Chatlo pukning braja vrindavanada
Katcharuro thawai hakchang
Hari magi charanda

Why remain fumbling O ignorant heart?
Go to Braja-Vrindavana where Hari sits
And throw thyself at His feet.

Free translation: O ignorant mind, O Human being, go to Vrindavana, offer your body and soul at the feet of Lord Śrī Hari.

Kakthatlamlo kallaba mayagi thouri
Atatpa leitana sonjaruro hari nam

Away from the nascent world,
Cut off all ties of attachment
And sing His praises ceaselessly.

Free translation: Detach the tough string of illusion by singing the rhyme of Lord Hari ceaselessly.

Ngasi ngasi haiduna ngasi kaya houkhre
Eigi haiba wakhanda luptuna leire

Imperceptibly days went by
While you remained indulged
In futile desires.

Free translation: Passed many days of life still clinging on your life in self-fulfilment,

Phangamdaba meeoiba hangjaraga kaobra
Khudum singna laklaga khubam tingna hangera

Why would you undo this rare human birth?
You came with a divine purpose,
Why are you trying to go empty handed?

Free translation: After attainment as human being you came with tight fists; do you intend to get back with empty palm.

Hari nam sonjabada matam charoi karamno
Hari ningna langam phiral thetpa yaokhina

It is never late in singing praises of the Lord.
Prayer in the heart and praises on the lips,
Many had come out with flying colours.

Free translation: There is no time bound in chanting hymn of Lord Hari and many got flying colours with devotion to Lord Hari.

Angang oina ningjakhiba prahladana kamdoukhi
Matam chadri khangjadaba dhruva kari phangjakhi

As a child devotee, remember,
What happened to Prahlāda?
And what became of Dhruva, the immortal?

Free translation: What happened to boyhood Prahlāda, what did achieve the innocent Dhruva.

Shiva mahadebamakna uphul waiphul teiduna
Harinam sonjabani mongphamda phamduna
Gopeswar haiba mingthol ama phangjakhi
Vrindavanada leiduna thongngapa oijakhi

Even Lord Mahādeva, painted in dust and ashes,
Sat in the grave in deep meditation
And, later known as Gopeśvara,
Became Hari's doorman at Braja-Vrindavana.

Free translation: With smearing ashes Lord Mahādeva by chanting Hymn to Lord Hari by sitting in the grave in deep meditation. Received the the of Gopeśvara and then became a door keeper at Vrindavana.

Chatlasira hanna hanna eeraknaba asida
Pokpa siba naidana magi nakta leijaba
Apambado ninglabadi phangjagani soidana
Phangjagani soidana kari pamba nahakna pinaheiba harini

Repeatedly drowned in the ocean of sorrow,
And full of frustrations is that what you are?
Surrender to Hari, you will find eternal bliss at His feet.

Free translation: To immerse in the mortal ocean of life, we shall get immortal life if we stay in devotion to Lord Hari, the kind-hearted Hari, pray.

Sadhu sangga touduna lambi mashak khangjahou
Lamjingbiba kanano sri-guruda hangjahou
Guru kripa nattanadi hallakkani soidana
Changjou naidraba eepak lanbigani kanana

Learn the right path from the seers,
Heed to the advice from the divine *gurus*,
Lest you will be thrown back once again into the churning ocean of life.

Free translation: What your desire is? Make friendship with esteemed mentor seek to know the true path, He will be your leading savior. Make an approach to *guru*; without his benignly blessing you will be retracted. He will help you in crossing the implicit ocean of earthly life.

A Few Words about Manaḥ Śikṣā

Manaḥ Śikṣā, literally translated as "Teachings for the Mind" is a genre of devotional songs composed and popularized by Raghunātha Dāsa Goswāmī, one of the six Goswāmīs who are the principal assistants of Caitanya Mahāprabhu. Tradition is that it was the six Goswāmīs who not only founded this holy city of Vrindavana but also firmly established the teachings of Caitanya through their various writings. They explained the doctrine and philosophy of Caitanya for the benefit of the whole world. The two brothers, Rūpa and Sanātana Goswāmīs were ordered by Lord Caitanya in the year 1516 to go and live in Vrindavana and search out all the lost holy places connected with Lord Śrī Kṛṣṇa's transcendental pastimes. He also ordered them to compile books on the great science of *bhakti-yoga*, the process of devotional service to God. In their sacred mission, Rūpa and Sanātana Goswāmīs were ably assisted by Raghunātha Dāsa, Raghunātha Bhaṭṭa, Gopāla Bhaṭṭa and Jīva who altogether formed the famous transcendental group, the six Goswāmīs of Vrindavana (https://www.radharaman.org/the-six-goswamis/#1590731729246-a664a3b2-17df).

Though born to a wealthy family Raghunātha Dāsa is said to have showed a particular disinterest in everyday pleasures and an interest in more religious pursuits from a relatively young age. This was much to the displeasure of his parents, who eventually took to hiring guards in order to prevent Raghunātha Dāsa from leaving the family home with the aim of having a simpler life elsewhere. Eventually Raghunātha Dāsa escaped their home and made a journey to Jagannātha Purī where he met his *guru*, Caitanya Mahāprabhu.

According to accounts in the *Caitanya Caritāmṛta*, written by Kṛṣṇadāsa Kavirāja Goswāmī, Raghunātha Dāsa led a life of extreme devotional practice. In this connection, Raghunātha Dāsa is quoted as saying:

> "If one's heart has been cleansed by perfect knowledge and one has understood Kṛṣṇa, the Supreme *Brahman*, he then gains everything. Why should such a person act like a debauchee by trying very carefully to maintain his material body?"

Raghunātha Dāsa Goswāmī served Caitanya for sixteen years at Jagannātha Purī. After which he went to Vrindavana in *c.*1543-44, where he lived for many years at a sacred lake known as Rādhā-Kuṇḍa (https://www.radharaman.org/the-six-goswamis/#1590743829879-6ca366c7-4ff2).

It is beyond the purview of this paper to dwell at length all the twelve verses of *Manaḥ* written and sung by Raghunātha Dāsa for the popularization of the *bhakti* cult, which is core to Caitanya's teaching; it would be suffice to say that it had a lasting impact in shaping the world view of Vaiṣṇavite Hindus more particularly in Bengal and beyond.

Khangembam Gulapi Singh and His Manaḥ Śikṣā

Khangembam Gulapi Singh (1919-81), popularly known as Guru Gulapi Singh Sangeet Ratna, was one of the most popular exponents of Manipuri *nāṭa saṅkīrtana,* which forms the core of Manipuri Gauḍīya Sampradāya. No ritualistic ceremony is considered complete without a *saṅkīrtana* performance, and it was through these performances Guru Gulapi earned not only a name and fame but also created a niche for himself since his youthful days. What makes Gulapi distinct from other artists of his time is his ability to sing and perform with īlan and his ability to render in the native language of the land, though there has been a tradition of performing through the Bengali language interspersed with Sanskrit texts. Most of the Bāsak performances one witnessed in the local language were the most important contribution of Guru Gulapi Singh. Apart from being a performer, Gulapi Singh was also a well-versed lyricist and composer. *Shri Shri Goura Govinda Thouram Sheireng*, written by Khangembam Gulapi Singh, is one of the remarkable books on the translation of *Vaiṣṇava Padāvalī* in Manipuri. His lyrics on *Manaḥ Śikṣā,* though based on *Vaiṣṇava Padāvalī,* are very popular among every section of Manipuri Vaiṣṇavites as in these lyrics, he could capture the nuances and intricacies of human nature in a simple yet beautifully rendered style which could be understood even by the common folk. Through this song, the artiste prodded people to give up pride and develop wonderful love and devotion to the spiritual master, the abode of Braja, the people of Braja, the saintly devotees only through one will get the ultimate bliss and free one from the false ego, deceitfulness, and crookedness.

Acknowledgements

The author is grateful to Shri Ngangom Iboton Singh and Shri Laishram Damudor Singh of Khongman Mangjil, Imphal East, respectively, for their help in making possible the English translation of Guru Khangembam Gulapi's nuanced lyric of *Manaḥ Śikṣā*.

NOTES

1. Gangmumei Kabui (1991), *History of Manipur*, Volume-I: *Pre-colonial Period*, New Delhi.
2. E. Nilakanta Singh (1993), *Fragments of Manipuri Culture*, New Delhi.
3. On Saturday, 4 April 1931, Bāsak singing in Manipuri (Meitei language) was performed at Mukhtyar *maṇḍapa* at Singjamei locality lead by Shri Waikhom Chaoba Singh who was a high ranking official of the kingdom. *Source*: L. Iboongohal Singh & N. Khelchandra Singh (1989), *Cheitharol Kumbaba*: *The Royal Chronicle of Manipur*, Imphal.

   "শজিবু থা ইরাইনা হল্লে । ২নি থাংজাদা শিংজমৈ মুক্তারগী মান্দোপ্তা ৱাইখোম চাওবনা মৈতৈ লোননা বাশোক শকপা হৌদোকএ"। চৈথারোল কুম্বাবা- লমায় ৬১১: ফোংবা চহী ইং: ১৯৮৯; ইম্ফাল ।
4. Aman Kashyap (2023), *The Six Goswamis of Vrindavana,* 18 May. https://vrajvrindavan.com/six-goswamis/#:~:text=Srila Prabhupada and Aindra Prabhu, pure unalloyed loving devotional service and text.
5. Khangembam Gulapi Singh (2010), *Shri Shri Goura Govinda Thouram Sheireng*, 4th edition, Imphal.

4

The Rādhā-Kuṇḍa of the Bhūloka-Braja-Vrindavana

The Tīrthasthāna of Manipuri Gauḍīya Vaiṣṇavas

P. Milan Khangamcha and *L. Bishwanath Sharma*

Introduction

For the last four centuries since the eighteenth century, as the historic contribution by the spiritual vision and royal patronage of Rājarṣi Bhāgyacandra, the Rādhā-Kuṇḍa of the Bhūloka-Braja-Vrindavana has been a holy *tīrthasthāna* of the Manipuri Hindus falling under Gauḍīya Vaiṣṇava religious denomination. The human world, including the so-called purely rational or scientific, reason-based modern world, is constituted by various mythical, cultural, spiritual, and philosophical ideas, values, ideologies, and thoughts. Hence, it is pointless to question the alleged historical facticity of the mythical stories related to the epical narratives of the *Mahābhārata*, which comes under the traditional Indian literary genre of *itihāsa* and its extended Paurāṇic *kathā* of the divinity of the Lord Kṛṣṇa, and the earthly manifestation of His transcendental histrionics of Nitya-Līlā and its central spiritual theme of Rāsa-Līlā in the Bhūloka-Braja-Vrindavana. The contiguity between myth and the real world is an ever-present structural component of every model of civilization in the history of the human world. The so-called modern world, which is accepted today as a universal, scientific, secular, liberal, and democratic colonial legacy, is the direct historical outcome of the Greco-Latin and Biblical, mythical narratives of the colonial West.[1] This is evident from the fact that, till today, every religion in the world has a "mytho-geographical" belief, wherein a particular geographical space is associated with some religious belief. This perhaps has something to do with the unconscious element in the finite human mind, which acts as the driving power of the works of those extraordinary personalities belonging to art, religion, philosophy, and science that brought sharp turning points in human history. In this context, as an ethnic reconstruction, and to that extent, a synthesis of local and incoming elements of an indigenously revisualized Gauḍīya Vaiṣṇava religious philosophy of Bengal which was not imposed from outside, but it was so ingeniously adapted by the eighteenth-century monarch of Manipur—Rājarṣi Bhāgyacandra (Meidingu Chingthangkhomba 1763-98 CE).[2] Yet, it had become a highly ethnicized, self-sufficient version of the *Devotional Religion* (that is, the traditional path of *bhakti* is its own end and not *mokṣa*) of the then kingdom of Manipur. Nevertheless, it is based on the totally aestheticized Bengal Vaiṣṇavism which was established on the basis of the God intoxicated Divine Persona of Śrī Kṛṣṇa Caitanya Mahāprabhu's (1486-1533) lifelong ecstatic rapture of a historically uncommon spiritual experience of bridal mysticism (*nāyikā-nāyaka bhāva*—the erotico-aesthetic symbolism of mystic experience). Till today, no contemporary Indian scholars in the field of Vedānta are aware of the fact that this unique form of aesthetic-devotional worship (*rasopāsanā*) of the spontaneous and eternal play of *rasa* as the self-expression of the bliss-potency (*hlādinī śakti*)—the innermost core of the potencies of the Lord Kṛṣṇa is the last easternmost cultural and religious frontier of the pan-Indian devotional religion of monotheistic Vedānta. This may be very well deemed as what has been missing in the pan-Indian collective spiritual and cultural consciousness. This has serious political implications in the matters of National Integration and the very idea of Bhāratavarṣa, which, as a matter of principle, is supposed to be inclusive.

Therefore, the Meitei Hindus today earnestly long for the national consciousness to give a respectable highlight to this religio-historical fact and to include it in the reimagined idea of Bhārata. If this historic phase of the then Manipur which is still a living spiritual and sociocultural tradition is reflected in the finale blueprint of the problematic task of accomplishing the still pending task of the national integration would go a long way in making it as the source of internal strength of the country. Since, even in this century of science and technology dominated global society, unlike the developed Western countries, Bhārata might be the only country where tradition and change have been so well weaved into its social, cultural, economic, and political systems in the absence of such a necessary condition the country's inner strength, the dream for Akhaṇḍa Bhārata may face innumerable obstacles. Before, Bhārata ventures out into the highly competitive process of globalization, first it needs to have a soul searching introspective insight of the said inner source of motivating its citizens. The saintly king Bhāgyacandra Mahārāja did certainly had a political vision of making his tiny kingdom to be culturally and spiritually connected to the mainland Indian Hindu kingdoms for ushering into an integral world of peace, harmony, and happiness. Thus, he had relinquished his earthly throne to Śrī Śrī Govindajī, was installed at the palatial temple as the Divine King of his kingdom, and carried on with the mundane task of ruling only as that of a trustee king of the Supreme Lord. This was not the fiction or the wild gaze of Bhāgyacandra. The *Gītā* V.29 supports it when the Lord Himself speaks in the first person as—

भोक्तारं यज्ञतपस्यां सर्वलोकममहेश्वरम् ।
सुहृदं सर्वभूमानां ज्ञात्वा मां शान्तिमृच्छति ।।

> Knowing Me as the enjoyer of all sacrifices and austerities, as the Supreme Lord of all the worlds, as the Friend of every being, he attains peace.[3]

The ingenuity, power of his spiritual persuasion, and depth of his faith lies in that it became so much of a naturalized form of religious practice of the people of the valley of Manipur despite its being located at such a remote and ethno-culturally so different north-eastern most corner of Bhārata. The chaste and faithful character of the Manipuri Vaiṣṇavas is only explainable in terms of the ways the dexterity and seamless nature in which the pre-existing elements of the aesthetic, spiritual performance of the Lai Haraoba were weaved into the very textures of the incoming aesthetic performance oriented Bengal Vaiṣṇavism. It was entirely based on the reimagined spiritual vision of Rājarṣi Bhāgyacandra. This explains the truth behind the fact that it was an internally generated spiritual process and not an externally enforced religio-cultural transformation, as the heralding of a new form of Vaiṣṇavism is what is described as "the Meiteization of Hinduism and not Hinduization of the Meiteis". Yet, it did not, and it still does not make the Manipuri Gauḍīya Dharma ethnocentric. This is evident from the expanding social, cultural, and spiritual consciousness of the chaste and pious Manipuri Vaiṣṇavas' seen in their seeking residence as the Rādha-Kuṇḍa of the Bhūloka-Braja-Vrindavana as their supreme abode (Rūpa Goswāmī and other followers of Caitanya calls it as the manifested—*prakaṭa* while the eternal play of *rāsa* at the original Braja-Vrindavana remains as unmanifested—*aprakaṭa* to the ordinary mortals). The well-known Meitei Hindus' expression—"the departed soul has attained at the Holy Dhāma of the Braja-Vrindavana—*vrindavana prāpta oikhre*" (printed on the invitation of the *śrāddha saṁskāra* of the deceased near and dear ones. Hence, it is quite understandable as to why the elderly Gauḍīya Vaiṣṇavas of Manipur used to visit the Bhūloka-Braja-Vrindavana—especially its spiritually significant Rādhā-Kuṇḍa as an accomplishment of their religious lives, and many have their spiritual longing to leave their bodies at this Holy Dhāma as a *sanctum sanctorum*. The co-author of this piece (P. Milan Khangamcha) had the rare opportunity to perform this rite for his maternal grandfather as per his death wish in 1988 at the Rādhā-Kuṇḍa during one of his visits to the Vrindavana for collecting Sanskrit texts of Jīva Goswāmī from Haridāsa Śāstrī at Kālīya Ghāṭ. Their frequent pilgrimage (*tīrthayātrā*) to this sacred place is a part of their form of devotional worship, which is more oriented towards an "inwardized spiritual movement of contemplative devotional worship" (*rasopāsanā* or *antaraṅga-sādhanā*) facilitated by the communicative aesthetic recreation of the unmanifest (*aprakaṭa*), eternal (*nitya*) Rāsa-Līlā/Krīḍā or the play of *rāsa* of the transcendental realm here on the earth in its visible or manifest form (*prakaṭa*) as the highest form of the spiritual state consisting in the play of *rāsa* as a transcendental histrionics of Rādhā and Kṛṣṇa's *prema-bhakti rasa* eternally played in the original Goloka Dhāma (*rāgātmaka-bhakti*).

No other denominations of Vaiṣṇava Sampradāya had ever carried out such a well imagined masterpiece and classical level reconstruction in the form of the aesthetico-ritual contemplative worship of *jagoi-rāsa* as the spiritual rendering of the Vrindavana Līlā here on the earth. This performative enactment as an "aesthetic-devotional contemplative worship" is telescoped within or projected from the larger framework of the form of the devotional worship of the millennium—*saṅkīrtana mahāyajña* as a highly ritualized aesthetic-devotional performance of *nāṭa saṅkīrtana* of Manipur. This is called as Navadvīpa Līlā where as *jagoi-rāsa* is the Braja-Līlā and they are conjoined by an episode ritual narrative called *tīna-vāñcha* in Gauḍīya Vaiṣṇavism. The first is centred around the five divinities—*pañca-tattva* led by Śrī Kṛṣṇa Caitanya, who leads the devotees to the innermost of worship consisting in the contemplation on the original Braja-Līlā recreated in its full form of devotional performance in Manipur as the *jagoi-rāsa*. The well-integrated but unfailing power of aesthetic communication is used in this contemplative worship. This performative act was never enacted in the land of its birth (Bengal) to benefit the Bengali Vaiṣṇavas. Their only access to this spiritual content was only via the highly authentic and powerful Bengali folk devotional songs. In this contemplative worship devotees are called *sahṛdaya* (spectator, "one of similar heart") and they are enabled to undergo the same *bhakti rasa* embodied in the *jagoi-rāsa* by its built-in power of "aesthetic communication". Hence, this is also called *rasopāsanā* as another expression of *antaraṅga-sādhanā*.

Nāṭa saṅkīrtana is the Manipuri version of Śrī Caitanya's *saṅkīrtana mahāyajña*, which has been in vogue since the eighteenth century. *Nāṭa saṅkīrtana* and *jagoi-rāsa* are religio-philosophically interrelated; the former as the outward ritual stage of life in general and the latter as the performance of its core spiritual essence. The said dynamic core spiritual essence portrayed in and through the aesthetic form of *rāgānuga-bhakti-sādhanā* is the earthly recreation of the eternal play of *rāsa* of Goloka. It is the highest *sādhanā-bhakti*, and it is modelled after the *rāgātmaka-bhakti* of the original eternal relation of devotional love between Lord Śrī Kṛṣṇa and his eternal associates (*parikaras*)—*gopīs* led by Braja-Sundarī and Brajeśvarī Kalaṅkiṇī Śrīmatī Rādhikā. Rāsa-Līlā or Krīḍa is the tasting of the pure delight or the disinterested joy of the highest state of the *madhurā bhāva-bhakti* in its *parakīyā śṛṅgāra prema bhāva. Rasa* is the pure devotional sentiment born out of this transcendental histrionics of the Braja-Vrindavana. *Jagoi-rāsa* as the re-enactment of Braja-Līlā is telescoped within or projected as a play out of the *nāṭa saṅkīrtana* as the recreation of the Navadvīpa Līlā of Manipuri Gauḍīya Dharma is an aesthetically enabled and historically unprecedented form of "contemplative devotional worship". The complicated ritual, aesthetics, and philosophical explanations are done in the light of the concept of *tīna-vañcha* (three theological episodes).

Three theological episodes of Gauḍīya Dharma of Śrī Kṛṣṇa Caitanya Mahāprabhu were established on the divinity of his spiritual persona and the nature of his uncommon mystic experience. These three religious phenomena also connect the Navadvīpa Līlā and Vrindavana Līlā in the theology of the Gauḍīya Vaiṣṇava Dharma of both Bengal and Manipur. They have become so succinctly visible in the social and cultural embodiments Manipuri Vaiṣṇava faith which have a continuity between Rādhā-Krṣṇa's dalliance during the epic period of the *Mahābhārata* and the advent of this Divine Love embodied in the androgynic form of Śrī Caitnaya's Divine Persona in the Navadīpa as it was and is still believed by His followers as such as internally Lord Kṛṣṇa who took His advent in the outward mood of the divine pathos of Rādhā's *viraha*. Therefore, Bhūloka-Braja-Vrindavana as the only spatio-temporal context of the advent of the Parama Bhāgavata in His Self-Same Form (Svayam Bhagavān) of being the Supreme Being Himself is related to the question as to why the Manipuri Vaiṣṇavas take the holy *dhāma* as the transcendental theatre of the Nitya-Līlā as the ultimate aim of life.

No human world is freed from some element of "self-transcendence" or the other. Myth or faith comes into the picture of every human world, ancient, medieval, and modern. It is this elemental human desire for self-transcendence in the form of a perpetual existence of partaking of the "pure devotional sentiments (*prema-bhakti-rasa*)" here and now and also in the future journey of their souls which is beyond the highest traditional Vedāntic spiritual goal of *puruṣārtha-mokṣa*. It is this spiritual journey that the devout Manipuri Vaiṣṇavas dream and their pilgrimage to Braja-Vrindavana and Rādhā-Kuṇḍa is a real expression of it. In the earlier times before Second World War, many of them took their spiritual journey on foot taking more than three months all the way to this holy place far away from the torturous wild animal infested difficult hilly terrains of the tiny hilly kingdom of Manipur. Many of them died on the way, and against all odds, those who were lucky to survive the dangerous journey made their way to the earthly Goloka of Braja. It was this spiritual spirit that, after the death of Rājarṣi Bhāgyacandra (1798), his third son Yuvarāja Chourjit[2] had visited the holy *dhāma* as the first of its kind by any member of the royal family of the eighteenth-century Manipur after the Gauḍīya Vaiṣṇava Dharma was established as a fully developed and institutionalized state religion to take pilgrimage to the Bhūloka Braja-Vrindavana. He had undertaken this *tīrthayātrā* as the fulfilment of both his spiritual aspiration and also to honour the last religious wish his father Rājarṣi Bhāgyacandra. He had carried out the wish of his father to perform the last rite (*śrāddha karma*) at the most scared pramagatism of the Manipuri Vaiṣṇavas — Rādhā-Kuṇḍa at the earthly Braja-Vrindavana. And many of the members of the royal family, as well as the ordinary Manipuri Gauḍīya Vaiṣṇavas had followed suit after that. And this religious tradition of taking residence, leaving one's body or spending the last days of life and performance of death rite at this holy *dhāma* became a very important part of the faith and religious practices of the Manipuri Vaiṣṇavas since the eighteenth century. The royal families of Manipur had established royal residences near the temple of Jagannātha at Purī (Odisha), in and around Braja-Vrindavana, Rādhā-Kuṇḍa and Navadvīpa. Many other devout Manipuri Vaiṣṇavas also had their different temples as the facilitations of worship to the state's Vaiṣṇavas on pilgrimage in the holy *dhāma*. This in fact was the first beginning of the ways how the socioculturally expressed religious consciousness of the valley Meities were taking shape well beyond their tiny kingdom in the eighteenth century and thereafter. But, the most painful thing is that it has been this community that holds the last and easternmost frontier of the cultural and religious frontier of the country well within the idea of the pan-Bhārata consciousness that is yet to be acknowledged by all concerns.

Some Highlights of Manipuri's Connection with Rādhā-Kuṇḍa

To a Manipuri Hindu, Rādhā-Kuṇḍa is known as the most holiest of all the religious places and it is known in an inclusive sense where exits different religious places like Govardhana, Vrindavana, Rādhā-Kuṇḍa, Śyāma-Kuṇḍa, etc. The importance of these places and their religious narratives reflected in the *Śrīmad Bhāgavatam* have imprinted in the souls of each and every Manipuri Vaiṣṇava. They are considered the ultimate goals in their lives. It is a strong faith that the people of Manipur particularly Vaiṣṇava who have a firm commitment in both hearts and souls to visit on a pilgrimage to Rādhā-Kuṇḍa for sanctifying their bodies and souls that have been polluted by the forbidden acts in the past lives. Manipuri Vaiṣṇavas always remember the story told in the *Śrīmad Bhāgavatam* for washing off the sins, including even a wrongdoing done to Lord Śrī Kṛṣṇa.

According to popular legend, when Lord Kṛṣṇa slew a mighty *asura* (demon) in the form of a bull, his consort Rādhā asked Kṛṣṇa to wash off His sins by taking dips in various holy rivers. Kṛṣṇa laughed it off and struck the ground with his foot, whereupon all the river goddesses emerged in front of them and filled the ground with their water. Kṛṣṇa bathed in this *kuṇḍa* (temple tank) to please Rādhā. Later, this water reservoir is called Śyāma-Kuṇḍa. Opposite to Śyāma-Kuṇḍa, Rādhā and her friends also dug out the ground which was filled with the holy water of Śyāma-Kuṇḍa, by Kṛṣṇa. This water reservoir is named after Rādhā and is called Rādhā-Kuṇḍa. Kṛṣṇa then took a bath in the Rādhā-Kuṇḍa and announced that whoever takes a bath in Rādhā-Kuṇḍa will be blessed with the intense love (*prema-bhakti*) which Rādhārāṇī has for him. Similarly, Rādhārāṇī also took a bath in the Śyāma-Kuṇḍa and announced that whosoever takes a bath in Śyāma-Kuṇḍa would be blessed with the love that Kṛṣṇa has for her. To this day, millions of pilgrims desiring to relish the selfless Divine Love between Rādhā-Kṛṣṇa come to this holy spot to take a bath in a reverential mood, bathing first in Rādhā-Kuṇḍa, then in Śyāma-Kuṇḍa, and then again in Rādhā-Kuṇḍa. This is the only place of pilgrimage where the auspicious bath is taken at midnight. The Manipuri Vaiṣṇavas also followed this practice since they embraced Vaiṣṇavism as their religion.

Many pious and devout Manipuri Vaiṣṇavas take a vow to visit the Rādhā-Kuṇḍa in the Braja-Vrindavana at least once in their lifetime, and many more still go on pilgrimage every year in the group by bus till today. The depth and scope of the spiritual involvement of the Manipuri Vaiṣṇavas with the inclusive ancient Indian spiritual heritage in every sense as an expression of the original holistic Vedic world view encompassing geographical spread, its contextual historico-cultural developments and its ever-growing dynamic "inner spiritual movement" in its form of Vedāntic monotheism which was launched by Śrī Rāmānuja Ācārya in the eleventh century Tamil Nadu is the natural expression of the pan-Indian spirit of synthesis. It is the historical precipitation of the sixth- and fifth-century movement of the Bhāgavata Dharma with Lord Kṛṣṇa as its Central Personal Absolute—the Divine Speaker of the *Śrīmad Bhagavadgītā*. This spiritual persuasion and its cultural expression, in some form or the other, more indirectly, entered the land of the ancient kingdom of Manipur. As a tiny geographical space surrounded by vast Southeast Asian countries and a highly mobile warrior people of Manipur riding on horsebacks with the skills of cavalry warfare which had travelled right up to southern China where the impacts of the inevitable influences of the sociocultural, spiritual, and philosophical ideas, values, and thoughts of the ancient Indian civilization were already felt in the form of Buddhism including Vedic religion (Hinduism), it is unthinkable that the cultural consciousness and its geographical embodiment were only explainable as per autochthonous reasons.

Therefore, it is highly unlikely that the eighteenth-century wholesome embracing of Hinduism in the form of its version of Manipuri Gauḍīya Vaiṣṇavism on the basis of the royal patronage of the eighteenth-century king of

Manipur—Śrī Rājarṣi Bhāgyacandra of Manipur who made it a state religion was a sort of historical accidence. That is, it a sheer impossibility to believe that the spread of Hinduism in Manipur was an external imposition as if it did not have any preceding spiritual, cultural, and philosophical contiguity with the highly versatile, ever expanding, ever growing, malleable, accommodative and inclusive ancient Indian civilization. These are some of the important points to be remembered while speaking about the reason as to why the holy *dhāma* of Rādhā-Kuṇḍa of the Bhūloka Braja-Vrindavana became a very important theo-geographical space called *tīrtha-sthāna* for the majority Hindu Meitei population of the State of Manipur.

Some Important Temples of Braja-Vrindavana Run by the Manipuri Vaiṣṇavas

The contemporary relevance of Śrī Kṛṣṇa Caitanya or Gauḍāṅga Mahāprabhu of Bengal, who was one of the medieval *bhakti* saints would be that it is only in his religion in which the Vedāntic *bhakti sādhanā* (*mārga* or *yoga*)—the path of devotional worship ceases to be a mere *upāya* or the means (*sādhanā-bhakti*) for the attainment of the highest spiritual perfection. It has led to the idea of the *sādhya bhakti*—"*bhakti* as an end in itself" in the form of *prema-bhakti* as the highest spiritual value. Jīva Goswāmī had interpreted the highest state of devotional love of Rādhā and Kṛṣṇa as the *pañcama puruṣārtha* or *parama puruṣārtha* of Gauḍīya Dharma and, thus *mokṣa* is not the highest spiritual attainment). Hence, *prema-bhakti* as the central theme of this form of Vaiṣṇavism makes Śrī Kṛṣṇa Caitanya's religion as a "*bhakti* religion" which applies only to Bengal or Manipuri Vaiṣṇavism. Krishna Sharma (1987) in his *Bhakti and the Bhakti Movement: A New Perspective—A Study in the History of Ideas*[4] puts forward this view. His view can very well be defended. Thus, it is no longer about a mere path of spiritual worship in the sense that traditional popular devotional worship has been in vogue in mainstream Vaiṣṇavism. This point is related to the plot of *prema-bhakti rasa* in its form of the bridal mysticism of the Rāsapañcādhyāya of the *Śrīmad Bhāgavata*'s Daśama Skandha as the fundamental theme of the Nitya-Līlā. The relish of the disinterested joy of the *prema-bhakti rasa* of the *parakīyā* form of *śṛṅgāra madhura bhakti* between Śrīmatī Rādhikā and Lord Śrī Kṛṣṇa of the Goloka Vrindavana is the ultimate spiritual aspiration of the Manipuri Vaiṣṇavas. This spiritual aim is the basis of the spiritual life and its pan-regional cultural expression of the valley population of Manipur in their desires to visit Bhūloka Braja-Vrindavana in UP. The most important factor is the larger spiritual, cultural, and geographical landscape of the religious consciousness of the people of Manipur as it is seen in the seriousness of spiritual intent with which the Hindus of Manipur had so far come live and its being majority religion of the state of Manipur. Hence, the conserving and taking care of the places of worship of the Manipuri Vaiṣṇavas in the holy *dhāma* of the Rādhā-Kuṇda and its adjoining geographical spread of the Bhūloka Braja-Vrindavana would go a long way in the interests of the ancient Indian spirit of holism which Akhaṇḍa Bhārata is all about. The geographical distance between Manipur, located at a remote corner of north-east India, and Rādhā-Kuṇḍa is so easily overlooked by the Vaiṣṇavas of Manipur. And losing this sense of geographical remoteness in their sense of cultural and spiritual nearness observed in the religious fervour of *tīrthayātrā*, permanent residence and wishing to die at the Rādhā-Kuṇḍa is the sign of the cross-geographical transfiguration of religious consciousness in the minds of the Hindus of Manipur. That it is something to do with their spiritual life as a historic reality would certainly contribute to the vision of the Undivided Future of India. And losing those temples of the *gaddi* of the Royal families and other smaller temples own and run by the devout Hindus for the last three or four centuries with permanent residences at the Rādhā-Kuṇḍa at the Braja-Vrindavana will be a serious impediment to their Vaiṣṇava faiths and religious practices. Without these temples of the royal families of Manipur in the Rādhā-Kuṇḍa, the Hindus of Manipur will lose their very heart and soul. The above points will be augmented by the following list of temples in the Rādhā-Kuṇḍa of the Manipuri Vaiṣṇavas, called *gaddi*, which have been serving the Manipuri pilgrims.

Gaddis of the Royal Families

1. Though, *nāṭa-saṅkīrtana* and *jagoi-rāsa* were the Manipuri reconstructions by Meidingoo Chingthang-khomba alias Bhāgyacandra Mahārāja as fully developed ritual theatrical performances—the first one as highly classical *saṅkīrtana mahāyajña* of Śrī Kṛṣṇa Caitanya Mahāprabhu and the latter as the visible rendering of the eternal Rāsa-Līlā of the Braja-Vrindavana, the king did not visit the holy *dhāma*. Thus, his unaccomplished desire to go to Rādhā-Kuṇḍa in the sacred place was fulfilled by his son Meidingoo Chourjit. As it has been already referred to, he was the first king of Manipur who had undertaken the *tīrthayātrā* to Rādhā-Kuṇḍa between 1798 and 1800 CE. His main spiritual mission was to carry out the last wish of his father, Rājarṣi Bhāgyacandra, to perform his *śrāddha-karma* at the Rādhā-Kuṇḍa.
2. Gambhīr Singh Mahārāja (1825-1834) constructed the biggest royal Gaddi or Boḍo Kuñja (with a temple of Rādhā-Govindajī near Śyāma-Kuṇḍa and Lalitā-Kuṇḍa.
3. Narasingh Mahārāja (1844-1850) constructed the Yuvarāja Kuñja with a temple named Naval Govinda near Rādhā-Kuṇḍa.
4. Sir Chudachand Mahārāja (1892-1941) constructed Śrī Gopālajī Mandira at the north-western corner of the bank of the Rādhā-Kuṇḍa.

Minor Gaddis run by ordinary and influential Manipuri

Vaiṣṇavas or nobles:

1. Śrī Vinoda Mandira
2. Rādhārājabihārī Mandira
3. Giridhārī Mandira (Nimaichand family)
4. Gopālajī Mandira
5. Ācārya Mandira
6. Nabīn Keśora Mandira
7. Gopīnātha Mandira
8. Giridhārī (Family of Mema)
9. Mahāprabhu Mandira
10. Rādhābrajavinoda Mandira (Sawaijam family or clan)
11. Viśvambhara Mandira (Hijam family)
12. Rādhārājabihārī Mandira (Bihārī, clan title is needed)
13. Sītānātha Mandira
14. Rādhāmādhava Mandira
15. Brajanātha Mandira (Irengbam clan)
16. Girirāja Mandira (Irengbam clan)
17. Gopīnātha Mandira (Chirom clan)
18. Śrī Bhagavad Mandira
19. Kāmon Kuñja Mandira
20. Chapak Kuñja Gopāla Mandira (Hodam clan).

After the Anglo-Manipuri War, locally called Khongjom Lān 1891 CE, out of the 23 prisoners[5] of the British Rāj were the princes and leading military officers of the then kingdom of Manipur, the following list had stayed or were later on permitted to shift to Braja-Vrindavana and died there. During the Anglo-Manipuri War Hinduism was the state religion of Manipur and the old palace Kangla Fort had the palatial temple Śrī Śrī Govindajī.

1. Mahārājā Kulacandra Dhaja or Singh was released by the British on 11 May 1895; after staying at Hajārībāg for some time, he shifted to Rādhā-Kuṇḍa and died there on 26 January 1934.

2. Major Chongtham Miya, or Iboton, was also released by the British on the same day as Kulacandra Singh, and

he also stayed for some time at the Braja-Vrindavana. Colonel Luwang Ningthou Maisnam Shamu Singh (also released on 11 May 1895) had settled at the holy *dhāma*.

3. Ayapurel Major Chongtham Nilamani Singh had died at Vrindavana in 1897.

4. Angousana Singh, Senapati, had shifted from Hajārībāg to Rādhā-Kuṇḍa and died at the place on 18 November 1911.

Till today, Rādhā-Kuṇḍa, in particular of the Bhūloka Braja-Vrindavana in general are the most important and sacred of the places as the earthly spiritual stage where Lord Śrī Kṛṣṇa had his childhood life and joyous transcendental sports—Bāla-Līlā and Rāsa-Līlā with the *gopī*s among which Śrīmatī Rādhikā who is also called as Rāseśvarī. It is believed in the Vaiṣṇava Dharma established by Śrī Kṛṣṇa Caitanya that Rādhā is the personification of the *hlādinī-śakti*—Bliss Potency of the Monotheistic Absolute—Svayaṁ Bhagavān Śrī Kṛṣṇa. As the earthly transcendental theatre where the personification of Rādhārānī as His most essential (*svarūpa-śakti*) and innermost (*aṅtaraṅga-śakti*) of the three potencies—*svarūpa śakti*s—*sandhinī-śakti* (potency of existence), *saṁvit-śakti* (potency of consciousness), and *hlādinī-śakti* as the playful expression of His Bliss potency in the form of *prema-bhakti rasa* is the highest possible state of Bengal Vaiṣṇavism and Manipuri Vaiṣṇavism. It is to relish this spiritual taste of the pure delight of the highest form of *bhakti rasa*, which had manifested (*prakaṭa*) in the holy *dhāma* of Bhūloka Braja-Vrindavana that, settling at this sacred place, to leave one's body and to visit this *tīrthasthāna* is the most essential aim in the lives of the Manipuri Vaiṣṇavas.

NOTES

1. Raymond Schwab (1984). *The Oriental Renaissance: Europe's*

Rediscovery of India and the East, 1680-1880, translated by Gene Patterson-Black and Victor Reinking, New York: Columbia University Press.

2. Lamabam Gojendra (ed.) (2017). *Meidingoo Chingthangkhomba: Rajarshi Bhagyachandra*. Śrī Śrī Anumahāprabhu Sevait Samiti, Navadvipa, West Bengal, pp. 61-62.
3. *Gītā* V.29. English translation by Swāmī Ādidevānanda. https://www.gitasupersite.iitk.ac.in/srimad?htrskd=1&ecsiva=1&etsiva=1&etpurohit=1&etgb=1&setgb=1&etssa=1&etassa=1&etradi=1&etadi=1&choose=1&&language=dv&field_chapter_value=5&field_nsutra_value=29.
4. K. Sharma (1987). *Bhakti and the Bhakti Movement: A New Perspective: A Study in the History of Ideas*. New Delhi: Munshiram Manoharlal Publishers.
5. Gunachandra Sharma (2022). "Kakchingtabam", *Andamanda Loi Thakhiba Athouba 23*, Imphal.

5

Glories of Rādhā-Kuṇḍa and the Permanent Residents of Manipuri Vaiṣṇavas

Sukadeva Das

Braja, Vraja, Brija or Brajabhūmi has a circumference of Brajamaṇḍala Caurāsī Kosa or 84 Kosa (1 *kosa* = 3 km approx.) region in northern India on both sides of Yamunā River with entire Mathurā district of western Uttar Pradesh, part of Palwal district of Haryana and part of Bharatpur district in Rajasthan. Rādhā-Kuṇḍa is around 150 km from the national capital, Delhi, and is toward Agra (65 km). Most important places within Brajabhūmi, like Vrindavana, Mathurā, Gokula, Govardhana, Rādhā-Kuṇḍa, Barasānā, Nandagrāma, etc., are only in the Mathurā district. Rādhā-Kuṇḍa itself is a very unique name of the same village derived from the Śrīmatī Rādhikā's personal and favourite *kuṇḍa* (pond) also known as Rādhā-Kuṇḍa.

> "The holy place known as Mathurā is spiritually superior to Vaikuṇṭha, the transcendental world, because the Lord appeared there. Superior to

Mathurāpurī is the transcendental forest of Vrindavana because of Kṛṣṇa's *rāsa-līlā* pastimes. And superior to the forest of Vrindavana is Govardhana Hill, for it was raised by the divine hand of Śrī Kṛṣṇa and was the site of His various loving pastimes. And, above all, the super-excellent Śrī Rādhā-Kuṇḍa stands supreme, for it is overflooded with the ambrosal nectarian *prema* of the Lord of Gokula, Śrī Kṛṣṇa. Where, then, is that intelligent person who is unwilling to serve this divine Rādhā-Kuṇḍa, which is situated at the foot of Govardhana Hill?"—*Upadeśāmṛta* Text 9

"Just as Śrīmatī Rādhārāṇī is most dear to Lord Kṛṣṇa, so Her lake, known as Rādhā-Kuṇḍa, is also very dear to Him. Of all the *gopī*s, Śrīmatī Rādhārāṇī is certainly the most beloved."—*Caitanya Caritāmṛta,* Madhya 18.8

"After Ariṣṭāsura had been killed by Kṛṣṇa, who acts wonderfully, Nārada Muni went to speak to King Kaṁsa. That powerful sage of godly vision addressed the king as follows."—*Śrīmad Bhāgavatam* 10.36.16

Purport

The term *deva-darśana* can be understood in many ways, all of which are consistent with the context and purport of this narration. *Deva* means "God", and *darśana* means "seeing" or "an audience with a great personality". Thus, *deva-darśana*, a name for Nārada Muni, indicates that Nārada has attained the perfection of seeing God, that getting Nārada's audience is as good as getting God's (since Nārada is a pure representative of the Lord), and also that Nārada's audience is as good as that of the demigods, who are also known as *deva*s. That there are all these meanings of the term *deva-darśana* reveals something of the richness of the *Śrīmad-Bhāgavatam*'s language.

From the Purāṇas, Śrīla Viśvanātha Cakravartī Ṭhākura has quoted twenty verses describing a joking conversation between Rādhā and Kṛṣṇa that took place after Kṛṣṇa had killed the demon Ariṣṭa. This conversation, so kindly quoted by the *ācārya*, describes the origin of Rādhā-Kuṇḍa and Śyāma-Kuṇḍa, Rādhā's and Kṛṣṇa's bathing ponds. The verses are as follows:

> "The innocent young *gopī*s said, 'Āh, Kṛṣṇa, don't touch us now, O killer of a bull! Alas, even though Ariṣṭa was a terrible demon, he was still a male cow, so You will have to undergo atonement, just as Lord Indra did after killing Vṛtrāsura. But how can You purify Yourself without going to the trouble of visiting every single holy place in the three worlds?'"
>
> "[Kṛṣṇa replied,] 'Why should I have to wander throughout the entire universe? I will at once bring all the countless pilgrimage places here and take My bath in them. Just watch!' With this, Lord Mukunda struck His heel on the ground."
>
> "[Then He said,] 'This is the water of the Bhogavatī River, coming from the Pātāla region. And now, O holy places, all of you, please come here!' When the Supreme Lord had spoken these words, all the holy places went there and appeared before Him. Kṛṣṇa then addressed the *gopī*s as follows."
>
> "'See all the holy places!'
>
> "But the *gopī*s replied, 'We don't see them as You describe.'"
>
> "Then those best of holy places, joining their palms in supplication, spoke up:
>
> 'I am the salt ocean.'
>
> 'I am the Ocean of Milk.'
>
> 'I am the Amara-dīrghikā.'
>
> 'I am the River Śoṇa.'
>
> 'I am the Sindhu.'

'I am the Tāmraparṇī.'
'I am the holy place Puṣkara.'
'I am the river Sarasvatī.'
'And we are the Godāvarī, Yamunā, and Revā rivers and the confluence of rivers at Prayāga. Just see our waters!'"
"After purifying Himself by bathing, Lord Hari became quite arrogant and said, 'I have produced a pond containing all the various holy places, whereas you *gopīs* must never have executed any religious duties on this earth for the pleasure of Lord Brahmā.' Then Śrīmatī Rādhārāṇī addressed Her girlfriends as follows."
"'I must create an even more beautiful pond. So go to work!' Having heard these words, the *gopīs* saw that Ariṣṭāsura's hooves had dug a shallow ditch just west of Śrī Kṛṣṇa's pond."
"At that nearby spot, all the *gopīs* began digging up lumps of soft mud with their hands, and in this way, a divine pond manifested in the short span of an hour. Kṛṣṇa was astonished to see the lake they produced."
"He said, 'Go ahead, lotus-eyed one. You and Your companions should fill this pond with water from Mine.'"
"But Rādhā replied, 'No, no, no, no! This is impossible since the water of Your pond is contaminated by Your terrible sin of killing a cow.'"
"I will have My countless *gopī* companions bring the pure water of the Mānasa-Gaṅgā here in billions of pots. In this way, I will fill this lake with My own water and thus make its renown unequalled in the entire world."
"Lord Kṛṣṇa then gestured to a heavenly personality who was an intimate associate of all the holy places. Suddenly, that person rose up out

of Kṛṣṇa's pond and bowed down to the daughter of Śrī Vṛṣabhānu [Rādhārāṇī]. Then, with palms joined and tears pouring from his eyes, he began praying to Her in devotion."

"O Goddess, even Lord Brahmā himself, the knower of all scriptures, cannot understand Your glories, nor can Lord Śiva or Lakṣmī. Only Kṛṣṇa, the supreme goal of all human endeavour, can understand them, and thus He feels obliged to personally make sure that You can wash away Your perspiration when You are fatigued."

"He is always anointing Your lotus feet with nectarean *cāru* and *yāvaka* and decorating them with ankle bells, and He rejoices and feels most fortunate simply by satisfying the tips of the toes of Your lotus feet. On His order, we have immediately come here to live in this most excellent pond, which He created with one stroke of His heel. But only if You now feel satisfied with us and bestow upon us Your merciful glance will the tree of our desire bear fruit."

"Hearing this prayer spoken by the representative of the full assembly of holy places, Śrī Rādhā was pleased and said, 'So, kindly tell Me your desire'."

"They then told Her plainly, 'Our lives would be successful if we could come to Your pond. That is the benediction we desire.'"

"Glancing at Her beloved from the corners of Her eyes, the daughter of Vṛṣabhānu replied with a smile, 'Please come'. Her *gopī* companions all agreed with Her decision and became immersed in the ocean of happiness. Indeed, the beauty of all creatures, both mobile and stationary, was enhanced."

"Thus gaining the grace of Śrīmatī Rādhārāṇī, the holy rivers and lakes in Śrī Kṛṣṇa-Kuṇḍa forcibly broke through its boundary walls and swiftly filled Rādhā-Kuṇḍa with their waters."

> "Lord Hari then said, 'My dear Rādhā, may this pond of Yours become even more world-renowned than Mine. I will always come here to bathe and to enjoy My water pastimes. Indeed, this lake is as dear to Me as You are.'"
>
> "Rādhā replied, 'I will come to bathe in Your pond as well, even though You may kill hundreds of Ariṣṭa demons here. In the future, anyone who has intense devotion for this lake, which is on the spot where You chastised Ariṣṭāsura, and who bathes or resides here is sure to become very dear to Me.'"
>
> "That night, Lord Kṛṣṇa initiated a *rāsa* dance at Rādhā-Kuṇḍa, generating a torrent of the greatest mood of splendorous pleasure. Śrī Kṛṣṇa resembled a cloud, and Śrīmatī Rādhārāṇī a brilliant flash of lightning filling the sky with abundant beauty. In this way their divine glories permeated the expanses of the three worlds."

As a final note, it should be mentioned that Nārada Muni, being a great sage, understood that the killing of Ariṣṭa more or less concluded the pastimes of Kṛṣṇa in Vrindavana. Therefore, Nārada, anxious to facilitate the transferal of Kṛṣṇa's pastimes to Mathurā, approached Kaṁsa and addressed him as follows —*Śrīmad Bhāgavatam* 10.36.16 commentary from Braja-*Vikas's-stava.*

> "The *gopīs* began glorifying Rādhā-Kuṇḍa by saying, O Śyāma! This Rādhā-Kuṇḍa is for your benefit and for your beloved friend Śrī Rādhā. It is purifying like the Ganges that flows from the feet of Lord Viṣṇu. A person gets liberation by its mere touch. As Pārvatī Devī appeared from the Himalayas, similarly Rādhā-Kuṇḍa appeared from the Govardhana Hill. Lord Balarāma defeated the pride of the demon Pralamba. In the same way, Rādhā's Lake defeats the pride of the great rivers—what else can we say to glorify this Rādhā-Kuṇḍa?"—*Gopāla-campū.*

Śrī Rādhā-Kuṇḍa itself is the *summum bonum* of all the holy *tīrtha*s and rivers not only from this earth but also from other heavenly planets. However, Vrindavana is a very important spot for Śrīmatī Rādhikā and Śrī Kṛṣṇa's divine past time.

Following this sacred tradition of Brajavāsa (permanently living) at Rādhā-Kuṇḍa village and the most sacred confidential narratives, many Manipuri Vaiṣṇavas built numerous Manipuri Vaiṣṇava temples at Rādhā-Kuṇḍa, which are explain the later part of the paper.

Lord Caitanya Mahāprabhu Reveals Rādhā-Kuṇḍa

After completing his *parikramā* Brajamaṇḍala, Lord Caitanya sat under a *tamāla* tree near Śyāma-Kuṇḍa. However, no one knew the location of Rādhā-Kuṇḍa and Śyāma-Kuṇḍa. Mahāprabhu revealed them amidst two paddy fields. The Lord joyfully bathed in whatever little water was there and glorified the *kuṇḍa*s in various ways. Then Gaurāṅga applied *tilaka* with mud from the *kuṇḍa*s. Amazed by the Mahāprabhu's behaviour, the local Brajavāsīs become maddened with attraction to His nectarian form.—*Bhakti-Ratnākara*. Later, under the supervision of Śrī Rūpa and Sanātana Goswāmī, Śrī Raghunātha Dāsa Goswāmī was entrusted with the divine instruction of Śrī Caitanya Mahāprabhu to excavate and extend the sacred *kuṇḍa*s. In 1545, Śrī Raghunātha Dāsa Goswāmī purchased the two paddy fields where the Rādhā-Kuṇḍa and Śyāma-Kuṇḍa are located. Thus, the present-day Rādhā-Kuṇḍa and Śyāma-Kuṇḍa twin lakes are being re-established.

A Brief Historical Account of the Manipuri Temples and Āśramas at Rādhā-Kuṇḍa

Śrī Śrī Rāsabihārī Mandira or Pūraṇakuñja, Parikramā Mārga, Rādhā-Kuṇḍa Bazar Road (1799 CE)

Śrī Śrī Śrī Rāsabihārī Mandira is the first and oldest Manipuri temple at Rādhā-Kuṇḍa founded by Prince Chourjit (1777

CE) in the year 1799 CE. It is also known as Pūraṇa-Kuñja. The presiding installed *vigraha* of Śrī Rādhā and Rāsabihārījī is made of eight metals (*aṣṭa-dhātu*). The temple is located near and toward the southern side of the main market in Govardhana Parikramā Mārga.

Rājarṣi Bhāgyacandra, during his last days at Śrī Paṭa Kṣetra, Murshidabad in Bengal, could not proceed to Brajadhāma Vrindavana due to ailing and ageing. He entrusted his third son, Prince Chourjit, who was very dedicated to his saintly king father, to perform the death anniversary ceremony at Rādhā-Kuṇḍa. Prince Chourjit and his nine-member party started their adventure from Murshidabad on 1 November 1798 CE. The journey almost took place two months and arrived at Rādhā-Kuṇḍa in the early part of January 1799 CE. Accordingly, as a Gāuḍīya Vaiṣṇava *paramparā*, Prince Chourjit performed the posthumous ritual ceremony of his Royal father Rājarṣi Bhāgyacandra at Rādhā-Kuṇḍa.

While at Rādhā-Kuṇḍa, by the blessings of Śrī Rādhā-Kṛṣṇa, there was an inspiration in the mind of Prince Chourjit for the establishment of a *kuñja* (bower/arbour) in a temple in which the deity of Lord Śrīmatī Rādhārāṇī and Śrī Kṛṣṇa be installed so that each and every Manipuri Vaiṣṇavite devotees who arrived and entered there in course of their pilgrimage might be in satisfaction. The present temple *sevāyata*s have renovated certain existing old structures within the premise. The temple is wonderfully rebuilt with expansion on the same old spot in a traditional model made from bricks and cladding with colourful marbles. New multi-story residential buildings are built with numerous traditional and modern rooms for hosting and facilitating devotees and pilgrims. Now, the temple is running under the care and management of a family trust descendant of Mahārājā Chourjit Singh, named Sri Sri Rasabihari Mandir Seva Trust, with Rajkumar Dusarigopal Singh as president of the trust.—*Sri Sri Rasabihariji by Dusari Gopal.*

Śrī Śrī Rādhā Govinda Devajī Mandira or Baṛī-Kuñja

Baṛī-Kuñja is the most magnanimous temple in and around Rādhā-Kuṇḍa, built with intricately carved red stone and fort-like walls surrounding the sprawling temple premise of Śrī Śrī Rādhā Govinda Devajī. Hence, the name is, the temple is located north-east of the Śyāma-Kuṇḍa—Rādhā-Kuṇḍa Parikramā Mārga near the Lalitā-Kuṇḍa. Beside the main temple, there are numerous residence quarters. In one of the *bagīcā* (garden), there is the memorial *samādhi* of patriotic Vaiṣṇava King Mahārājā Kulacandra Singh (1854-1934).

Śrī Śrī Rādhā Govinda Devajī Temple was founded by one of the most powerful Vaiṣṇava kings, Mahārājā Gambhīr Singh (1788-1834), the youngest scion of Rājarṣi Bhāgyacandra. Although he never visited Śrīdhāma Brajabhūmi, he deputed his most trusted members of the royal family to construct the temple according to his desire. The total amount for the whole construction project work, including acquiring the temple premise land, was sent through *huṇḍī* (a kind of money-gram system of those days) from time to time as required. His firm intention for establishing the temple in Śrīdhāma Rādhā-Kuṇḍa is known from the *Gambhir Singh Nongggaba* (The Heavenward Journey of Gambhīr Singh) by Dayaram Louremba and Nabashyam Ningthoujamba which deals with the closing days of Mahārājā Gambhīr Singh mentioned that:

Mahārājā Gambhīr Singh, a great fighter and a devout Vaiṣṇava, having sat on the throne for about eight years, made up his mind to make a pilgrimage to Vrindavana after entrusting the state and his little son to Nara Singh against the pleas of his brother, nobles of the court, the royal priest, other brāhmaṇa *paṇḍita*s for whom the king had high regards, the surviving wives of Mahārājā Bhāgyacandra and the king's step-mothers, and lastly the queen and other spouses of the king himself. However, when all preparations were over, the king's ailing health suddenly took a turn for the worse, and soon, he passed away amidst the heart-rending cries of his people. When he says to the brāhmaṇa *paṇḍita*s, one can realize that he was venting to the yearning that throbbed in every Manipuri Vaiṣṇava's heart.

After the Anglo-Manipur War of independence in 1891, Mahārājā Kulacandra was arrested on 8 May 1891 and was tried before a special commission under the presidency of Lt. Col. St. John Mitchell on a charge of waging war against the Queen Empress and transported for life with forfeiture of properties. He was released in 1885 from Andaman and was residing at Hazaribagh Jail. On his release from Hazaribagh, he spent the remaining part of his life at Rādhā-Kuṇḍa (Vrindavana) and died on 26 January 1934 at Rādhā-Kuṇḍa Uttar Pradesh.—*Unsung Anglo-Manipur War Heroes at Kalapani* by Sukhadeva Sharma.

In the last few decades, one unique story of Rajkumar Manishana Singh, a descendant of Mahārājā Gambhīr Singh, was performing the regular daily *sevā-pūjā* of the Śrī Vigraha Śrī Śrī Rādhā Govinda Devajī personally as a *pujārī*. His last cremation was done at Rādhā-Kuṇḍa village crematorium, known as Śivaghara.

Śrī Śrī Naol Govindajī Mandira or Yuvarāja Kuñja (1849 CE)

The temple is located near the western bank of Rādhā-Kuṇḍa Lake adjacent to Śrī Gopalajī Mandira in the east, near the tri-junction of Govardhana Parikramā Mārga and Choṭā Parikramā of Rādhā-Kuṇḍa-Śyāma-Kuṇḍa. The existing original temple is built from bricks and cladding with intricately carved red stone slabs. The temple premise is surrounded by compound walls with simple residential quarters.

Yuvarāja Nara Singh (1792-1850) personally established the presiding Śrī Vigraha of Śrī Śrī Naol Govindajī and the temple itself. In the history of Manipur royals, he was considered the most dedicated Yuvarāja to his elder brother Mahārājā Gambhīr Singh, and the narrative goes like that of Prince Bhorot to his elder brother King Rāma of *Rāmāyaṇa* epic. It is said that he was one of the important royal team members from Manipur, deputed by Mahārājā Gambhīr Singh, who moved to Rādhā-Kuṇḍa in the early second half of the nineteenth century to establish the Śrī Śrī Rādhā Govinda Devajī Temple. Although Mahārājā Nara Singh ruled the kingdom as regent from 1834 to 1844 and then reigned as king for a period of six years from 1844 to 1850, out of humility and dedication to his brother Mahārājā Gambhīr Singh, he chose to remain Yuvarāja. Therefore, the temple he established is named Śrī Śrī Naol Govindajī (Naol means New), derived from his brother's temple and also known as Yuvarāja Kuñja (prince bower) so that the original name of his brother's temple remains original but follows in a derivative scaled down version.

A family trust of the king's descendants maintains the regular *sevā-pūjā* of the temple by deputing deviates. In the last few decades, royals who left their bodies while serving as *sevāyata* caretakers are Rajkumar Agentshana and Rajkumar Sanaton Singh. Recently few years back, one of the elderly *sevāyata* Rajkumar Mohendrajit Singh who was a very dedicated to the Ṭhākurajī and caretaker of the temple left the body in Śrīdhāma Rādhā-Kuṇḍa.—*Narratives from the King's Ffamily Members.*

Manipuri Śrī Gopālajī Mandira or Churachand Ghera

The original deity of Śrī Gopālajī is presiding inside the Śrī Gopālajī Mandira located just on the north-western bank of Rādhā-Kuṇḍa known as Gopāla Ghāṭ, where there is a large sandstone gate and tri-junction of Rādhā-Kuṇḍa-Śyāma-Kuṇḍa 1 km Choṭā Parikramā Mārga along the 21 km Govardhana Parikramā Mārga. The humble temple is entirely built with bricks and cladding granite slabs within the in-house complex, and a towering temple dome is situated in the front section of the premises. The temple premise is completely enclosed by a residential building. The back side of the temple premise is an open courtyard in the centre of a residential building in four directions where the *samādhi mandira* of H.H. Bhaktisvarūpa Dāmodara Swāmī (1937-2006), a Manipuri Vaiṣṇava saint and scientist is also located.

Once, young Mahārājā Churachand Singh KCSI, CBE (1896-1941) was visiting Rādhā-Kuṇḍa to pay a visit to his uncle Mahārājā Kulacandra Singh, the ex-regent of Manipur, after attending a seminar at Princes Chamber in Delhi. The uncle, who is permanently residing at Baṛī-Kuñja, was in exile after returning from Andaman at Kālāpānī. While staying there, one night, Mahārājā Churachand Singh had a very wonderful and particular dream of his future *iṣṭa deva* of Laḍḍu Gopāla, an infant form of Lord Śrī Kṛṣṇa.

Lord Gopāla instructed the king to build an east-facing temple on the bank of Rādhā-Kuṇḍa so that the Lord could give an audience to Sūryadeva, the sun God, and also view His favourite lake, Rādhā-Kuṇḍa. The location of the temple and altar would be in such a position that the rising sun's first rays fall directly on His face, especially during the spring season and Kārttika (October). Lord Gopālajī also told the king that he was being worshipped by a Brajavāsī brāhmaṇa *pujārī* in a temple on the *ṭillā* (small hillock) near Rādhā-Kuṇḍa Lake. The king related the dream to local elderly Brajavāsīs. As per the direction of Lord Gopāla, the present location was found to be exactly suitable. So the king acquired the land from a Manipuri Vaiṣṇava known as Thengbai Bābā, who already had his *bhajana āśrama* there. The king related the dream of Lord Gopāla to Bābā and requested for the purpose. Bābā was happy to know the intention of Gopālajī and agreed to trade another piece of land nearby and build an *āśrama* for the Bābā accordingly. Thus, temple construction was completed under the supervision of the king. It is said that the temple was specially designed and built with secret underground rooms and passages that lead from the temple directly to the sacred waters of Rādhā-Kuṇḍa. The bathing waters of Gopāla would enter via these routes. According to scripture, the north-west corner of Rādhā-Kuṇḍa is the location of Śrīmatī Tungabidyā

Sakhī's (one of the principle eight *sakhī*s of Śrīmatī Rādhārāṇī) personal *kuṇḍa* in the original spiritual platform. Again, on the pretext of a dream, Gopāla instructed the Brajavāsī brāhmaṇa *pujārī* to take Him to the temple built by the king, saying that he felt very cold and that the king could arrange for better care and regular worship. The brāhmaṇa, whose family had been worshipping the deity for generations, brought Him to the king, who had installed him in a grand ceremony and requested the brāhmaṇa to perform His regular worship.

During the first half of the twentieth century, there were already regular train and air services to various destinations within India. Unlike his predecessors, Mahārājā Churachand Singh paid regular visits to Rādhā-Kuṇḍa on many occasions, and therefore, many important events also happened in his life at Rādhā-Kuṇḍa. As a Vaiṣṇava king, he shunned wearing the *rājā veśa* and instead adorned a simple traditional *dhotī-kurtā* whenever he visited Rādhā-Kuṇḍa.

The king had committed to adorn the deity with gold ornament but could not fulfil it due to not being permanently based at Rādhā-Kuṇḍa. Therefore, one substitute temple, *pujārī*, had verbally offended the king. It is said that when the king returned back to Rādhā-Kuṇḍa, Śrī Gopālajī was worshipped by adorning gold ornaments like crowns, necklaces, earrings, nose studs, armlaces, bracelets, waist belts, anklets, and flutes adorned with various precious gemstones. One day, when the same *pujārī* who opened the deity altar, there was a snake in the altar, and it bit the *pujārī*. Because of the opulence, once, two thieves were sneaking into the temple but were intercepted by the king's security, and one of them was shot while in the encounter. It was the first temple in Rādhā-Kuṇḍa and nearby to be illuminated by a power generator.

Mahārājā Churachand Singh laid the old pavement around Rādhā-Kuṇḍa Choṭā Parikramā Mārga with massive-sized red stone slabs. However, it was covered up by modern PCC slabs recently in 2009 renovation by the state government. The first few steps of the total nineteen stone steps inside the

Rādhā-Kuṇḍa Lake were also laid by the king in a concentric manner. He also renovated and beautified the Julan *sthalī*, which is located on the western side of the lake, by erecting massive size stone slabs at the entrance gate of the *sthali* where his designated name, etc., were engraved in Devanāgarī and Bengali scripts. The monumental entrance gate of the *sthalī* still exists in the exact location. He was fond of playing chess in his leisure time with the elderly local Brajavāsīs.

Once, there was a crocodile sneaking into the Śyāma-Kuṇḍa Lake during the rainy season from the nearby moat, but it remained there unnoticed during the summer season when the water level became very low and started showing the *khambā* (flat top stone column) in the middle of the Brajanava Kuṇḍa inside Śyāma-Kuṇḍa Lake. Village folks were fetching water from this lake for regular household uses. One day, this massive crocodile was sunbathing by lying on the top of this stone column and became scared to go to the lake to fetch water. Elderly Brajavāsī brāhmaṇa acquaintances were requesting Mahārājā Churachand Singh to eliminate the crocodile for the safety of the village folks. So, as a kṣatriya duty, he shot the crocodile with his double barrel gun to safeguard the village folks from the beast. The brāhmaṇa acquaintances advised the king to perform a *śrāddha* ceremony for the animal as per customary Sanātana (Hindu) tradition. Although it was a beast, it was regarded as a Vaiṣṇava since it resided in the holy Kuṇḍa. Thus, Mahārājā Churachand Singh observed the *śrāddha* ceremony for the crocodile by engaging brāhmaṇas in performing rituals and inviting village folks to the *laṅgara* feast.

Later, Mahārājā Bodhacandra Singh also visited Śrī Gopālajī Mandira at Rādhā-Kuṇḍa on many occasions. He was also acquaintances among the Brajavāsī brāhmaṇas, especially from the Goswāmī Paribās, living near the affinity of Śrī Gopālajī Mandira. The temple management was engaged by *kāmadāra*s from time to time but not by the royal family. In due course of time after the departure of Mahārājā

Bodhacandra, temple maintenance money transferred from the palace in Imphal became scarce. The *kāmadāra* started misusing the power of attorney by selling many valuable assets, including a portion of the temple premises. Thus, the temple became inhabitable, although it was once like a palace. By the will and arrangement of the same Ṭhākurajī Śrī Gopāla who once appeared in the dream of Mahārājā Churachand Singh, in the year 1994, Mahārājā Okendrajit Singh had permanently transferred the temple sevāyataship to a group of senior Manipuri Vaiṣṇavas headed by HH. Bhaktisvarūpa Dāmodara Swāmī of ISKCON temple at Sangaiprow, Phurailatpam Jagadish Sharma of Sayang Pukhri Mapal, and Rajkumar Dusari Gopal Singh of Keishamthong Top Leirak for the sake of safeguarding the Manipuri Vaiṣṇava tradition at Rādhā-Kuṇḍa. A trust formed by the above Manipuri Vaiṣṇavas is now taking care of the temple management under the supervision of Rajkumar Dusari Gopal Singh and the disciples of Bhaktisvarūpa Dāmodara Swāmī do Ṭhākurajī's regular daily *sevā-pūjā.—Narrated by Ramswarup Gosai, Mangal Gosai, H.H.BS Damodara Swami* and *R.K. Dusari Gopal Singh*

Śrī Ṭhākura Gopīnāthajī Mahārāja Mandira or Chirom Mandira

It is a family temple located on the northern side of the Rādhā-Kuṇḍa Lake toward Konai and Sūrya-Kuṇḍa Road. The temple is enclosed by residential quarters and is nearly a hundred years old. It was established by one Chirom Gopal Singh (aka Govinda Das Babaji, who died in 1978) and his wife, Chirom Ongbi Leihao Devī. The presiding beautiful deities of Śrī Rādhā Gopīnāthajī are brought from Manipur and are featured in Manipuri tradition. In the name of *virājamāna* Ṭhākurajī Śrī Gopīnāthajī, the husband and wife also acquired about 12 *bighā*s of paddy field to maintain the temple's regular *sevā-pūjā*, including *sevāyata*s and *pujārī*s. The family had no issue or descendant but adopted one son named Chirom

Labanga Singh, and the son also died. One Brajavāsī *pujārī*, Gopalprasad Shergaria, was very dedicated to the Ṭhākurajī and to the owner of the temple, who served as a *sevā-pūjā pujārī* from the establishment of this temple. After the old *pujārī* died, his son Kaluwa Shergaria inherited the *sevā-pūjā* of the Ṭhākurajī, and now his descendants are continuing the *sevā*.

Mahāprabhu Mandira

It is a family temple of one Manipuri brāhmaṇa family, located on the northern side of the Rādhā-Kuṇḍa Lake toward Konai and Sūrya-Kuṇḍa road. The temple was recently rebuilt on half of the original old temple, which was dismantled. The presiding Śrī Vigraha of Śrī Caitanya Mahāprabhu, featured in Manipuri tradition is brought from Manipur about 150 years ago by one Manipuri brāhmaṇa simply called him as Eigya Idhou (respected grandfather) by his descendants and the original temple was also established by him. Eigya Idhou was serving in this temple during the reign of Mahārājā Churachand Singh of Śrī Gopālajī Mandira and Mahārānī Dhanamañjarī Devī was in favour of this brāhmaṇa family. After the Eigya Idhou passed away in Rādhā-Kuṇḍa itself, his son Hidangmayum Gouranitai Sharma and four children, two sons and two daughters, continued the *sevā-pūjā* of the Ṭhākurajī. The elder son, Nandakiswor Sharma, was once elected as one of the local commissioners of the Radhakund Town Committee. Hence, Manipuri Vaiṣṇavas are also known not only as simple residents but also earned a name as local administrators. Elder daughter Brahmacharimayum Ongbi Chandani Devi and younger sibling Gurumayum Ongbi Kunjarani Devi are the present *sevāyata*s serving the temple as caretakers.

- Śrī Giridhārī Mandira: Ema Kripadasi, Ema Memma
- Śrī Gopīnātha Mandira or Bhani Mandira
- Van View Cottage or Bhani Mandira
- Śrī Śrī Navin Kishor Mandira: Sapna Vavan Gopi Das Babaji and other two siblings

Śrī Śrī Rādhā Mādhava Mandira or Śrīnivāsa Ācārya Prabhu Āśrama

The temple-*āśrama* is located in Shergharia Mohalla, Konai Road, just opposite Śrī Śrī Navīna Kiśora Mandira on the western side. A narrow alley known as Damodar Galli leads from the Choṭā Parikramā Mārga in front of the Rādhā Śyāmasundara Mandira toward Konai Road, where there is a trijunction that is the exact location of the temple from another direction. The present temple was rebuilt recently with white marble cladding on a brick structure surrounded by an RCC structure, a stories *āśrama* building having numerous rooms for hosting devotees and pilgrims. There is also one legendary Pushpa Samādhi cum Bhajana Kuṭīra of Śrīnivāsa Ācārya Prabhu right in the temple. Presiding Ṭhākurajī Śrī Rādhā Mādhava is the original Estha Dev of Hemalata Ṭhākurānī, the daughter of Śrīnivāsa Ācārya Prabhu. Her descendants continued the *sevā-pūjā* and, later, the father of Ema Endumukhi Devi, a Manipuri brāhmaṇa *pujārī*, inherited as *sevāyata*. They continued the *sevā-pūjā*, later led by his daughter Endumukhi Devi and her husband Aribam Ibomcha Sharma, then their son Govardhana Sharma. Out of good gesture, Eigya Govardhana Sharma permanently transferred the sevāyataship to the same trust as Śrī Gopālajī Mandira in 1995. The inspiration of H.H. Bhaktisvarūpa Dāmodara Swāmī for having a Lady's *āśrama*, under the careful supervision of Shri Rajkumar Dusarigopal Singh, to fulfil the desire of Swāmījī the project for facilitating destitute women, especially from the Manipuri community and lady disciples of H.H. Bhaktisvarūpa Dāmodara Swāmī was fulfilled in 2016. In the last three decades, one elderly husband and wife from Tripurā, simply known as Ene and Mamma, and one Ema Dhani, who were facilitated in this *āśrama* for years, left the bodies. Ema Tungabidya Devi, a senior lady disciple of Swāmījī from Ngaikhong. In Manipur, was serving in this *āśrama* for more than a decade and also left the body around 2013. Another Ema Lakhi Devi from Tripurā, a soft-spoken, very humble, sweet old lady who was also serving in this *āśrama* for more than 25 years, left the body in this *āśrama* around 2015. Presently, there are few elderly single lady *mātājī*s who are sheltered for their life long. The same trust as that of Śrī Gopālajī Mandira is taking care of the *āśrama* and temple *sevā-pūjā*.

Kripa Dasi Bhajan Kutir: Nimai Baba

Ṭhākura Nawala Gopālajī Mandira

The temple is adjacent to Yuvarāja Kuñja on the western side and Gopālajī Mandira on the northern side along the Govardhana Parikramā Mārga. It is about a 100-year-old family temple built with bricks, and the interior is clad with red stone slabs. One Gopal Sharma who established the temple where *virājamāna* presiding Ṭhākurajī is Śrī Nawala Gopālajī. Three daughters, Rādhe Devī, Kiśorī Devī, and Lalitā Devī, continued the *sevā-pūjā* of the temple after their parents departed from this world. The elder sibling, Rādhe Devī, married a Brajavāsī brāhmaṇa and had a daughter named Munni Devi. While growing up, Munni Devi married Shyam Kaushik, a reputed local Brajavāsī family's son. Munni Devi's sons, Tarapanchi and Pankaj Kaushik continued the *sevā-pūjā*. Other descendants of the Rādhe Devī are living at Sugnu in Manipur.

Śrī Brajanātha Mandira

The temple is located on the southern bank of Śyāma-Kuṇḍa, near Caitanya Mahāprabhu Baiṭhak or Tamāl Tāla along the Choṭā Parikramā Mārga. It is a multi-story building with a modern RCC structure, having numerous rooms for hosting family members and pilgrims. Presiding Ṭhākurajī Śrī Brajanāthajī and the old temple were established by Chaoren Kamdar. Erengbam Brajagopl Singh Singjamei, Imphal in

Manipur, rebuilt the present temple. A family trust takes care of the temple and the regular *sevā-pūjā* of the Ṭhākurajī.

Girirāja Mandira (1943)

The temple building is a modern RCC structure and multi-storied with numerous rooms for hosting pilgrims, while the Ṭhākurajī Girirāja Mahārāja's altar is on the ground floor. The temple is located on the Choṭā Parikarmā Mārga toward the entrance alley of Rādhā-Kuṇḍa-Śyāma-Kuṇḍa Saṅgama, or the meeting point of the two *kuṇḍa*s. The temple was established by Erengbam Anganghal Singh of Singjamei, Imphal, in Manipur. The late Erengbam Tompok Singh, the ex-deputy chief minister of Manipur, was one of the family members of this temple. A family trust maintains the regular daily *sevā-pūjā* of the Ṭhākurajī by deputing family members occasionally. One Eigya Ningthem Sharma, Manipuri brāhmaṇa, a *pujārī* who was serving in the temple, left his body in Rādhā-Kuṇḍa around the late twentieth century.

Śrī Śrī Rādhā Braja Binoda Mandira or Narottama Mandira (1945)

The temple is located on the foothill of a small hillock known as Ṭillā, adjacent to Pūraṇa Kuñja on the eastern side and inside a small alley called Pachouri Gali from the Govardhana Parikramā Mārga. The brick temple, along with numerous quarters and rooms for hosting pilgrims, are there. Presiding Ṭhākurajī Śrī Śrī Rādhā Braja Binodajī is apparently a traditional feature of Manipuri that was established by Śrī Narottam Dās Bābājī. Bābājī was brought up in a very well-to-do family, but how he became a renunciate *sādhu* is a mystery to many. During his mature age, Bābājī inspired every Manipuri Vaiṣṇava community, and his decision was final without a second. He was a lifetime celibate Bābājī and never married. He entered the Rādhā-Kṛṣṇa's Nitya-līlā in the late twentieth century. One of the present trustees, ex-chief minister of Manipur Radhabinoda Koijam, is Bābājī's younger brother. A family trust is nicely taking care of the temple and the Ṭhākurajī's regular *sevā-pūjā* by deputing care takers and *pujārīs*. One Nataraj Das Bābājī, disciple of H.H. Bhaktisvarūpa Dāmodara Swāmī served in this temple for many years as *pujārī* left the body just before the COVID-19 pandemic.

Gītā Gaṅgā Gāyatrī Govinda

Originally, this small family *bhajana āśrama* was part and attached to the front section of Pūraṇa-Kuñja or Śrī Śrī Rāsabihārī Mandira. Once, there was an agreement with the caretaker of the temple to set up their own family relationship, although the family was not from the royals.

Kṛpādāsī Bhajana Āśrama

The *āśrama* was located near the *saṅgama*. Ema Kṛpādāsī was from Khangabok in Manipur. She was a self-reliant and apparently neat and tidy elderly lady of light stature. She left her body in the early twenty-first century.

- Opposite Rāsabihārī Mandira, no name.
- Ṭhākura Śrī Kamala Bihārījī Mahārāja Mandira or Kamala Kuñja.
- Śrī Śrī Bishambhar Mahāprabhu Mandira.
- Śrī Śrī Rādhā Binoda Mandira or Saugaijam Kuñja: Sawaijam Ibomcha Singh.
- Śrī Rādhā Brajamohana Mandira.
- Śrī Sītānātha Mandira.

These temples or *āśramas* are no longer under the care of Manipuri Vaiṣṇavas anymore.

Personal Descriptions of the Manipuri Vaiṣṇavas Living in Their Own Accord till 1st Quarter of the Twenty-first Century

Kṛpāsindhu Bābājī

Bābājī was from Khangabok in Manipur and was staying at one of the Pancha's cottage right in front of the Śrī Gopālajī Mandira on Vetnama. He also hardly mingled with any Manipuri Vaiṣṇava community on any occasion other than individual interaction. He left the body around the late twentieth century.

Bamsi Das Bābājī

Bābājī was from Cachar in Assam. He once stayed at Śrīnivāsa Ācārya Prabhu Āśrama as a caretaker but later moved to his own Bhajana Āśrama at Radhanagar colony. He was another head of the *saṅkīrtana pala* and a good *nāṭa saṅkīrtana* singer. He left his body at the beginning of the twenty-first century.

Rs. 2 Bābājī

Bābājī was from Khangabok in Manipur and is known for their humble, unique way of asking *madhukarī* for just Rs. 2 only when necessary; otherwise, he would never accept anything. He was staying at Ema Kṛpādāsī's Bhajana Āśrama Near Saṅgama and passed away around the last of the twentieth century.

Rādhāramaṇa Bābājī

He was from Sylhet in Bangladesh and lived at a Pancha's cottage in Vetnama near Vyasdeva Ghera on the eastern bank of Śyāma-Kuṇḍa. He had a very unique lifestyle of complete renunciation and hardly mingled with any community gathering or ceremony other than personal interaction. He always carried a mild sweet smile on his old but radiant face. He left this world before the COVID-19 pandemic at a very mature age.

Ema Keinahanbi

She was from a Manipuri brāhmaṇa family from Imphal and had a very strong, courageous personality. She was switching on staying in various Manipuri temples. Once, in the early 1990s, she was one of the leaders of two factional Manipuri communities while Narottama Bābā was still on this planet. She left the body while she was staying at a local Brajavāsī's house around first decade of the twenty-first century.

Ema Keng Keng Baṛī-Kuñja

She had a small stature frame but had much wonderful information about Rādhā-Kṛṣṇa's pastimes. She was a very sweet elderly lady who was originally from Sylhet in Bangladesh. She lived at Baṛī-Kuñja on Vetnama while Jambung Manishana was the *sevāyata* and left the body in late twentieth century.

H.H. Bhaktisvarūpa Dāmodara Swāmī

Once during the month of Kārttika/October of 1972, Shri Thoudam Damodar Singh, also known as Svarūpa Dāmodara Dāsa Brahmacārī (a celibate's *dīkṣā* name), a Vaiṣṇava devotee native of Manipur, was visiting Śrīdhāma Rādhā-Kuṇḍa for the very first time. He was returning for the first time from the United States after leaving India in June 1965 to pursue PhD in Chemistry under the UGC scholarship scheme. Co-incidentally, by the will and arrangement of Lord Śrī Kṛṣṇa, Damodar Singh met Śrīla Prabhupāda, his future spiritual master, who also left India around the same time in June 1965 for the United States, and both of them met for the very first time at Rādhā Dwārkādhīśa (ISKCON) Temple in Los Angeles in April 1970. Later, he was initiated (*dīkṣa*) into Gauḍīya Vaiṣṇava Sampradāya in the lineage of Śrī Narottama Dāsa Ṭhākura, from whom Rājarṣi Bhāgyacandra Mahārāja was also initiated by Mahāsoi's grand disciple Paramānanda Ṭhākur Mahāsoi. He was actually visiting his spiritual master,

A.C. Bhaktivedānta Swāmī Prabhupāda, the founder *ācārya* of ISKCON (International Society for Krishna Consciousness), who was presently residing at Śrī Kṛṣṇa-Balarāma Mandira in Vrindavana for observing *niyama-sevā* month of Kārttika. While he was already in Vrindavana, he narrated the event one day by recalling the tradition of Manipuri Vaiṣṇava devotees. Whoever visited Vrindavana Dhāma on their pilgrimage journey also definitely paid a visit to Śrīdhāma Rādhā-Kuṇḍa.

At first sight, Svarūpa Dāmodara Dāsa was extremely enchanted by the breathtakingly beautiful ancient twin lakes of Śrī Rādhā-Kuṇḍa and Śyāma-Kuṇḍa with crystal clear water, spiritually-oriented trees of many different species growing on the banks of all directions, and their branches laden with leaves into the lake. He was absorbed in the thought of Śrīmatī Rādhikā and Śrī Kṛṣṇa's regular pastime in this transcendental lake mentioned in the holy scriptures. While Svarūpa Dāmodara was doing an *ācamana* (sprinkle of holy water for spiritual purification), he heard a friendly voice indicating him by a saint Bābājī in English enquiring whether he was a Manipuri Vaiṣṇava. It is a unique feature for the Manipuri Vaiṣṇava community. If anybody who appears to be in Mongoloid features is always considered to be Manipuri Vaiṣṇava by general populaces also, even nowadays. It is a legend here for this community other than the Brajavāsīs. Few decades ago, one Manipuri Vaiṣṇava was elected to the Radha-Kunda Town Committee as a commissioner. The Bābājī, who introduced himself as Madrāsī Bābā, was an educated saint from the southern state of Tamil Nadu, a disciple of Siddha Bābā Śrī Gopāla Dāsa Bābājī, also a native of Manipur, having his *bhajana āśrama* at Sūrya-Kuṇḍa village. In the later part of Svarūpa Dāmodara Dāsa became a permanent resident and *sevāyata*s of Śrī Gopālajī Mandira in 1994, paid a visit to Madrāsī Bābā, who was ailing due to old age, staying at Rādhāramaṇa Temple at Rādhā-Kuṇḍa. Bābā was so happy to see his old friend, and they were conversing on many other spiritual topics and about their well-being.

The visit to Rādhā-Kuṇḍa was an important moment to recall. Svarūpa Dāmodara had conceived the idea of establishing an *āśrama* for destitute (women) Vaiṣṇavī, especially for the Manipuri Vaiṣṇava community, which comprised not only from Manipur but also from different parts of Assam, Tripurā, including Sylhet in Bangladesh. In 1995, he became the permanent sevāyataship of one Manipuri Vaiṣṇava temple of Śrī Śrīnivāsa Ācārya Prabhu Āśrama. His desired was accomplished posthumously by his disciples and followers in the year 2012. One portion of the old *āśrama* was reconstructed into a multi-storied building with numerous rooms with modern brick structures. Now there are already several senior Vaiṣṇavīs being permanently facilitated in this *āśrama*. Till now, one old Vaiṣṇava and three Vaiṣṇavī had left their body due to natural old age in this shelter *āśrama*.

Once again, in October 1993, H.H. Bhaktisvarūpa Dāmodara Swāmī (His Holiness Bhaktisvarūpa is a title being honoured after accepting the *saṁnyāsī* order or sainthood in 1979) with many disciples and followers from different parts of the world, including two buses full of Manipuri devotees visited Rādhā-Kuṇḍa. The whole pilgrims were being hosted at Saugaijam Kunja where one of Swāmījī's lady disciple is also a family member from this reputed temple *āśrama*. While the rest of the pilgrim devotees were still at Saugaijam *mandira* enjoying themselves, in the afternoon, Swāmījī secretly paid a visit to Śrī Gopālajī Mandira with a few confident followers. With the blessings of Śrīmatī Rādhārānī and Śrī Gopālajī's arrangement, the visit was a historical moment in the future of Swāmījī's life here at Rādhā-Kuṇḍa to follow up. The following year, in September 1994, Swāmījī became a resident of Śrīdhāma Rādhā-Kuṇḍa by becoming a permanent sevāyataship of Śrī Gopālajī Mandira. Afterward, Swāmījī visited Rādhā-Kuṇḍa several times, stayed at Śrī Gopālajī Mandira, and permanently lived at his Samādhi Mandira from 4 October 2006 onward.

- Śrī Śrī Rādhā Gokulānanda Mandira.
- Śrī Śrī Rādhā Mādhavajī Mandira.
- Śrī Bihārījī Mandira.

These three temples belong to the Viṣṇupriya community from Assam, Tripurā, and Bangladesh. They also have a close affinity with the Manipuri Vaiṣṇava community of Rādhā-Kuṇḍa.

Section II
Literature (Manuscript)

6

Chingthang Khomba Maharaja Ganga Chatpa

Rajkumar Jhalajit Singh[1]

Another literary achievement of Lābaṇyacandra's reign is a travelogue describing Mahārājā Jai Singh's pilgrimage to Vrindavana. On 5 February 1798, i.e., 20 Phairen 1719, Śakābda, the king, started for Vrindavana from what is now the compound of the Raj Bhavan. He reached Navadwip, and from there, he proceeded by boat towards Vrindavana but died on the way at Murshidabad (approximately latitude 24.11 N; longitude 88.19 E) in West Bengal. A book covering the entire journey in detail from Imphal to Murshidabad, the ceremonies for the spiritual benefit of the departed king, and the return journey of the retinue from Murshidabad to Imphal was written in the reign of Labanya Chandra. The book is *Chingthang Khomba Maharaja Ganga Chatpa.*

Chingthang Khomba is one of the many names of Mahārājā Jai Singh. His other names are Kartā and Bhāgyacandra. His descendants usually call him Kartā, Vaiṣṇavite circles usually call him Bhāgyacandra while historians prefer to call him Jai Singh. Women of the valley and his hill subjects lovingly called him Chingthang Khomba. The word *gaṅgā* occurring in the title of the book, of course, means the River Gaṅgā and *chatpa* means "to go". The title of the book means Mahārājā Chingthang Khomba's going to the Gaṅgā.

The book is the joint work of three writers, Navachand, Haricharan, and Madhav Ram Wahengba. We have already noticed some books of Madhav Ram Wahengba. The laborious task of actually handling the pen was done by four juniors. Jai Singh went on the pilgrimage as the king of Manipur with full royal powers and privileges. Yuvarāja (crown prince) Labanya Chandra ruled Manipur on behalf of his father. Madhu Chandra, who was the *senāpati* (commander-in-chief), accompanied his royal father to provide security to him and the large retinue. Jai Singh was accompanied by his queens, five sons, three daughters, and a large number of pilgrims. The pilgrims including the king, queens princes, princesses and nobles numbered about 200, and their porters about 300. The king took with him arms, and ammunition and the royal insignia. On occasions, it was necessary to fire guns to keep dacoits away. Now, let us have a bird's-eye view of the pilgrimage.

Bird's-Eye View

King Jai Singh, in the evening of life, thought that he had reigned too long and decided to go on pilgrimage to Navadwip, the birthplace of Caitanya and the centre of the Bhakti movement. His ministers and nobles led by the prime minister requested him to change his decision. But he was determined to go on the pilgrimage. Learned brāhmaṇas and devotees of God also requested him to postpone the pilgrimage. He entreated them not to press their request. Rather, he asked their blessings for the success of the pilgrimage. Then old brāhmaṇa women and young and old ladies of the realm requested him to give up the pilgrimage as the long journey of the pilgrimage through forests and plains would be too hard for a king. He did not change his mind. Then, his wives, sons, and daughters requested that he give up the pilgrimage. He did not agree.

One day the king talked to Labanya Chandra in private. He asked him to administer the realm and handed over the sword *khagemba* and the royal *pān* bowl (a bowl with a lid for keeping pellets of betel, areca, etc.). Jai Singh then apologized to his ministers and nobles for the sufferings of the people during the frequent Burmese invasions in his reign. He appealed to them to give full cooperation to Labanya Chandra, who was now going to administer the realm in his absence. He then sent Kumudananda Haobamcha and Nava Thokchomcha at the head of a large gang of roadmenders. They were accompanied by a contingent of the Manipur Army to give cover to the engineering operation.

A few of his wives and some of his sons and daughters were eager to join the pilgrimage. Respecting their religious sentiment, the king allowed them to join. On Monday, the 20th day of Wakching at the auspicious hour of Mahendra, the king started on his long journey with his retinue in the midst of chanting of Hari's name, striking of cymbals, beating of drums, blowing of conchs and *shingas* and playing of *sanai*.

Women stall-holders at the Royal Market and women who came for marketing wept, "What a man of firm determination! Come back to your kingdom after the pilgrimage!" The king proceeded towards the south through the area between the rivers Imphal and Nambul. At every gate there was a lamp and burning of incense. Men and women of all ages thronged the road and bowed to the king as he passed. These words were on their lips: "Be pleased to return quickly after the pilgrimage". The king reached Kanchipur and spent the night at the site of the old palace.

The next day, he resumed his journey at dawn. At this stage, the women who came to Kanchipur to see him off returned to Imphal weeping. Jai Singh proceeded along the course of the Chandra Nadī and reached Bishnupur before nightfall. He spent the night there at the site of his former palace. The next morning, he resumed his journey and proceeded along the foot of the western hill and easily reached Khujairok. He spent the night there. Resuming the journey the next day, he crossed the Loijing range and, passed through the hill village of Urangpai and crossed the hill stream the Tonnan to reach the Leimatag River. He spent the night on the bank of the Leimatag. While staying there, he said to Labanya Chandra,

> "Your birth signs tell me that you will surely become a king. Become the king of Manipur. You shall follow the four policies: *sāma*, *dāma*, *daṇḍa*, and *bheda*. The wide sea never boils. Never boil over with rage. Keep yourself from favouritism. You must not give undue favour to your relatives by blood or marriage. The people are like the body. The king is like the soul. The body and the soul live in harmony. Likewise, the people and the king must work in close cooperation. The brave, the wise, the learned and those that excel in their respective professions are gems of the kingdom. Bestow favour on them according to their merit and you will reign successfully. Persevere and rule well to the best of your ability".

Labanya Chandra returned from Leimatag and met Chourajit at Khujairok. Chourajit was coming from Imphal to join his father. Labanya Chandra and Chourajit spent one night together at Khujairok. Labanya Chandra reached the capital and assumed regency. Under his orders, there were readings of the *Bhāgavata* at the palace everyday for the success of the king's pilgrimage.

Jai Singh proceeded following the course of the Leimatag, passed through a village of the Chirus, and crossed a hill range. He reached Tuyang and spent the night there. While he was there, he sent a message to Labanya Chandra to send fresh supplies of rice for the pilgrims. Envoys from the ruler of Tripurā also arrived there with presents and requested Jai Singh to give a Manipuri princess in marriage to the ruler of Tripurā.

King Jai Singh, comparable to Janak in relinquishing worldly pleasures, proceeded from Tuyang and crossing the Irang River, a hill range and the Gwai River, reached the territory of the king of Cachar. The king of Cachar learnt that the ruler of Tripurā was now in alliance with Jai Singh. There was some enmity between Cachar and Tripurā. The king of Cachar sent a message to Jai Singh that no Tripurī should be brought with him to Cachar. Jai Singh, therefore, procured boats from Lakhipur. He sent away the Tripurī envoys with instructions to wait for him at Bhaṅga with ample foodstuffs. He and his retinue proceeded by boat on the Barak and reached Jiri. From there, they proceeded by boat on the Barak and reached Ruparbari and, from there, Sonai.

Jai Singh and his retinue halted at Sonai. There was a problem in getting milk. But a servant of the king hit on a brilliant idea. He made a raft, crossed the water, and brought some milk for the king. A pilgrim following the king died at Sonai. Jai Singh, with his retinue, proceeded from Sonai and reached Hilisar. The youthful younger brother of the king of Cachar had built a nice camp at Hilisar for the Manipuri king. Jai Singh spent the night there with his retinue. The Cachar king's brother presented him with a great quantity of essential foodstuffs. The next morning, the king of Cachar greeted Jai Singh with presents of coins, gold and cloths. He requested Jai Singh to halt one day more as his mother wished to see his face. Jai Singh thought that this would be incompatible with the aims of the pilgrimage. So, he declined and presented one horse each to the Kachari king and his brother. He left Hilisar and reached Bhunbari. He spent the night there.

The next morning, Jai Singh and a part of the retinue proceeded by boat on the Barak River towards Bhaṅga. The remaining part of the retinue proceeded by land. As a fresh team of oarsmen rowed the boats, they proceeded swiftly. Those who proceeded by land reached a village called Udan. There, two sepoys armed with daggers held up their advance.

Prince Chourajit went to his father, riding a horse at full gallop, and reported the matter to him. On getting the news, an official from Tripurā named Mohan Singh sent two sepoys armed with muskets. These two sepoys summoned the sepoys who obstructed the advance of the pilgrims. The matter ended there, and the pilgrims proceeded without further hitch. They joined the king at the town of Bhaṅga.

At Bhaṅga, Jai Singh found that the Tripurī envoys had brought much essential foodstuffs for the pilgrims as he had ordered at Jiri. He found that there were some weak and ailing men who would not be able to undertake the arduous pilgrimage further. From Bhaṅga, he sent them back to Manipur under the leadership of five able men. He sent with them a large quantity of betel-nuts as his presents to ministers, nobles and women in the palace in Manipur. The weak and the ailing men started for Manipur under the leadership of the five men. At this stage, some messengers from Manipur sent by Labanya Chandra arrived with Rs. 444 and some gold. The king was pleased to learn that his son was ruling Manipur well. He told the messengers to return to Manipur after some rest and tell the regent that all the pilgrims were doing well. While at Bhaṅga, Jai Singh sent two men to Sylhet to see the British commissioner's reaction to his coming to Sylhet and also to know the price of essential commodities like rice and salt in the bazar of Golapganj. The bazar was about two days journey from Bhaṅga.

The king's men returned in time and reported to him that the British commissioner of Sylhet had waited for him for a few days and that a minister of the chief of Jaintia was waiting for him with presents. They also reported to him the price of foodstuffs in Golapganj bazar. Before starting the pilgrimage, Jai Singh sent messengers to the commissioner of Sylhet to inform him of his coming to Sylhet on pilgrimage with a large number of pilgrims. But now the king found that another person had become the commissioner of Sylhet. So, Jai Singh wrote a formal letter to the commissioner of Sylhet informing him, in detail, of his pilgrimage. He sent two messengers to Sylhet with the Jetter.

About this time, Khetri Gouradas arrived from Calcutta. Before beginning the pilgrimage, Jai Singh sent him from Imphal to Calcutta to inform the governor-general of his pilgrimage through British territory with a large retinue. Gouradas brought the message that Jai Singh and his retinue could go through British territory without let or hindrance. The two messengers who were sent to Sylhet also arrived. Rabat Sabib[2] asked Jai Singh to come to Sylhet without hesitation. He added that the change of the incumbent was immaterial and that he was as good as his predecessor. The wise king was happy with this news from Calcutta and Sylhet.

The next day, the king left Bhaṅga for a village in the territory of the chief of Jaintia. Only a small part of the retinue accompanied him. The major part of the retinue was sent to Golapganj bazar by land. When Jai Singh reached the village in the territory of the Jaintia chief, he found that the chief had built no camp for his stay. He and his retinue were, therefore, obliged to spend the night in their boats on the River Barak. The king's boat had a weatherproof shelter. Night came. What a stormy night! It hailed copiously. The banks were swiftly covered with hail. Then rain followed with high wind. It was a downpour. Blazing lightning and deafening peals of thunder! The Barak was now in spate. What a dangerous night! There was no casualty, however. The king's men changed the moorings five times during that night, bringing the moorings higher and higher on the bank.

The next day, a minister of the chief of Jaintia brought, on behalf of his chief, the presents to Jai Singh. The king and his retinue were obliged to spend one more night in the territory of the chief of Jaintia. The king got a disquieting report. In that locality, there were dacoits who were in the habit of committing dacoity with murder. The king ordered Lakshman Nameirakpa to fire guns around the perimeter of the camp every now and again. Because of this arrangement, no dacoit dared come. When it dawned, the king and his retinue started for Golapganj.

When Jai Singh and his men reached Golapganj, he found that those members of his retinue he sent from Bhaṅga had already reached there. After resting for a while, all the Manipuri pilgrims assembled together. The king called Prince Madhu Chandra and told him to go to Tripurā with some men as an advance party. They were to go on horseback. The king himself crossed the River Barak in a boat with some men and reached Sylhet. Mr Robert, the commissioner of Sylhet, had struck two tents on the bank and was waiting for him. Mr Robert had made arrangements for a formal reception. All the things needed for such a reception were there. Twelve sepoys guarded the place day and night. King Jai Singh, accompanied by Prince Vishwanath and Prince Gambhir Singh, entered the British tent with all the royal insignia. Mr Robert stood up, took off his hat, and held the king's hand.

The commissioner of Sylhet asked the king why he went on pilgrimage, leaving behind his kingdom. Whom did he leave as regent? The king replied that he had appointed his son Labanya Chandra as a regent. The king added that as he was advanced in age, he came on a pilgrimage to give up his mortal body in a holy place. The commissioner of Sylhet gazed at him and said, "O great king! king of Manipur! You are an embodiment of virtue. No king has ever spoken like this. I think there is no parallel also in the stories in the scriptures. But let the other pilgrims return to British territory after the pilgrimage is over." After the conversation, there did was exchange of presents. The king presented him with costly cloths of silk. The commissioner of Sylhet presented the king with a telescope that was three cubits long and two tents. Two British officers were present with the commissioner. They gave presents to the other pilgrims. The king and his men returned to their camp on the other side of the Barak.

Jai Singh sent a part of the retinue to Tripurā as the second batch of an advance party. Princess Harisheshwari was included in this batch. They proceeded by boat. The commissioner of Sylhet provided an elephant to carry the Manipuri king's luggage and two sepoys for escort up to Tripurā. Jai Singh took a Tripurī guide and went to Dhaka Dakshin, the ancestral home of Caitanya. He held a religious feast and a Manipuri-style *saṅkīrtana* (devotional songs) there. While returning to his camp, there was an incident. There was a bottleneck as the road passed over a hillock. Men and ponies could pass easily, but an elephant could not. Jai Singh and some of his men passed without difficulty, but the elephant carrying the tents was held up near the hillock. Without the tents the Manipuri pilgrims would be in difficulty at the camp. The king's storekeeper, old in age but young in spirit, led a team of roadmenders in cutting the hillside and broadening the road. The elephant could now pass easily. The king and the other pilgrims reached their rest camp along with the tents.

At the camp at night, it rained heavily. It hailed also. But four nobles led by Bhadra Singh kept vigil all the night and made every endeavour to protect the king from rain, wind and cold. After leaving this camp, the king and the other pilgrims spent some more nights on the way and reached the town of Tarop in Tripurā. Meanwhile Prince Madhu Chandra, the commander-in-chief of Manipur, was anxious in Tripurā. What had happened to his old father? Madhu Chandra sent two persons to see what had happened to the king and the other pilgrims. They met the king and the other pilgrims at Tarop.

After getting the message sent by Madhu Chandra that the ruler of Tripurā had made nice arrangements, Jai Singh and his retinue left Tarop and reached Makara Bazar via Champapur. At Makara Bazar, a minister of Tripurā received Jai Singh with presents. A certain Madan Sai, who had lived in Tripurā for some years, also joined the reception. After this, the king and his retinue reached Agartala.

At Agartala, the king and his retinue and the two batches of the advance party sent earlier to Tripurā assembled. Here, Jai Singh saw that it would be a great problem to feed so many people. So, he sent back most of his followers to Manipur under the leadership of two officers. To provide cover to the returnees, he sent back most of the armed personnel also. At Agartala, Jai Singh gave his daughter Harisheshwari in marriage to Rajdhar Manik, the ruler of Tripurā. The actual ceremony of *kanyādāna* (giving away a girl in marriage) was performed by Prince Tulajit as Jai Singh had given up family affairs.

Jai Singh made preparations to resume the pilgrimage. Rajdhar Manik requested Jai Singh to spend the monsoon in Tripurā as the journey to Navadwip would be very inconvenient in the rainy season. Jai Singh had a premonition of death. He somehow guessed that he might die the next autumn. So, he declined and prepared for the next leg of the pilgrimage. He rewarded the warriors who protected the pilgrims from dacoits. He ordered Purushottam Chiromcha to purchase firewood and bring it in a boat for use in the pilgrimage for cooking and keeping the pilgrims warm at night. He left one woman and five men in Tripurā to remain with Harisheshwari so that she might not feel lonely in her hew surroundings. The woman was Devamallika Hidamcha, and the men were Narayan Laishraba, Tulasi Shyam Shanglakpa, Chudamani Thiyamcha, Parashu Ram Lairikyekteiba, and Caitanya Thingujamba. He ordered a servant of his to hire a few boats and bring his belongings, which his fleet of boats could not hold. On an auspicious day at an auspicious moment, the king resumed his journey with his retinue.

The king reached the town of Makaran. He ordered a servant of his to bring in a few boats and his goods. These boats were to come in the rear. Then he sent ten persons to Manipur to deliver to Labanya Chandra the message that Harisheshwari had been married to the ruler of Tripurā and that he had left Tripurā for Navadwip. He sent 23 men to go to Navadwip by land and provided each of them with a horse. At this stage, Purushottam Chiromcha, who had left Agartala to buy firewood, arrived. The king and his retinue had a good meal with fresh vegetables, including blossoms of plantain tree and pumpkin seasoned with green chilies.

The king and his retinue resumed the journey in a fleet of 67 boats. Out of these, the ruler of Tripurā contributed 15. Of the remaining, one was a big boat purchased by Jai Singh, and two belonged to the queens who bought them there. All the Manipuri pilgrims reached the village called Goshaipur. The king's servants could not build huts to spend the night in. So, tents were struck, and the king and the other pilgrims rested comfortably during the night.

The next day, they reached the River Meghanā. At nightfall, they made arrangements to spend the night on its bank. At night, they heard land loud human voices, accompanied by the beating of drums coming from the east. What was it? The king sent a few men to find out its nature. The men returned and reported to the king that it was a usual affair occurring every day at this locality.

The pilgrims resumed the journey and reached the River Brahmaputra. They offered *tarpaṇa* (offerings to the manes) in the Brahmaputra with rice, sesamum, *bermuḍā* grass, and flowers. Resuming the journey, they reached the village called Dhakeshwar. Here, the king received 700 British Indian Rupees sent by the ruler of Tripurā. Leaving Dhakeshwar behind, the pilgrims proceeded further and reached the Padmā River. Here also they offered *tarpaṇa*. Among the pilgrims, there were some who brought the ashes of their ancestors for immersion in the Gaṅgā. The king sent them to Balicharan Ghāṭ, a *ghāṭ* (a bathing place with or without stairs at the bank of a river) of the Gaṅgā. They were to immerse the ashes there. He also sent with them a daughter of Garib Nawaz, who came all the way with Jai Singh to perform a religious feast on the bank of the Gaṅgā for the spiritual benefit of the departed king.

Here the king found that the boats which carried tusks and beeswax to be sold in Calcutta did not arrive. According to his orders, the boats came in the rear. But what had happened to them? Did they sink in the river? Or did dacoits attack them?

The king sent some men to find out what had happened. They found the boats safely moored to the riverbank and waiting for the high winds to subside. The boats and the men who were sent to find them arrived and reported to the king. After this, the king reached Jalaki Ghāṭ. From there, he wrote a letter to Ganga Govinda Singh, the Dewan of Navadwip, requesting him to find a house for him to stay in during his stay at Navadwip. He sent Khetri Gouradas, who knew Bengali well, and two others to carry the letter to Navadwip.

A serious problem faced the pilgrims at Jalaki Ghāṭ. They found that from there, there was no navigable channel up to Buṛhī Gaṅgā. So, the king sent back the 15 boats of the ruler of Tripurā to him. The hired boats also departed. What about the remaining few boats? The Manipuris carried them, except the biggest one, physically on their shoulders till they reached Buṛhī Gaṅgā. It took two days. The king, however, went on a palanquin.

The king and the other pilgrims went for one day by boat. They found that the 23 men who were sent by the king from Makaran to Navadwip on horseback had not yet arrived. The king felt for them. He feared that they might have gone short of money. He sent two men with Rs. 35 to wait for them on the road and give the money to them. The two men met the 23 men coming on horseback and gave them the money. Because of that, food did not run short, and they and the two messengers arrived safely and reported it to the king.

The pilgrims who came by boat and the pilgrims who came by land joined one another. The king now wished to go by land. But he told those who came by boat to go to Navadwip by boat. Likewise, those who came by land were to go to Navadwip by land. All the pilgrims spent one night together.

The next day, the pilgrims proceeded as directed by the king. The king himself, going by land, reached Krishnanagar. The *rājā* of Krishnanagar had built a township called Gangabas for himself to spend his last days in. He offered it to Jai Singh to stay in. But the Manipuri king thought that to live there in luxury, even for a short while, would be incompatible with the ideals of the pilgrimage. So, he declined and left for Navadwip.

The king and those who came by land reached the Gaṅgā, and they bathed in it. Some held religious feasts for the spiritual benefit of their ancestors. A Manipuri pilgrim died here. The pilgrims now crossed a branch of the Gaṅgā and reached Navadwip, the birthplace of Caitanya. The advance party of the Manipuri pilgrims sent by the king to Ganga Govinda Singh had built two huts in which all the Manipuri pilgrims could stay. They were modest, neat, and clean. King Jai Singh liked them very much. All the Manipuri pilgrims who came by land or by boat stayed in them happily. A descendant of Nityānanda and a descendant of Advaita came there and saw Jai Singh. The Vaiṣṇava community there, led by Gourachand, a descendant of Gouridas, presented rice, salt, milk, ghee, and sugar to the Manipuri king.

The Manipuri pilgrims visited Ambikā, a nearby place of pilgrimage. There the king arranged a Manipuri *saṅkīrtana* of women. The star singer was Devahuti. She was assisted by seven women singers. The drummers were, of course, two men. The site was packed to capacity. It was a grand success. The mother of the *rājā* of Bardhaman requested the king through a brāhmaṇa *paṇḍita* to repeat the performance at her residence. The king declined, saying that the *saṅkīrtana* was not for performance at the residence of mortals for their amusement. The pilgrims returned to Navadwip. They spent some days at Navadwip. During their stay, they had a busy programme visiting different temples. Jai Singh went to the temple of Rādhā Ramaṇa, an image of Kṛṣṇa worshipped by Gour Shyam in Manipur, but taken after his death to Navadwip and worshipped there by the dowager queen. Jai Singh offered a Manipuri gold coin and a cloth for the dress of the image. When the king returned, he found that Khetri Gouradas and Ganga Govinda fell ill. He called his physicians and told them to treat them. Then he left for Soudabaji. The place was at a distance of a few days only, but during the journey, he had much difficulty on account of the incessant rain. On one occasion, he had no firewood to cook his evening meal. At this critical time, Jagadananda Haobamcha presented just one bundle of firewood to the king. After visiting many temples at Soudabaji, the king returned to Navadwip.

The pilgrimage to Navadwip was now over. So, Jai Singh sent back to Manipur under most pilgrims two officers, Kumudananda Haobamcha and Birasingh Oinamcha. Jai Singh sent this message through these officers: "In administration, do everything now according to your discretion. Don't reserve matters for my consideration anymore." He also sent Khagindra Nandeiba and Sujan Laipik-yekteiba to Tripurā to see his daughter Harisheshwari and to allow those left in Tripurā to go on a pilgrimage to the Gaṅgā. The pilgrims, after bowing to the king, started for Manipur.

Jai Singh now shifted to a house of Ganga Govinda on the other bank of the Gaṅgā. The king presented two swords to him. Throughout this long journey up to this time, measurement of time was done by Hari Thokchomcha. The king asked him to continue to attend to the clepsydra well and keep time carefully as before to enable the remaining pilgrims to be punctual. He also asked the conch-blower of the Khoisnam family to blow conchs as before on reaching temples and holy places. He asked the pilgrims not to fear that food would run short.

The king purchased wood, bamboo, and other building materials. Madhu Chandra, the commander-in-chief (*senāpati*), built houses for the king and all other pilgrims. He also built a parlour for the king from his own pocket. Then, the pilgrims fenced the compound of their resting place, dug the soil, sowed pulses, and planted banana trees. Using this place as their base, the pilgrims visited nearby holy places. On one such occasion, they went to a place called Kunworpur. There at the temple of Rādhā Mādhava, they got among other things, sugar-candy (Manipuri *sitamisarī*), then a novelty to the Manipuris. On another occasion, they spent a night at a village

Jnanjan. Dacoits were active. Four gunners were placed round the perimeter of the resting place. They fired guns now and again with loud bombs throughout the night. No dacoit dared approach the Manipuri camp. The Manipuris returned safely. The boat left at Jalaki was fetched.

The king was aware that he had not yet reached the holy place for which he came. He sent Shri Ni Thokchomcha and three others to Murshidabad to find out Śrīpat Kṣetra, where Narottam Ṭhākur of hallowed memory lived. After finding the place, Shri Ni was to return promptly and report to him. The other three were to remain at Murshidabad and build a rest camp for the king and all other pilgrims. The king also sent four persons led by Lokanath, a brāhmaṇa of Soudabaji, to Calcutta to sell the tusks and the beeswax. The money would be utilized for meeting the expenses of the pilgrimage.

One of the men sent to Śrīpat Kṣetra returned and reported favourably. The king sent two more men there with a message to begin construction of the camp. He also sent seven persons on horseback led by Prince Chourajit with the necessary funds. He also told them to sow seeds of vegetables in their camp. On Friday the 5th of Thawan (about August), the king left Jnanjan for Śrīpat Kṣetra in a boat on the Gaṅgā. The king's boat could not hold all the pilgrims. Prince Chourajit was to bring more pilgrims in other boats. On the way, the king's boat was caught in a storm and narrowly escaped being capsized. The boat went upstream further. Near the second bend of the Gaṅgā downstream from Kamila, there were rapids. All the men in the boat managed it carefully and with fine teamwork, and the danger was passed. After some days, the king's boat reached Śrīpat Kṣetra. The boats which followed the king's boat were not so fortunate. Campakalatā, a junior wife of the king who went in one of these boats, was drowned in the Gaṅgā. The other pilgrims arrived safely at Śrīpat Kṣetra.

The king seemed to know that his earthly existence was coming to an end. He sent for Prince Madhu Chandra. He also sent for all those Manipuris still remaining at Jnanjan.

When all the Manipuri pilgrims assembled before him, he gave clear instructions. He sent two men to buy a standing timber, a tamarind tree. A temporary hut for him to stay in was to be built with the timber. Prince Madhu Chandra felled it and cut it into sizeable pieces for the hut, and the first post (Manipuri *jātrā*) was erected. But the king fell seriously ill.

Seeing the sorrow of the five princes—Madhu Chandra, Chourajit, Vishwanath, Tulajit, and Gambhīr Singh, the king said, "The love between father and son, between brothers and between husband and wife is but a temporary worldly affair. Devotion to Kṛṣṇa, the Supreme Being, is the greatest wealth. Do not grieve for me." To the other pilgrims, he said, "You have served me with devotion and to the best of your ability. When you reach home, serve Labanya Chandra likewise."

To Madhu Chandra, Jai Singh said "My son, Madhu Chandra, you have served me without the least reservation, I am satisfied. I have also attained most of my objectives. The end of your devoted service has come now." Return to Manipur with your mother and the other pilgrims, saving them from all troubles and looking after them well. Entrust them to Labanya Chandra. Following me, your mothers have visited many holy places that no woman has ever had the facility to visit.

> "Your little brothers Vishwanath and Gambhīr Singh are like the prints on your body, the prints of holy names and marks made with blocks from these places of pilgrimage. Carry your brothers lovingly. Carry to Manipur these four articles of royal insignia—the *hookāh* decorated with gold, the vessel of gold for drinking water, the receptacle of gold for betel, and the platter of gold for keeping towels on. Place them before your beloved brother Labanya Chandra, to whom I have given the throne."

He told Chourajit to go to Vrindavana with Tulajit, who was carrying a part of his ashes for immersion. The remaining part of the ashes was to be taken to Manipur. Then Jai Singh listened to the reading of the *Bhāgavata*. He offered gold to seven brāhmaṇa *paṇḍitas*. His sons placed *prasāda* from temples on his lips. Jai Singh's last words in this world were "Śrī Rādhā Kṛṣṇa". He breathed his last on Friday, the 3rd day of Mera[3] at about 1-30 p.m.[4]

The timber of the tamarind tree mentioned above proved to be very handy. Madhu Chandra cut the timber into smaller pieces, and Jai Singh's funeral pyre was made of these pieces. Sandalwood, *ghee*, and incense were added to the pyre. Prince Tulajit ignited the funeral pyre amidst the chanting of God's name, blowing of conchs, beating of drums, and firing of salvoes. Brāhmaṇa *paṇḍita* and people of both sexes of Śrīpat Kṣetra joined the funeral.

A few days after his death, the money sent by Labanya Chandra arrived. The price of his tusks and beeswax mentioned above also arrived. Then, the *śrāddha* ceremony of Jai Singh was performed on the 13th day of the demise according to Manipuri custom. Then, according to the custom prevalent at Śrīpat Kṣetra, an *ahorātri kīrtana* (singing of God's name for 24 hours without stopping) was performed. Three teams of singers of Śrīpat Kṣetra, one team from Navadwip, and one local team from Manipur performed the *ahorātri kīrtana*. The pilgrims spent about one month more visiting different holy places. Then Chourajit left for Vrindavana. Tulajit could not accompany him on account of illness. The Manipuri pilgrims began their return journey. They returned by boat, and the pilgrims reached Makaran. From there, Madhu Chandra sent messengers to Labanya Chandra to inform him of the death of their father and of their return journey. The pilgrims reached Agartala and spent ten days there. From there, a letter was sent to Labanya Chandra requesting help with the return journey. Without difficulty, the pilgrims reached Badarpur. After staying there for five days, they reached Hailakandi. Then they reached Lakhipur via Udharban and Khaspur. From Lakhipur, they reached Bishnupur in the Manipur Valley. They reached the capital of Manipur on the 20th day of Lamda 1799.

Critical Appreciation

This is a good travelogue. But the date of the beginning of Jai Singh's pilgrimage given in this book does not agree with the date given in the Royal Chronicle. There is a difference of one month. This has to be looked into. This book does not give the dates of many important events, such as Harisheshwari's marriage, the arrival of Jai Singh at Navadwip, and Śrīpat Kṣetra, etc. If it mentioned these dates, the usefulness of the book would be much greater. While giving an account of Jai Singh's listening to the reading of the *Bhāgavata* before his death, there is an allusion to Parīkṣit's listening to the *Bhāgavata* for seven days immediately before his death. The allusion is very apt. Jai Singh also listened to the *Bhāgavata* for seven days immediately before his death. But there is an error. *Chingthang Khomba Maharaja Ganga Chatpa* makes Vaiśampāyana relate the *Bhāgavata* to Parīkṣit. But it was Śuka and not Vaiśampāyana who related the *Bhāgavata* to Parīkṣit.

In spite of these drawbacks here and there, we appreciate the book much.

NOTES

1. R.K. Jhalajit Singh (1998/November). *A History of Manipuri Literature* (Volume II, 1709-1819), Imphal, pp. 136-53.
2. Mr. Robert.
3. 12 October 1978.
4. Local Time of Murshidabad.

7

Mahārāja Gambhīr Singh and Śrī Vrindavana

Manindra Konsam

Around the end of the seven-year Burmese occupation of Manipur since 1819, the combined determination and brotherhood bonds of Gambhīr Singh and his cousin Nara Singh liberated the valley of Manipur, and Gambhīr Singh ascended the throne of Manipur for the second time on 12 June 1825; and dispelled the Burmese completely from Manipur in February 1826 and started building a strong sovereign Manipur.

After 1826, peace prevailed in the political spheres of Manipur. King Gambhīr Singh, after the completion of the renovation and reconstruction of the palace at Langthabal, where his father Chingthangkhomba (Bhāgyacandra) (1763-98) reigned, shifted the capital from Bishnupur. The idols of Śrī Govindajī and Śrī Vrindavanacandrajī, which were evacuated to Cachar during the Burmese occupation of Manipur, which is known as "Seven Years Devastation", were brought back to Langthabal via Bishnupur and reinstalled with pomp:

> *"Mutum khombagi kum shak 1749... mera thaadi thaangjana halle . . . kuntaruk ni leipaakpokpada shree govindajee okpa chatle . . . . khwairaakpa eerenta shree govindajeebu khurumba phangladuna shree govindaga shrijutka shri maharanisu yaona hallakle . . . poynu thaati leipaakpokpana halle . . . . mapan ni leipaakpokpata leibaakki angam athounachingba thaana thaana mapham khudingta govindagi laishang shaiye. laphu yunge lambi lam ahum paakna bishnupurtagi langthaban faona yaanle. brahman vaishnav lamboiba pumnama matam kuina khurumpa phangtarapapu shree govindajeegi padavalipu premka loinana louchaiye. meite leipaakta leingampaki nahaanupi hanuba naha nupi pumnamakna premdhaara ichenna khutaang pipham teituna maana maana ngamba potpu shree govindajeegi khuyaada katcheiye. lei chai dolai pujeiye.... numitaang yuthak matungda langthabal konungda thungle. . .".* (The year of Mutum Khomba, Saka 1749 . . . . the month of Mera starts on Saturday . . .)

On the 26th Tuesday proceeded to receive Śrī Govindajī. Received Govindajī at Khwairaakpa Eerel and the king, queen along with Govinda returns. The month of Poynu begin on Tuesday. . . . On the 9th Tuesday, nobles and the public constructed temple huts for Govinda in every village. Three arm-length wide roads were made from Bishnupur to Langthabal, and plantain trees were erected alongside them. All brāhmaṇas, Vaiṣṇavas, monks, and devotees who had been obviated from worshipping heartrendingly and emotionally touched the feet of Govindajī. All the young and old of Manipur offered whatever they could afford to Śrī Govindajī. They showered flower petals, carried palanquin. . . . Reached Langthabal palace in the late evening. (*Cheitharol Kumbaba*).

Other than reinstallation and worshipping of Śrī Govindajī Mahārājā Gambhīr Singh, being a devout Hindu, also revived worshipping of Śrī Hanumān Ṭhākurajī in 1828 CE by repairing the old temple, which was ruined during the Burmese occupation:

> "Śaka 1750, the year of Yanglem Khunchao . . . Monday starts the month of Poynu. . . . On 27th Friday, engaging the Mahārāja himself started repairing of Śrī Mahābali Ṭhākura Hanumān." (*Cheitharol Kumbaba*).

Also, in 1832 CE, he introduced the Ratha Yātrā festival in Manipur by installing the idol of Śrī Śrī Jagannātha,

> "Śaka 1754 the year of Thangjam Uraba. The month of Kalen starts on Tuesday. . . . on Sunday the 20th, a brāhmaṇa who came from Jagannātha Kṣetra started carving the idol of Jagannātha. . . . The month of Ingen begins on Friday. On the same day the idol of Jagannātha was installed. On the 2nd, Saturday the festival of Ratha Yātrā started." (*Cheitharol Kumbaba*).

On the other hand, the valiant of Mahārāja Gambhīr Singh as a true Sanātanī Vaiṣṇava can be seen in an instance that took place in 1829 CE during his sojourn at Sylhet (of present-day Bangladesh).

In 1829 CE, Mahārājā Gambhīr Singh went to Sylhet as the British approached him to help them out in subduing the Khahi (Khasiyas of present-day Meghalaya) and indeed, Mahārājā Gambhīr Singh, along with his Meitei Armies defeated and captured Khahi king and handed over to the British. During that brief sojourn at Sylhet, a day happened to be the same day of the Ratha Yātrā festival of Hindus and the Muharram festival of Musalmans. At such happening a conflicting situation came up between the two parties of Hindu and Musalman opting to celebrate their festival first before one another; in which the British sided with the Musalmans by ordering the Muharram procession to take place before the Ratha Yātrā procession of the Hindus. In that conflicting situation, Mahārājā Gambhīr Singh came forward and stood valiantly to lead the Ratha Yātrā procession of the Hindus before the Muharram procession. That gesture of Mahārājā Gambhīr Singh was all praised by the Hindus of Sylhet:

> "The year of Thiyam Antram, Śaka 1751. . . .The month of Kalen starts on Monday. . . . On the 22nd Monday, Śrīyut Mahārāja proceeded for Sylhet to help the British as informed of having failed in subduing the Khahis. The governor received the Mahārāja at the riverbank and marched together to subdue the Khahi. The British army from Assam and the Meitei army were divided to attack differently. Meitei army first plundered villages. Captured the Khahi king and handed it over to the British. A conflict aroused out of a day when the Hindu festival of Ratha Yātrā and Musalman festival of Muharram falls on same day and one group preferring themselves to celebrates their festival first before another and whereas the British authority taking sided with the Musalmans ordered Muharram procession to take first before the Ratha Yātrā procession; however, Śrīyut Mahārāja came forward and led to performed the Rath Yātrā procession, whereby the king was all praised by the people of Sylhet for his courageous act of keeping Sanātanī Dharma." (*Cheitharol Kumbaba*).

Mahārājā Gambhīr Singh was known for his devotion to Śrī Govindajī and love for Gauḍīya Vaiṣṇavism; it is said that Gauḍīya Vaiṣṇavism in Manipur flourished to its zenith in his time. He introduced Gosta Līlā, a form of dance-drama based on cattle herding days of Śrī Kṛṣṇa, in addition to three forms of Rāsa, *viz.:* Mahā Rāsa, Vasanta Rāsa, and Kuñja Rāsa, introduced by his father, Mahārājā Bhāgyacandra.

Above all, Gambhīr Singh planned for himself to spend his last days at Vrindavana in the service of Śrī Rādhā-Kṛṣṇa; as such, the king confided his yearning to his confident brother-in-law Langmaithem Kirti Nongthonba and deputed him with a big amount of money for acquiring a convenient place inside Vrindavana to construct a temple and also a separate building for dwelling. The task of acquiring land and constructing a temple and dwelling house was successfully completed, for which material evidence still exists in the form of a temple complex at Rādhā-Kuṇḍa near Vrindavana.

Immediately after the demise of Gambhīr Singh on 9 January 1834, his infant son, Candrakīrti (Ningthempishak), was enthroned as the king of Manipur while the uncle Senāpati Nara Singh shouldered responsibilities of ruling affairs. However, by the turns of a few events within royal affairs, the dowager King Mother fled from Manipur on 27 January 1844 with her young son Candrakīrti, leaving the throne empty. However, yielding to persuasion from nobles and subjects, Nara Singh ascended the throne on Thursday, 8 February 1844, and reigned till his death on 10 April 1850.

During his reign, Mahārājā Nara Singh assigned two of his court's *paṇḍita*, Dayaram Louremba and Nabashyam Ningthoujamba, to write a book about Gambhīr Singh, describing their love of brotherhood bond, their endurances in liberating Manipur from Burmese occupation, unbearable sufferings by the peoples of Manipur during the Seven Years Devastation; moreover, all about Gambhīr Singh's devotion to Śrī Rādhā-Kṛṣṇa and love for Gauḍīya Vaiṣṇavism and his yearning of spending his last days at Vrindavana in the service of Śrī Rādhā-Kṛṣṇa. Thus, the two *paṇḍita*s wrote *Gambhir Singh Nonggaaba* (Demise of Gambhīr Singh) is one of the finest literary works of that period.

The two *paṇḍita*s, Dayaram Louremba and Nabashyam Ningthoujamba write in their *Gambhir Singh Nonggaaba* (Demise of Gambhīr Singh). The gist of the text as relevant to the paper is explained below:

(1) After reigning fruitfully with ardent devotion to Śrī Rādhā-Kṛṣṇa in his heart, the judicious king, considering his age, acknowledged himself that he will no more be able to fulfil all his wishes.
(2) Unseen in front as of a different face, but the inner eyes which can easily see through seven heavens above and through the darkness of seven earths down below sans the worldly joys and sorrows with pure heart, my devotion to the ultimate Gauḍīya Dharma is the only thing I have achieved.
(3) Abstaining from all worldly pleasures and not seeing any of the human contempt, I shall leave for Śrī Vrindavana, the heaven on this earth and the harbour of human salvation, where the incarnation of Rādhā and Kṛṣṇa confluence as in the form of the creator Brahmā, with ornamentation of six seasons of the west along the enchanting cuckoos coo as the harbor of human's salvation.
(4) Thinking Śrī Rādhā-Kṛṣṇa, who was born in the house of Nanda-Yaśodā, may embrace him warmly and disclose his desire to nobody, the king confides his yearning to his confidant brother-in-law Langmaithem Kirti Nongthonba.
(5) And deputed with a large amount of money, saying: Oh, my brother-in-law Nongthonba, you choose a convenient place inside Śrī Vrindavana and construct a temple and a separate dwelling building. (p. 3)
(6) My yearning for Śrī Vrindavana, the land of bliss where one Brahmā (creator) existed in two separate forms of Śrī Rādhā-Kṛṣṇa, may be granted sooner. (p. 37)
(7) Langmaithem Kirti Singh Nongthonba, brother-in-law of the king, with an injunctive command, proceeded to Śrī Vrindavana after acquiring appropriate land and started planning to construct the temple and others. (p. 45)

(8) At the place where the centuries-old *pīpal* tree is called *śyāmabaṭa*, where the king of cowherds Śyāmakanhai is, the sun is setting with a cool breeze. (pp. 45-46).

(9) Keeping the *śyāmabaṭa* inside the compound wall a temple and a storied building along the corner of the compound is beautifully constructed with fine plastering floors. (p. 46)

(10) And another storied building for store and other purposes is also separately constructed, and the floor of the precinct of the temple is tiled with white marble. Four idols of gods sculpted from white marble are installed in each of the four corners of the compound. After the completion of the construction of the temple, the idol of Śrī Kṛṣṇa was initiated and installed. (p. 46)

(11) After complying with everything his brother-in-law, King Gambhīr Singh, wanted and entrusted to him, Nongmaithem Kirti Singh Nongthonba returned to Manipur and faithfully reported to the king. (pp. 46-47)

From the above-cited contents in the book *Gambhir Singh Nonggaaba*, the devotion of Mahārājā Gambhīr Singh to Śrī Rādhā-Kṛṣṇa and his love for Śrī Vrindavana can be clearly seen. The present *akhāṛā* still existing at the Rādhā-Kuṇḍa near Śrī Vrindavana, though now fallen in the hands of outsiders due to mismanagement from the side of descendants; will remain ever as an epitome of Mahārājā Gambhīr Singh and his love of Śrī Vrindavana.

Section III
Pilgrimage (Yātrā)

8

Pilgrimage to Brinam

Ashangbam Minaketan Singh
(Translated from Manipuri to English by Mayanglambam Sadananda)

Since it is the sacred abode of Bṛndādevī the Vrindavana is called Brinam by the Meiteis. The word Brinam is derived from Bṛndām. Travelling to Vrindavana is thus known as travelling to Brinam.

Bṛndādevī was the consort of Śaṅkhāsura, the demon king of Jalandhar—being a *satī*[1] lived only for her husband. Because of her ethical principles anyone said to be powerful belonging to the heaven, the earth, the underworld—the three worlds could not touch her husband. Having reigned tranquilly once Śaṅkhāsura, just rose up gradually the arrogence day by day. The heaven doubted him in fear of approaching towards the throne of Indra perhaps. As they doubted approached as thus. No sooner than the Viṣṇu stepped down listening to the anguished voice of the heaven and obliterated the ethical principles of *satī*, vanished the life of Śaṅkhāsura.

The heaven just escaped, the Viṣṇu himself extremely yeilded to *satī*, when listening to the umbrage of *satī* "the stone you are, not the image of love", the Viṣṇu became stone image into the form of today's Śālagrāma. Sanctioned the leaf of *tulasī* as the attribute of Bṛndā, be the holy leaf for *Bhāgavata*[2] worship while the water of coarse be the holy water in attribute of Śaṅkhāsura. Viṣṇu remained completely suppliant on Bṛndā, never moved for a single step from Vriṇdavana, performed his eternal devine pastimes. Also in Dvāpara,[3] even the earthly pastimes were performed on this sacred place.

That was towards the end of Dvāpara age. The quality of arrogance reached its limit, not only it touched the limitation but extremely excessive. In subsequent, disappreared exceedingly the quality of *satya.*[4] Being dependent on *rajo guṇa*[5] and *tamo guṇa*[6] a fair space for it was found. Turned over surplusly from the earlier thoughts, ethics, perspectives, destination, and perception of life's meaning. Miserable aspects of selfish and ego-centric attitudes became the ethics of the age. Failed to feel the night and day although it remained, the sin and virtue were remained invisible although they were existed. The intolerable tortures from monsters who were withstand strongers like Rudra[7] in strength, possessed immortality in lives—the powers of uncountable number of demons, terrible behaviours of the devils, the kings who possessed the unacheivable power from meditation altogether compelled the mother earth to call on the Almighty by transforming herself into a form of a cow running on all sides with a tragic voice. The lament of mother earth was blown into the mercious ears of Almighty.

The burdens of earth to redeem
To save the saints
Descended the Almighty on earth immidiately.
The miscreants to annihilate
The principles of religion to re-establish
Was descending himself the Almighty
The sorrows of the ages
In mind to redeem
Was descending Almighty in the form of human.

The very first anchorage of Almighty was Mathurā, landing on the prison of Kangsha. That was exactly at the time of ringing the bell of midnight. Sooner kept aside to Gokula. Dwelling twelve years in the abode of Nanda by hiding his identity with illusion. Hence, known to be the son of Nanda and Yaśodā by all and even by [Gokula] themselves. Played several eternal pastimes, not a single but in series. Tested the multiple tastes of friends, devotees, parents' affections, and melodious love. By the series of those earthly pastimes manifested the paths for participating in his cheerful eternal recreations to the world.

Gokula is also called Braja, a land situated under Brajamaṇḍala. The Brajamaṇḍala refers to a line of grazing ground, a name of boundrical area covering 84 *kosa*[8] around the *mahānagarī* of Mathurā. It is thus called [Gokula] as it is the site for cowherds. As espoused in the family of a cowherd the child Kṛṣṇa is called Gopāla-Kṛṣṇa. Since Brajamaṇḍala is the place for childhood pastimes of Lord Kṛṣṇa, it has been holy place for the sacrament of Gopāla-Kṛṣṇa's devotees.

Vrindavana is in Gokula. Therefore it is called Braja-Vrindavana. Hence, travelling to Brinam is said to be travelling to Braja. This place did remain in darkness for a long time. Śrī Kṛṣṇa Caitanya[9] did ascertain it anew. Most of the temples are of the school of Caitanya's scholars. Therefore, as it is purified by the footprints of prophets, in spite of being the holy place for Lord's pastimes it has moreover been a sacred place for the devotees of Gauraṅga. The prayers of the noble brāhmaṇas also extend a heavy influence on them. Pilgrimage to witness the Vrindavana has been a legitimate religious obligation to all of them. Vrindavana has always been a holy place for years since the time the millions of devotees travelled on foot upon a hope, "an opportunity to participate in the ceremony having occurred on a calendrical day is obtained".

Today, it has already been more than 200 years the Meiteis professed to follow the Gauḍīya school of Vaiṣṇavism. Even the formulation of Govinda has already been awfully prolonged. Since the practice of worshipping Gopāla-Kṛṣṇa started before the advent of Caitanya school, in the reign of Nīlāmbara Sana, it seems completing 300 years. However in the early period, having encountered with the political, the economic, and the social hindrances most of the people could not visit Vrindavana although the wishes had there been. From the beginning of around the nineteenth-century people started pilgrimaging despite of having the hindrances. Subsequently, during the time of monarchy, some kings and princes were constructing the temples as extending the devotional service to the middle Vrindavana and the Śrī-Kuṇḍa also towards providing a sort of shelters to the pilgrims. In Śrī-Kuṇḍa, the Purānī Kuñja of Mahārājā Chourjit, Baṛī-Kuñja of Mahārāja Gambhīr Singh, Naol Govinda Mandira popularly known as Yuvarāja Kuñja erected by Nara Singh Mahārāja while he was the prince, as thus Naol Govinda popularly known as Yuvarāja Kuñja set up by Suracandra Mahārāja in madhya Vrindavana during his tenure of princeship are seemingly the early major temples during kings' period. These temples are still in existence. The signs of ownerless situations are clearly visible—miserable in witnessing.

When we were in preoperational stage of age the Grandmother Yaiskul Lakpi looked after the service of Naol Govinda. Sanaibemma Yumshangbi was also there. Khakashi is born to Mahārājā Nara Singh. He is the brother of Yaiskul Lakpa. Frequently heard about their livings but never known in person, hence always wish to see them. Moreover, the IAS Phalguni's grandfather who loved me with care had also gone there, hence just eagered to see them once. Having about a gap of one year grandpa and *eigya*[10] usually used to visit and it had been a long durable dreamt for me to join them. The saying, if there is a will there is a way had really come to heppen. Few days later just after the completion of my 4th standard examination Grandma Thoidingjambi and *eigya*, both mother and daughter were in preparation like gazing of materials-clothes to take along. As it was not a new thing, I had understood that it was done for pilgrimage to Vrindavana. I asserted as "the repeated promises nor ever translated for taking me with could not be entertained this time I would go definitely, will just run after you", but instantly replied before completing my submission, "your grandpa has messaged to come with you, hence being commented to take you with". Touched once the zenith of pleasure when listened to the recommendation, "Go to order for shoes along with Grandma to Yaiskul Lakpam".

Went with Grandma to Yaiskul Lakpam in the evening. Yaiskul Lakpam was not simply prominent in the royal families of Manohar Sai but the family of Sanamacha who had been in the position of *guru*. They were the decendants of Daujee. Daujee was the very first son of Bhāgyacandra, he should have been the inheritance of the throne. Being a *Bhāgavata* devotee sacrificed his right unto the feet of Almighty. Since succeeding to the position of Yaiskul Lakpam[11] their family came to be known as Yaiskul Lakpam. The Sanamacha's Grandma was well experienced in sewing sleeper, shoe, and boot, most of the shoes and sleepers were made by this royal mother.

The royal mother had taken the measurement of my boot. As per suggestion of gramdma within few days a red boot with a little thicker sole was made, so as to reach the time of the trip, yet to guard from the hill's gravels, and to protect the outsole also. It was my first shoe to have in life. If Brinam was not gone, there was no any particular reason to get acquanted with shoes as early. Some smells that our intramoral and extramoral cocurriculars activities of student were persisted by the use of shoes, had already been perceived from our family's attitudes.

Departure

Departed for Vrindavana, altogether we three, the grandpa, *eigya* and I. That was in the early evening. Mother's teams followed up to Kwakeithel. What is mentioning is that of today's Kwakeithel. In early days every betal nut whichever brought in by the Mayang (Indian) or improrted by the Meiteis were sold here for which it is called Kwakeithel (betal nut market). Most of the elderly people always pronouced it by keeping silence the *kaa*. Grandma Tondonleima and uncle Sanajaoba were waiting in the market. They were the parents of Professor Rajkumar Tarasana of Manipur University. Few things about their family had already been written in the first volume. They all were closed relatives to both grandpa and grandma—as always as ever.

All of us had entered the house and took rest for a while by taking fruits and packet of betal. All the mother's team got ready to reach home as early as the sunset. Hard to say its accomplished, by walking through day and night over each graveyards; the sense of dwindleness kept in mind; since the living beings we were who had always been encountered with segregation, as if said to be separated it would be ascertained that the tear to follow just having emotional ahead. It's only for few days was seemingly not recognizable, everybody shedding tears in the eyes. I also wept, for what reason "got unease" was unknown. Well! did it seemingly integrate the world.

No sooner than the mother's team left grandma just went for cooking. Many items were made, that was vegeterian foods. Among the benefits gained in travelling to Vrindavana was the eating of the vegeterian foods also the one. Since eating of fish was stopped just for a short period of time no violence had been committed. As cooking was just over the dusk also simultaneously set over. Just after completing the chanting of the holy name the preparation for having dinner was soon started. A bullock cart had come. The bullocky also joined the dinner.

The dinner over. That was early of the post-nightfall. Decided to flag off the cart at the earliest since that was to be a long journey. It is not ignorable too, as there had been a mountainous terrain. As many defficulties were there in travelling alone, some reasons had been there to join the folk in the journey. Scoundrels might have been found and encountered with wild animals perhaps. Boarded in the cart.

The *ghumṭī*[12] was there, the space for sleeping inside was made. *Eigya* and I laid down, whereas the grandpa was chanting with *mālā* beads. For me I didn't ever feel homesick as grandpa and *eigya* were with me. By watching the oscillation of the *ghumṭī* that happened in accordance with the wheeling of the cart that made me unaware of asleep.

A sound, "Oh Choṭe wake up" was being heard—it was of *mamoyai*[13] who had already advanced with two engaged hillmen. Suddenly the eyes were opened and wake up as like as pulled up by *mamoyai*. There had only been an anrora of the dawn. *Eigya* and grandpa were in making warm on fire. As led by the uncle sat closed to *eigya*. Grandpa and *eigya* had already done bathing while uncle also finished cooking. So I had been awaken. All the people started leaving already as they used to eat at Tairenpokpi. That was on a side of the bank of Thongjaorok wherein I responded to the call of nature being guarded by an engaged helper. The uncle had bathed me with warm water. As wished by grandpa some *tilaka*s were also put on face.

Although we made preparation very fast, most of the people already left, it seemed that we were in the last troup. However, no one was upset as uncle was to see off us up to *jillā* apart from the two helpers we were found not a weaker team. Having remembered the advice for recalling the Narsingh on the hill track, Rāma in jungle and vast land, Barah in lake, river and drains, moreover for prosperity with chanting the holy name of Mādhava by crossing the river we climbed up the hill by holding hand with uncle and guarded by grandpa in the last.

On the Lap of the Nature (For Few Days)

Since childhood I never stepped out from my native environment. Whenever I played-in the yard, for roaming—in the locality, gone to the school, visited—to the Govindajī Temple on sacred days by following the paths of *eigya* only—kept dwelling amongst our people never encountered with the outside environment so long. It's happened landing on today;

it was so sudden, when the sun just arose, into a complete new world, never seen before, never known, never seen even in the dreams also. It's the lap of nature—land of wilderness, garden of trees and plants, reaping ground for the birds, dwelling hub for the insects, an incredible charming site for the nature herself. With blue colour roofed over the sky stretching all over the loops. To the down the masses of cloud spread throughout all directions with roaring. Behind the east mountain the light began to flooding—coming the sparkle lights. The eastern sky glittered abreast. The blue and the red were in contending with for nectar. The eastern blue sky turned over bluest besides. In different corners, the mountains remained standstill—fewer were being covered with circlet of cloud. Saliently, the darkness and light were in playing all through the cliff, middle, foot, and top of the mountain. Changing into shades of hundreds every instant every object. Gratifies the heart with grace and beauty, overwhelmingly fascinated with one view. Visibly germinated all the trees with bunches of diamonds and pearls, showering over piedmonts with the brightness of pearls. The flock was tweeting, the clans of grasshopper and cricket were singing, twittering, and making noise. Chirring the groups of cicada—the echoes strike on every façade of mountain slopes, running through the three layers of sounds the seven reverberations made noisy. Having recalled suddenly an excerpt from the beginning of the poem learnt in second standard—

> The rhythm of night has passed
> Has appeared the dawn
> The *pal* bird begins to tweet.

In the lawn of nature I have encountered face to face with the day break today which remained unknown but heard only the locution, thus the appearance has clearly been recognized. It seemed that on her face something was felt or seen but could not recognize what was that. As the colour of the day break kept changing in minutes all have immediately been merged with ever changing in every single step of an infant's mind.

However, when grown up, achieved some lights of knowledge with a higher level of study, gradually it had likely been understood through the words of scholars.

There are two schools in this world—one is the school of nature, another is of the men's school established by the people. From among these two, the knowledge has generally been achieved from the first one. Towards earning the knowledge the second one has been the subject for studies. The subject studied in the school of men except for those who has upright tradition no distinctness is found in general until they are sharpen in the school of nature—although becomes literate but impossible to be educated. Therefore, people are living with the contributions made by the men who have learnt from the school of nature. Our Vedas, the storehouse of India's knowledge system is the contribution of the school of nature. As the depth of Vedas, the core of Siddhānta are known as Āraṇyakars and *Bṛhadāraṇyaka* respectively have been the legitimate proof for this discourse.

Clean, beauty, and sacred are the qualities of flowers. It is used in the worship of *Bhāgavata*. The people who dwell in peace and prosperity also use them in decorations for the house and the homestead. Luxuriate themselves with—in adorning, wearing, hanging, and holding. By emulating the colour the clothes are being dyed. The patterns are also carved and sewed in clothes and used as the items of gift, display and for award. Even the patterns of pollen grain like ironwood flower have been the colour of adorning turban. Several are also used as medicines by the folk medicinal practitioners. Research has extensively been conducted on their genesis, nature and characteristics by the researchers and enriched the storehouse of knowledge. The health professionals are of the disparagement that the smell of flowers is harmful to the body. How far it is true or wrong is known to the Almighty. India which has continually been using flowers in social, political, religious, and economic sectors is remained prosperously alive and still existed. While studying the qualities of plants by the

Āyurvedic science it is said that the *tulsī* can cure 108 diseases. Since it has to be associated with in worship inseparably and perhaps it may be because of some reasons that about the smell of flowers are not presumably mentioned. However, the opinion of health professionals is also found to be an aspect of wisdom. As such this has been a vast area of discussion as to love the flowers, as to search for the genesis. Nobody knows that what does the flower tell, whose glory is sung, what message is delivered to the world. These secret messages are grasped, seen, listened by those who have dwelled in natural world, educated in the school of nature and enriched their knowledge through the experiential school like sage and the sage like people, covered only by them such huge chasm if the people are found to be unfamiliar with. All have witnessed the ocean, widening as touching the skyline, rippled amazingly, happy with its charming mode to see. Everything has been accomplished with it. However, Mahākavi Bairan witnessed the progenitor of universe all-powerful Almighty's image and attributes on its face which lies touching over the skyline, playing incautiously with heavy amazing waves, the physiognomy and the power of Almighty were subsequently described through the attribute of ocean. As thus only the Viśvakavi understood the attributes of flower, heard all messages extended by flower. The flower said to the sage, "you think I am gorgeous but I am not gorgeous one, one is there—gorgeous he is magnificently". What I have brought is just a little piece of his beauty. For me, it's only for delivering his message by taking this piece of beauty as instructed, read the message written on my petal. Watching into the petal immediately the sage, seen the notes written as "come if wish to have the beauty, there I am". There are two faces of Almighty—one is *raudra* (anger) and another is *madhura* (pleasant). The face of *madhura* is said to be incredibly beautiful, singing hence, "Satyam Śivam Sundaram". Thus, Viśvakavi Ātmadarśi calls him *sarbāṅgasundara*. In sum, the school of nature has given the knowledge and hence it is natural truth that the message of that knowledge has been the subject for the study in the school of men.

Went on some digressions, now it is fair to come to the central point, however, coming before to it mentioning only one point is thought to be legitimate. What Makar Singh has said in the first part of the poem mentioned above is not of his own but written after having listened to a Bāṅglā poem. It is the original Bengali of the lines—

Pakhi Sob
Kore Rob
Ratri Pohail

How far Bāṅglā literature contributes in shaping the practice of our modern or contemporary literature and how many influences are entranced in us have strongly been proved.

Walking happily thus from one range to another successively by watching the new frame of the new world which is seemingly changeable in every instant. Again, following the sound of sticks of two helpers, step on with their tunes. Enthralling once enough on seeing a bird never witnessed before elsewhere. As the stepping gone through ups and downs, rising the sunny henceforth, although exhausted the body, nor is there receding in the heart and mind's pleasure. Walking through as such got reached Tairenpokpi, there met most of the advancers. Rice abreast was being cooked by many; wherein some were eating, those who had finished were having betel nuts, smoking *hookāh* and cigarettes and again getting prepared the belongings to continue the journey. Having chosen a comfortable site we took respite. Uncle had prepared *phola* (*phalāhāra*)[14] mixing with sugar and banana after having cleaned the flattened rice with fetching water. We all have eaten something of it and had a fair few fruits and *laḍḍū* (sweet item) also apart. As waiting for the helpers to eat their tiffin, grandpa was in smoking *hookāh* while *eigya* and uncle were in areca nut chewing. Soon they got ready. There had started walking again along with the others. However, fewer had just soon gone ahead. Nor found staying in the dormitory—never met again ever. Some people like them were seen everyday—as gone ahead—came to know finally that they were going to Mayang (Cachar), a troop for the purchase of fish (dry fish) and betel nuts, it was about three days to reach the Mayang. Continued travelling by waking up before the dawn appears—not being unbent as afraid of unknown, animals and tiger. No sooner than the noon came all had taken the lunch—in a particular place together, inseparably. Walking had been continued again until the daylight came to the close. As the eyes fell on light, preparations were made for eating and sleeping. Travelling as such, on the sixth day we reached Lakhipur (Lakṣmīpur), on the next day advanced towards *jillā* (Silchar).

During these six days of mountainous journey much fierceness, panicky and peaceful enjoyments were met and some images went falling in heart, existing still today—remained unvarnished. We never travelled only on the right track but went through the shortcut also. It was said that one of the shortcut tracks was called Nungthabi, treading down on the stir of stones as highly steep as quietly long. The place was dense, got water springs too, the stepping stones were also wet, were overgrown the mosses, nor was it as slippery, had there been heavily greasy too. The levels never remained on a balance; the taller had also been there. Remained the fear of trodden down on that still today. Being so scary it was so petrified and startled even after uncle led me by holding and lifting me yet in every single step. After having descended when looking back with a fondest wish it was terribly dismay. The Khoubum Tampak was the one that had more been fearful. Had the dinner what was to be eaten. There had been started setting fire by finding some woods and bamboos. By making beds around all had lain down. I was already in asleep. Little sleepy am I, since being exhausted apart intolerable when touched the pillow with head, just fallen asleep. It had been broken however abruptly. Having heard a voice as illusively, "Dear folk, today Loudraobi"[15] is frocked on, just focus on fire. Sound lines sprinkled with—*uṁ, hu, uṁ, hu*, were subsequently heard as sounding as roaring of landslides. Frightened the mind and shaken the heart.

We have listened to many tales from the elders. All are of the ancient time, of the period once gods and human live together. While Laikhutshangbee pushed her hand through the hole of wall attempting to capture the child, the chopping off the hand by child's father, the coming of the chinless Goddess disguising herself as a yeast's seller as to eat child, escaping of the two brother and sister by pretending to be emergence for peeing, having eaten by capturing men by the Mee—*maraam*, eating of the men plucking from the fingers as being disobedient by Kabui-keioiba, having private relation to have childbirth along capturing man by the Loudraobi, when arrested on having the notice of footprints to the families throwing out the child by tearing louder, so on are there. As soon as they heard the roaring of Loudraobi the last narrative were being recalled. It was too startle on the fear of abduction. Throughout the night noisy they were, thus there had indeed been stressful in sleep. Frequently sweating, neither having nor eupnoea, undergone the whole night as such. The fear of that night seems to be felt till now, whenever get to recall.

Never know what kind of creature they are! It is said to grow its body hair with great reed, to have legs which are opposite to the normal position. Neither is animal being eaten nor birds (!), it's being eaten snails enough. It is said to be alert—if the pile of eaten snails is found in brook, on the bank of canals, it is not to be their abode perhaps but definitely the home range it is. The Loudraobi of our land does remain like the snowman of the Himalayas which existence is lightly experienced along, not understood in nutshell as nobody is there who has confronted with in day time. However, it is definitely true that the sound and echo of their laughing are almost the same with the human. A laughing creature indeed though it is an animal, it has been a laughing creature which being the half-non-humanlike.

As like confronting with the fears and startle, lovely and beautiful things were also met. Kabokchaibi was the name of a waterfall, located just nearby the road. The name of the hill was not known. The way had progressively been entered. The Laimatol Phourung of Khoubum Valley was located on crossing the Laimatol Achouba. One of the boundaries of this valley was the Tayal ranges. The longer as the way while the timing also frequently been fallen at the sun raises high after having crossed to reach in which there was a saying "the challenged would have been made there with the Tayal palm". Could not remember whether had Irang been crossed or not but seemed to be so closer. The beautiful creation of the nature it was, amazing natural deposition they were. In rainy season ever there flawed crossing over the road, people went through under it. At the time we went the strength of water was dwindled as it was at the end of the winter. However, it might not have diminished the beauty perhaps, still magnificent. On the other, while coming through hardship in heat wave, the sprinkling fallen of gems colour like water from the middle of the hill with burble and having witnessing the happiest dancing of the drops of water on the foothill made me afresh indeed, could not understand what kind of nectar were being poured. The sky's dew absorbers fruits and flowers they are.

No travellers were to call for each other, just seated nearby the waterfall of their own wishes. The brow of the mountain from which waterfall has been hailed was the stone. It is not the structure covered only by one huge stone but an accumulation of stones in layers. It is not to be fallen apart, as run as cement coating. As steep as wall, the height was also too high, might it be about the height of two houses perhaps. By looking intensely at the brow the *mamoyai* himself had mourned inaudibly—has it been climbed by wearing wooden sandal!

> I—*Mamoyai*, who was the one climbed on this by wearing wooden sandal?
> Mamo—Mahārājā Bhāgyacandra.

I—How to climb on this, it's too steep, sleeper and high!
Mamo—The God, the Mahārāja was.

Hence, there accomplished for that day. Neither the questioner I was also wrong nor the responder Mamo was mistaken too, was the narrative of climbing also found being truth after a long period of time.

Having often invaded by the Ava; couldn't stand, instantly thought to be guarded by staying outside of Manipur; stepped way towards the northern side as presumed as easier. No one was there to share the responsibility as usual as would there be limited friends for the king in hard times; all had stood against, taking the enemy's roles immediately. Since Jai Singh was the God's incarnation escaped thus from the tigers, bears and so on, set trodden on the way to Mayang (Cachar). While approaching to the aunt Induprabha's palace took respite on the foot of this waterfall, decided in mind to make try at least once. There surrendered his life immediately unto the Lord Govinda. Having said "Do save whether there is the possibility to render your service perfectly in this life or do finish if no", climbed up on this brow wearing the wooden sandal chanting along the *mālā* beads betwixt the scary watch of the people.

So wonderful the world is, is surprising the God also, amazing the more his pastime has been. As per the instruction of Sant Gyaneshwar the buffalo recites the Vedas. Being suppliant on the love of Mīrā, following her wishes performs dancing Giridhārīlāl. So as to keep the vow of Mādhavendra offers milk the Gopāla-Kṛṣṇa disguising as cowherd boy. As holding the hands of lame as crossing the mountain being led Jai Singh was also. The devotee goes unique from the other. To him either possible or impossible is not there—God is for the devotee, gracious being to the devotee.

To the western mountain ranges of Manipur the Oinamlong being the highest. As being the higher, the bigger in size also along, has occupied much area too. While finishing the taking of dinner and yet to prepare the beds properly someone did announce, "Dear folk, it's not too dark, if something has been progressed, there would have been less busy tomorrow". All have agreed, "Ok, get prepared to go". Collecting the materials from elsewhere the torch was also made hugely. Started walking all as led by one torch and followed by another. On the decent roads I went on foot whereas on uninvited road uncle carried me on his back. Trodden as pretty longer, ascended as exceedingly the higher. As there likely be existed a suitable place to halt the night all had decided to have respite. There whether fire making or preparing beds were in proceed. I was sleepy enough, getting hard to wait for the completion of bed preparation. However, the napping eyes got soon alert as the extension of the hundreds of melodious echoes multitudinously fell on ears. The uncle asked, "What's the tweeting these are". Got immediately the answer, "it's *Tamna*".

The mountain located in our surroundings was too high. The brook was also big and deep. That was hard to grasp how numerous they were, throughout from the top of the mountain to the brook seem to be lined up by hundreds of group. A single echo vibrated hundred sounds. The sounds were hence coming through ups and downs of the levels situated from the up-hill to the down dale of the mountain to the brook. The Tam's squall lines that started coming down from the top through the mid and cliff of the mountain along, and then uplifted just from the deep of the brook through passing its façade, Tam's squall lines overflowed from surroundings of far and near altogether looked like singing the songs of peace in hundreds, my infantile heart was impressed. The flow of utterance—*tam, tam, tam, tam, tam, tam, tam*—carried me to an unrevealed—indeed to a peaceful place.

After a long time, while reading some books, a song of Vishwakavi was found one day—

Tripto tumi amargeerage
Bhalo lage tomar bhalo lage,
Jani ami eai ganear bole
Basi giye tomari samukhe.

(Thou art pleased at my song
Utterly satisfied with my song
Thou art found through the song
Seating on the front facing with thyself.)[16]

The quality of song came to be understood. My infantile heart was known to the *tamna running* to the place with singing on *pañcama svara*.[17]

Life in Mountain (Few Smells)

There stayed in the village one day. Having told Luwangkot was its name. Whether that was an old or a new village is forgotten. The sunlight was there to perfection, at a hill's slope that was, when we reached. I could not but surprise as the lives in the mountain had extremely been different from the valley, exceedingly wonderstruck there. The having mentioned lives in the valley are also of only about a few for Imphal which are known to me. I haven't known the whole facets. I haven't ever known the countryside also. With a mercy ever since there encountered with the life in mountain. Finding village after having climbed up the hill high, being the houses also a fewer, all the houses being existed inside a bund, having kept only one opening, the trees grown in around like being reserved as far as not in thick, inside the bund, constructed the houses in a same design, keeping restraint in a line appropriately, with only the thick, the bigger plank fenced the wall, hanging the deer and mithun's heads at the middle of the house, having made the skull alike of human by sculpturing, curving on the plank itself in veranda, putting hanged the branched horn, dissimilarities in the size were the things witnessed at first. As everything was new, instantly it was highly surprised. When we reached the centre of the village a villager asked, "Do you have friend(?)". As replied as "off course not" being led into the veranda of the house in which the branched horns were hanged the largest. No one was there—door was being closed. However, all men and women came soon one after another. As asking as "are you from Imphal" concurrently said with the "sooner rather than the sunset you please have your dinner in the water canal". Perhaps I could have understood the generous hospitalities of the hill dwellers as ever being a child although.

The chief's family seemed to have about six-seven members. When we came back after having dinner they were yet to finish eating. Hence we seated on the veranda, as soon as finished eating being called us inside. No light were there inside. Set fire with a lot of longer woods. Some blazing came out, the heat made seemingly warm albeit not heated directly even there. By making beds around the fire the majority got slept. Somewhere in and around, on the mortar in the room there had been set to reside the night. All had thus got asleep without having hesitations.

No bird was yet to tweet, being found waken the housewife. Those who slept on the mortar and nearby had been awaken. As pounded the rice, the sounds of the pounding shaken along the floor of the room did everybody thus awake. While we were getting ready he also proceeded with wood cutting after having done the rice pounding. That was also inside the house. No sooner than finished the wood cutting started concentrating on cooking. Hence we also started walking. As walking as my infantile heart itself was silently humming, "lived as difficult as tight the hill".

On the Long Way (Few Days Again)

On the sixth day we reached Lakhipur. On arrival at Lakhipur all had been separated. Started leaving on their owns will. We did spend in a brāhmaṇa's house. As travelled with getting no human connection but a few companies through the wilderness along mountainous track for six days, today the heart likely felt some respites. In the mountain several wonderful and pretty things were found day by day, witnessed with the intensified eyes, swigged satisfactorily. However, since being born and grown up among people, there was always a fear and startle with all the time. As not being blessed as Vishwakavi—

Nutnera majhe tumi puratana
(Old you are among the new)[18]

I am the innocent child as not to be capable of having cheerful rest whenever saw new things whatever they might be.

In the early evening of the seventh day we reached the *jillā*. What has been mentioned here is the Silchar. The district is the Cachar. Today no one knows the reason for naming a town of a district in such a way. Perhaps it might be the consequence of the wrong perception to subdivision as district, the Silchar subdivision was known as Silchar district. Still today most of the elderly people of the Cachar used to call the Silchar as *jillā*. In those days in the centre of *jillā*, not even a single family of the Meiteis was there except the family of Khelendra Subedar.[19] Even the Subedar's family was not also in the proper town but in a corner. Even today also in the proper stands solely my years ago loved one of collegiate time Irungbam Chandra Singh to whom all of the own community people who lived in and outside of Cachar were reliant on for amity. Therefore, in those days, the pilgrims of Vrindavana, Navadwip and Kṣetra would have to struggle for survival of their own in such place. As no approving place was there for accessing sheltered for a while thus reached the station. Since *eigya* and grandpa had to take fasting as they were in against of hunger with the strong trust in sacred behaviour even though getting tired and hungry enough. From the snacks shop uncle had bought some snacks and milk. At the place where water was available nearby and in a roughly clean place by taking sugar and pounded rice out prepared *phola* nicely and eaten over there, didn't understand either that was just for the night or for how many days!

For me the entire normal regime was being happened contrary, the body was also highly exhausted, dieting also thoroughly in deficient. However, as the new series of amazing sequence stood in against of misery and hungry there would have likely never been exhausted at all. Today itself started from Lakhipur Khunman, travelled a quite along passing through Baskandi crossing the Barak River at Belenga, but wherein full of amazing glimmer had been there when entered to the station. The longhouse, iron bridge, verandas, crowd, different people, set of peddlers, groups of bagger, lines of cart, rows of compartment and the most enjoyable was the carrying of compartment by hissing of smoke with the engine's locomotive pulls, all these left no spare time for hungry, for tiredness. Having gone through a state of mind got deserted in eating and drinking.

Eating had been finished. The residues had been cleaned out. Washroom had been done. Uncle was buying the tickets. People a few started boarding on. The two helpers were Chirus[20]; they all were the regular friends of uncle and grandpa from the Ningthoukhong anterior. As being the attendants and having associated with the traditions of royal families for a long time the behaviours were so majestic. Nor to be the engaged helpers, as being closed to the heart, an emotional relationship were seen. Their remaining money was paid, told to associate with uncle up to Ningthoukhong and then extended greetings to each other. After finding an unconfined board all the belongings was uplifted. A bed was prepared for *eigya* and me. Another was also made for grandpa. Signaling the hoot blare of the train, the uncle had bowed down unto grandpa and *eigya* and the grandpa advised as needful. Putting hand on uncle's head, the *eigya* said, "Chaoyaima, get home without even having headache, do not away from home unnecessarily, we will come back soon" but in the eyes full of tear was in set. As attended me uncle just called, "Choṭe". As insisted by God I also just bowed down to him. When facing with after having pulled up by uncle heavy drops of tear started flowing from his eyes and said, "my dear Choṭe, don't ever be sick". Quite nervous I was, flowing tears in the eyes. The train begun to run, uncle went out from the board, as reached where the two helpers stood looked over again at us. Three of them stayed by looking towards our way, we also left over just keeping gazed at them.

During the sun was still at sight marching was continued by enjoying the serpentine and tediously running of the train.

Once getting darkness, having gone through again looking surprisingly at the ways of the train's lighting, the manner of fan's moving and the racks to put on the belongings. However, at the stumbling of the cart had fallen thereby a lullaby of the nature perhaps, started searching pillow as hence being napped with shaking, got asleep on finding the same—landed on dreamt but got soon interrupted. It's worth confusing to say whether it was happen because of the people's noise or the noisy sounds of the cart on the one hand and on the other, were the eyes opened up as coincidence—had being interrupted sleeping so. No sooner than the interruption a much cheerful glimmer was found. That was at Badarpur junction. At the long hut, in the long veranda, on the lengthy courtyard, crowded people along the shining row of light—running up and down, back and forth in tiers as the cart ran up, kept pushing, colliding with descending tiers in all the spaces with noise voicing out aloud. Again the peddlers ran back and forth announcing the names of item—another group were calling aloud in lengthy scale—*pān, biṛī*, and cigarette, another set of people were also calling the attention in shorten with heaviest tone—*cha cha*, apart from these by pushing small carts some people were also in progress with "*pūrī, śāk*,[21] and snacks", there was no end, the things were uncountable. Everything was surprising and pleasing glimmers for me.

Observing to the end of the people's wax and wane moving, two fieriest *pūrī*s along with *śāk* and one piece of sweet were being bought by grandpa. Having eaten—the stomach was completely full as *phola* had also been taken. Just started going by watching the chains of light being shone around the junction which looked like to me as the uncountable stars of the sky were installed. As the stomach was full along the lullabying run of the cart with shaking in abandon gay never had the notice of asleep.

That was about the time to sunrise. The grandpa had waked up me, "Oh, Choṭe get up, and let's move". That was in Chandpur wherein we landed down there. Kept marching led by a porter. That was something like as riverbed but couldn't understand in precise. By crossing a bridge and transiting through a house we entered into a mansion in the water. Grandpa arranged a bed finding a worthy place, all of us got seated. As being seated still *eigya* got to find tobacco leaf and *ṭīkī*[22] with which the grandpa rested smoking with a small Vrindavana *hookāh*. Being attending still *hookāh eigya* and I were suggested to wash the hand, foot and mouth by grandpa. Ship was not anew to *eigya* at all, she knew everything. Very frequent the ship had always been. While marching towards the washroom I asked the *eigya*, "*Eigya*, whose house is that there constructed in the water (?)". Thus replied, "Oh my dear, that is not a house, that is the ship and the river is called Padmā—when the cloud comes to disappear everything will be seen". Extremely got stuck in mind, could not understand why it was so surprising.

The ship also began sailing and the sun also arose. As to have paying salutation to the sun grandpa led us to the upper deck and made bowing. While in performing salutation started watching the beauty of Padmā surprisingly. On its extensive span, was wonderstruck extremely although it was said to be a river. As the cloud was less obliterate completely and being widening furthermost itself the opposite bank was not being seen. The shadow of the sky was appeared on its foreseen part. Since the water ran with forceful leap, it was being seen as waved the sky. Being the light of rising sun laid and also the shadow of crimson sky set—as glorified as running in leap with effect of back stream from the northern sacred dale, showering the pair with the golden drip came instantly through a chamber of earth. The grandpa was also slurping the aesthetic view with the eyes brimfully, I was also as same as such. The soul is God and the God is the image of beauty. On that day every soul experienced the beauty, no differences among old and child.

While watching the beauty of the river grandpa was opening, "the Padmā is met up with three rivers. All are in great extent. What we have witnessed right now is the course of Meghanād. After having some steps the Brahmaputra's course in the mid, then on the extreme verge shall find of the Gaṅgā. The colours of the water will not find matching; the streams will also remain different. Meghanād is originated from our land. About 40 miles from Imphal towards the north in the mountainous region there is the place called Karong. That is the origin of this river. It's the Gwai River that you saw in the lead. The Gwai was the Barak which the huge river you crossed when came to *jillā*. Hence, the Barak flown into Sylhet as being known as Surmā and here it comes with the name Meghanād. Since the stream is exceedingly forceful and the sound of current is being raucous, it has been named as Meghanād. While we were in war refuge frequently roamed places these are. It is also said to have called Kīrtināśa too. Perhaps, that was Gaṇeśa but fail to recall exactly, by whom the entire palace of a king unearthed in a night. As being his father it is seen as exuberance today.

Having stepped down there near to *eigya*. Some pounded rice was eaten with sugar and some water also drank. Having seated and lying down prolonged there with stopping over by watching the wheeling and the running of compressors of engine operated in the centre to sail the ship. The river however remained unmoved. Left behind the engine and proceeded to the edge of the ship for watching the river again.

The sun was shining utterly, hence cleared all the clouds. All the tributaries were seen. The other side of Goyaland was seen at a very far distance. Even the trees grown on the bank and the nearby were also seen as small enough. As the ship entered into the mid it seemed to be widening gradually the more. The capability to reach there easily was being uncertain. Much time was also being taken still. Started sailing from little darkness at the early morning, reached the Golaband at afternoon behind time. If went with looking at the watch it might have been more than eight hours. When looked back towards the northern direction the infantile heart was wonderstruck in witnessing wherein the right bank seen to be distant and the left too remained far away—in between the two banks adjoining the three large rivers flown with guarding the colours of their own and streams. The Meghnā (Meghanād) ran greeny over the right bound while the Brahmaputra tenderly in the middle wherein the water as light greeny as possessed the colour of gems liquid and the Gaṅgā flown calmly far way on the left, having less excitement by embracing the yellowish water on the lap. There could not turn over the view—forgotten the hungryness and thirsty.

Far and near sailing the hundreds of boat—didn't understand for why and what was being done there! The hundreds of boat remained striking each other—there lived men, women, and children together but could not grasp what was there and what's going on. Again hundreds of boat also were taking much longer net along—screaming and contending, never knew what was happening. As like worried for them there hissed the *nashubi*[23] turning over its head and tail. As looked at the south as it was thus. The water sounded as the roaring of rain. The boats sailed slim and slender, dip and down throughout the stream spreading every loop.

When witnessing the enormous creation of God, the lives of man, heavy struggle for living, weal and woe, tired although wished to live happily as delightful, the living things around, the infantile heart was seemed to smell "so lovely" as the smells of fruit and flower brought by the air even though not to be understood thoroughly because of the age—when some studied had been in progress sometimes sung thus a poem of Viśvakavi—

Marite chahina ami sunder bhubne,
Manber majhe ami wachiware chai.
(Wish not to die in this beautiful place
Wish to live thus amongst these people.)[24]

It became quite late. The ship reached in the mid, another ship was on waiting. Being said that it was of Dhaka Narayanganj. When just heard this name having recalled soon the two betel nuts quite popular in our time. One was something pointed, called Koirenganj; another was longer in shape and called Narayanganj. It was seemingly convinced that from among these two betel nuts, one was coming through the ship which being awaited to be left. Thus found as true. It had come to know from the grandpa that the longer one was from here and another pointed one was from Karimganj situated near to the Badarpur which I did not see as I got asleep.

Several people who travelled together with us also shifted to the awaiting ship. While shifting many boatmen came for peddling with milk, curd, and *rasagullā*. The grandpa bought a curd pot along with some *gullā*s. Changing over their attitudes when the ship gave signal, at the rising of the wave with the flagging of the two ships off one after another wherein the state of endurance in the conditions of sinkable oscillation the infantile heart was much being worried and panicked for the boatmen.

Having much hungriest condition and tiredness touching its limit of the body thereafter many hours reached the Goyaland. A cart was there but didn't pick up. There had to go after taking bath and some foods. Among the big rivers Padmā had been exceptional in terms of futility in water. Living there covering with the refuse of huge impure dirtiest things brought down by the three unpleasantly polluted big rivers of India through the overhead stream along which blocked by the sea. Subsequently by finding a fairly clean place some foods had been taken there and took rest for a while in spare time.

On the cart being seated there. That was in the late evening. By sleeping in I went throughout the night thus. The night had passed and reached Calcutta. That was in Sealdah, perhaps the time might have been at around midday. Getting dumbfounded there when witnessed the flood of crowd. My infantile heart could not but wonderstruck when witnessing the tight shouldering with each other that was unfamiliar in every aspect in terms of dress and address having no matched with us at all. However, it was useless to me as like failed to enter the fear and the nervous into a child having guarded by the grandparents and found to be a simply occurrence even though they got entering. When *eigya* just took hold of the wrist every fear and nervous had thus been atoned abruptly. However, no decrease of the crowd, meanwhile as the people crowded hectically the pulling rickshaws were also increased up. The rickshaw of the time was pulled by man and ran with ringing a bell. On a rickshaw *eigya* and I went together while grandpa on another along with the belongings, longer a while it was, finally reached and stepped up to a dormitory. That was also found utterly crowded. After getting bath at the dormitory took meal and had rest for a while peacefully. It was quite late, went again on a rickshaw confronting accordantly with the powerful stream of men's cart and reached the sea of people in *Habra* (Howrah) again. When got entering inside and thus found as a wonderland for me. Left dazing to see—whether to look at the people, the peddlers, to the vendors or to focus on the rows of the office and the traffic, was totally wonderstruck indeed. Having been born in hushed land and grown up in a still environment, the noise happened together with the awful people's din and the scary emanation of vehicles made me so jarring—by lying on the lap of *eigya* endured with the closing of the eyes.

Having seated again in the cart. That was seemed about the time of nightfall. The whole night was spent asleep. The dawn began to crack. The brushing was done in a station. I ate some *pūrī*s and sweets. *Eigya* and grandpa ate nothing as not done before bathing and chanting the *mālā* beads but used the *hookāh* very frequently. The day was also in travel on the cart around the clock. Enchoring either seated or laid on prolonged there over by watching the landscape, anon as getting sleepy lying down again and thus went instantly sleep-in. On the next day reached the Kanpur at daylight. All of us had done bathing and took meal very comfortably. As soon as moved up to the bus for Mathurā. It became very dark at Hathras. By the time we reached Mathurā it was quite late—hence stopped over the night at the station. Before the dawn yet to shine went to Tangam and in ahead of lunch time reached Śrī-Kuṇḍa.

All the exhausting of journey had been atoned in a second. Every weary for not having eaten, drunk and slept had thus been forgotten as being met with all the yearning and loving ones. However, there happened a surprise. The grandmother, Khaka and royal grandfather who stayed already there and our grandpa and *eigya*, got shading tears in the eyes. Said to be natural as sharing themselves the tears each other, my eyes also shed with tears. When maturity got to arrive just came to know, "the tear has been associated in both weal and woe". Only the difference is that the tear of woe is hot while the weal's tear remains cool.

At Śrī-Kuṇḍa (About a Month)

During my stay in Śrī-Kuṇḍa for about one month I used to reside mostly at outside rather than inside. The reason behind this was that I was the monument of peace and treasure for five heads. Whenever I was unseen the grandmother, Khakashi, *eigya* and the two grandpas—these five heads would just asked, "Where is Chothe (?)". Whenever anyone from among them went for market or anywhere else I was always accompanied with. In every conduct of devotional service far and near, I had never been left behind.

The Old King

The meaning of the term is the abdicate king—it refers to Mahārāja Kulacandra. In consequence of the Khongjom War's[25] catastrophe lived the king in Śrī-Kuṇḍa after sixteen years of exile in Kālāpānī residing at Baṛī-Kuñja established by his grandfather Mahārājā Gambhīr Singh and hence passed away at Śrī-Kuṇḍa itself. By the time we visited it seemed to have arrived quite a long before. He had fair complexion, endomorphic figure and fat body.

That was in the morning of the next day of arrival. The worship of Govinda had been done. Putting a clean *khudei*[26], some dry things along with some *laḍḍū*s made with *heitup*[27] and *heimang*[28] on a small tray; letting the Dohaliya's son of Govinda who was about twelve-thirteen old to carry with, *eigya* and grandpa along with me went to salute the old king at Baṛī-Kuñja. In Kālidās's *Śākuntala* the denotation of Śakuntalā at the *paśya śakuntalābhyaṅga* was taken as by Sarbadaman to Śakuntalā, I also denoted to the king whereby the saying "salute to the old king". With the assumptions that the armed personnel would have stood on the door; many gardens might be there inside, behind the residence the big tiger, tigress and leopard, horse riders' troop, Arabian horses and many others would be there perhaps—went happily in hope of seeing them on the day. However, there landed on a place which was being completely contrasted to. The entrance was being set as exterior and interior ways. No single personnel stood on the doors. Not a single sepoy was there and even a troop was not also seen. Neither a garden nor a cage and the one being known as tiger were not also there. There was no horse, no vehicle and no men as usual. Finally reached the courtyard, some monks and nuns were seen at the loop of the temple forepart, some titled like women dressed with complete sacred clothes at the corner of the temple's veranda and behind ouch cart. Stepped on the stir with extending respectful obeisance and entered to the veranda by opening ouch cart. The women who were there found to be the prominent personalities. When we were seen, asked by receiving well and warmly, "When did both of you arrive and who is the boy". Dear-in-laws, just arrived yesterday, could not visit yesterday, hence come today to make prayer to Govinda and to salute the Mahārāja. Being attending still with the response, prayer had been made to the Govinda and thus continued, "This one is born to the eldest daughter-in-law". Hence replied, "It's so good, having said thus as not a single *iya*[29] is there but now the boy should have to perform the kindness". Another one asked again, "What's the name has being kept?" *Eigya* replied looking simpler at me, "Choṭe Pakhangba". "So closely matched with the grandson", all were laughing by watching at me affectionately.

By the time we came down from the temple, he was already there in the veranda of the residence. All were marching led by *eigya* along holding of the tray which was taken with. "When did you come dear Sanajaobi, oh, the brother-in-law you are also herewith and then who is the boy", the then highness address was being extended thus by and by instantly, holding *mālā* bead in hand welcomed each and every person quite warmly. "Just arrived yesterday, could not offer the salutation unto you yesterday ..." having mentioned as such did offer the salutation by putting the tray before him. Conversations were held for a while with grandpa and *eigya*. At the end, expressed sentimentally with tears, "when glancing back only you are the one left behind me dear sister and brother-in-law". Grandpa and *eigya* were also in sentimental, shed tears, I was surprised with the full of tears in the eyes.

Understood today that he was a king who had completely been stolen all the power and grace by the time. In his life completed playing the tragic drama of a king—having fallen the last curtain. Marking the dream for the next day remained the dusk as dignified and the shutting day ever it was. Just remember an excerpt from one of the prayers of Viśvakavi—

Pathey yar phuraye ase pather majhekhane,
Kshater rakhe uthese yar phute,
Basanbhusa malin hal dhulai apamane,
Shakti yar parite chai tute—
Dhakiya dik tahar kshatbyatha
Karunaghan gabhir gopnata,
Ghuchaye laj phutao tare nobin usa-pane
Jurye tare adharsudhanjale.

(The tiffin was to over on the crossroad,
Scratching the line of stray on face,
Blushing with the dirtiest wearing
Touching the graveyard with the decline of strength
Please close the agony born by him
The furthest hidden mug of eternal blessing

Let be blossomed anew into the dark afresh
To dwell tranquilly yielding with the unlit.)[30]

Birds and Animals of Śrī-Kuṇḍa

The animal which was closely associated with Śrī-Kuṇḍa was the monkey whereas in terms of birds peacock and parrot had been.

In Śrī-Kuṇḍa men and monkey thus ever lived together. The monkey used to rob and stolen things, man chased them by holding sticks and throwing mallet with shouting, *lagae lagae*. There was not to be in the intension of beating and wounding. The monkeys although were big and strong hence just ran away if said *lagae* and the men also never continued chasing as thought to have come crazy child perhaps. The monkey also never greatly hatred the men and the men were too living together with the monkeys as usual. Never was there seen but the cheerful glimmer. Once a monkey happened to be hungry then it would enter into the house discreetly and search for eatable items, if found nothing, would take anything else whatever it might be a cloth or a utensil and would be sitting over high where the people could simply see. They would pretend to tear the cloth and to break with pounding the utensil whenever just the people were seen. After having offered some chickpeas or anything else by saying *le le* on a vessel only then the thing would be returned. By mistaken if only one vessel was offered by the man of unmindful—would have taken over both the vessel and item together. It was so funny when the mirror was robbed away. When came to see its own image a hand would grope on the back side of the mirror as anyone was there perhaps. Being played still jumping from the trees whenever there had been hot sunny in Śrī-kuṇḍa, in the evening a big monkey taught wresting to the infants. In the childbirth of the monkeys there had usually been a midwife. One surprising thing was of that the alpha recognized all the sounds of each and every small and big monkey of his troop. When extended screaming in encountering with a frightening alarm just readily arrived ahead of. While eating the mother pushed over the hand of infant aside if robbed by competence did never taken back—seemed to be taught robbing. Indeed a cheerful glimmer it was.

The peacocks were simply lived whether among the people or in thicket. As nobody had done any harmful things, the people were not ever hated at all. The parrots also candidly dispersed over the foot of the trees in Śrī-Kuṇḍa's surrounding, never flew away in people' coming, by moving aside a bit took their foods. Did not understand what was doing whereby putting its head and remained staying quite a long time into the hole of the squat wood!

In our time in most of the *maṇḍapa* and at the home of noblemen there was a tradition of listening to tales and religious texts recited. Following the elders we the children also listened to them. The narratives about living the human, the animals and the birds in saints' *āśrama* and in deep forest altogether were being listened frequently. That was seemingly witnessed in Śrī-Kuṇḍa clearly. Anyone never hurt even to a single bird and animal, whether fish or tortoise was not being touched. Hence, our perspective was thus changed over due to the place albeit a boy born and grown up in a place wherein the habits of trapping birds, harvesting of the *polylecithal* and larva of honey bee, fishing, crab catching, and digging for eel as associated with. It's so amazing that the place and the behavioural influence of the land.

The People of Śrī-Kuṇḍa and Its Surroundings

They were the groups of saints moody renounce persons and people who were born in Śrī-Kuṇḍa. The first group survived by begging, while the latter being lived by the professions of their caste wherein weaving by the weavers, ceramic by the pot makers, cattle husbandry by dairy farmers. Existent of wealthy people in the latter group were seen as unusual. It seemed that most of people lived as beggarly. Their hearts were also uncomplicated, as being much uncomplicated remained as not having blenching at all. Nevertheless, the God was being seriously believed. Whenever any religious day was occurred letting the family and village came together along. The specific possessed items which were not wanted to leave behind had been brought bearing on the head, sometimes even the goat was also brought by pull. When seen the performing of Śrī-Kuṇḍa *parikramā*[31] along chanting the holy name by the women bearing things on the head and the men carrying a child on the shoulder who were as poor and dirtiest as much wearing, had the filthy bodies and loose hairs—an inexpressible pleasure was felt in the heart.

Having found by the time we were grown up and started reading some books—wherever the places descended by the Almighty for the welfare of the world the Mother Nature poured the sacred pollen grain and holy water and sprinkled the nectar also in the air. Therefore, there had not been mis-spent at all whenever spent even for a few hours in these places. Could not understand how far it was true! However, it was at least understood that there had been some qualities of these holy places which were felt only by the heart, and a drop of peace was seemed to be sprinkled.

Govardhana Parikramā

It was just started from the Śrī-Kuṇḍa. Since we lived in Śrī-Kuṇḍa, being started itself as thus. It was so early that remained still twilight. We were altogether five which included uncle, royal grandfather, grandpa and I. the grandmother stayed behind in attending the service of Govinda, remained unmoved.

That was the time of Holī. It was the season of beauty for Govardhana touching its zenith. It was the period of sprouting for all the trees being married to the brow, grown at the foothill and its adjacent. Sprouting as just out, grown up the new leafs on every plant with the brightness of crimson. Being fallen the game of colours' steam of Rādhā-Govinda, having drunk with the pleasure of colours game by the inner eyes, the satisfied heart of devotee sung as—

Lāl Yamunājala,
Lāl Tamāla Tāla,
Sabu Lāl Hī Lāl

It was the Govardhana of this episode itself wherein we were performing *parikramā* on this day. Again, on the other, there had been an aspect found as stacking pearl on the gold. There 'As like the moon beamed when the sun arose' was being much coordinated in saying. The sky of dusk shining reddish having the light of sun hurled over the airspace, on the earth being handsome the Govardhana with brightening crimson by possessing the light of spring. It seemed contending each other the two in terms of coolness, calmness, and softness.

Neither knew the quality of Govardhana nor the mightiness of *parikramā,* just went as I was a plaything for all. Watched the beauty of Govardhana, saw surprisingly the face of Hanumān sitting on the trees, having dark face and long tail—jumping by waiving tail, having watched the peacock whether sitting on the branches of tree or walking on the ground, forgotten to march—just stopped if the dancing of peacock was seen. It was last but not the least—the rabbits of white, black, and yellow colours kept jumping jerk from dense to dense. Kept singing the *koel* there on the branches of the tree and running the squirrel up and down over the tree.

Someone else the monk was in perform *parikramā* hastily and the legs were also moving on hot headedly—the *mālā* beads in hand while in lip, didn't grasp what the holy name was being mumbling! Other else a devotee kept offering *daṇḍavata praṇāma*[32] repeatedly in a same place to complete the number stipulated with counting of stones to decide the numbers. No carefulness was seen in them for time, for stance—not being worried for the future but the counting of the number of steps could have not been interrupted. The stones that carried the numbers of his score were picked up one by one and continued instantly. On which day the 14 *kosa* would be covered was known to God. Amazing glimmers all over existed there. When recalling all these things now it is understood as true with the sayings that the Indian lives for the future, not for the present. Cannot but remember the remarks given by Swami Vevekanada,

> "If India does concentrate not only on the spiritual dimensions but also focuses on the material dimensions, and again if the Europe focuses not merely on materials growth but also earns spirituality to some extent, the light of paradise would definitely fall on earth."

Got reached and offered obeisance unto Rama-Krishna. I had eaten some *pūrī*s. Now, started returning back from the *parikramā.* The sunshine was also becoming hotter spell. As all were aware, no much conversation held, just went as usual, whether together or alone had done whichever was to be done. Mānasī Gaṅgā had been reached. Being decided there to offer obeisance unto Rādhācaraṇa Bābājī.

Rādhācaraṇa Bābā

He was also known as Manipuri Bābā. Born in Moirangthem family, and once heard as perhaps being the brother of Moirang Ningthou[33] in relation. By leaving the birth place during the period of Mahārājā Candrakīrti came to Brajabhūmi as early as quite young. Taking initiation from the Siddha Bābā Kṛṣṇadāsa he possessed the path of a saint.

There were three Kṛṣṇadāsa in Brajamaṇḍala who had been the prominent saints. Three of them were all *siddha bābā*s. Therefore, it had been very hard to know in clear that who was the *guru* of Rādhācaraṇa Bābā. However, there is a saying about this Bābājī Mahārāja *guru.* When walked down to the Mānasī Gaṅgā one day for taking bath he just sank into the water, failed to find in search by all. Being thought it was the confiscation of God. The floating over of the body one day was awaited disappointedly. However, it was not the confiscation of God; just came up spotlessly from the water on the seventh day of the sinking as like nothing was happen at all. Everybody got wonderstruck, came to know that just went as summoned to pick up the ring of Rādhārānī's ring finger being fallen in Naukābilash.

Maṇipuriyā Bābā was an entitled disciple of *guru*, the one who caught the divine appearance and kindness of Brajeśvarī[34]. He did grace in Mānasī Gaṅgā by taking the in-charge of *siddha bābā*'s hermitage until 105 years of his age. Rāmacaraṇa Bābā was a reputable saint who had been known as *siddha bābā* in his tenure of mentorship and later became familiar as Maṇipuriyā Bābā spending his living almost in the cave.

The Bābājī Mahārāja was a tall man. Due to the principle of the faith he was moderately thin; the complexion was nice-looking. If not being skilful it was difficult to grasp the words speaking wherein Bāṅglā, Brajabolī, and Maṇipurī by mixing the three dialects. Having become old by the time when crossing the age of hundred years the eyes vision was something low. However, a specific quality of him was that once a heard sound never forgotten even it was too long ago, just said putting the head down for a while, "isn't that". So auspicious it was indeed catching the divine appearance of such a diocesan character.

Holī

As it was the time of *yaoshang,*[35] it was the moment of colour festival. In Brajamaṇḍala, the Holī of Nandagrām and Barsānā were famous. Didn't go to Nandagrām but the Barsānā was gone. Over the hot sunny it seemed to die in climbing the temple constructed on the top of the hill likely to have 108 stirs perhaps. Many people were there—it seemed that the monks and nuns were maximum in number. Some *khañjanī*s, *ḍapha*s, *ḍholaka,*[36] and *jhallarigā*[37] were also seen. Two monks were dancing in their own wills, by and by enchored the attitudes of woman also. Since the image of God had already been brought out, seated over there by watching the deportments of the monks after doing obeisance. In enquiring after having a long rest it was confirmed that the *halaṅgkara*[38] would be performed in the evening at around four. As we didn't have the plan to stay the night there, had to go right back. Having departed instantly unwatched. However, it came to know from the narrative told on the way by *eigya* that the *halaṅgkara* was central to the Barsānā's Holī, chasing for beating the male performers of Holī by the women who took the roles of *brajamāī*s in the *halaṅgkara* of Bijaygovinda[39] was adapted from this Barsānā's tradition. Not performed as done in Manipur by having identified performer and wearing signified costumes rather it was informally participated and sung by the folk in casual, our home grown Holī had more been critical was instantly known.

Utsava

During the season of Holī many pilgrims had ever come, not only from Manipur but several from Cachar, Sylhet, Tripurā and Shivsagar also. In the temples, the *utsava*s[40] were offered as not being collectively but rather individually. The *utsava pakkā, kaccā* and *kṣīrapuwā*, these three kinds of *utsava* were prevalent. The numbers of individual were fixed for invitation and hence known as being invited and inviting individuals. The share of reasonably non-attending invited individuals might have been taken by a closed person. If there performed *kīrtana* that associated with *adhivāsa* the *kīrtana* singers got an extra dish apart from eating and being taken away to home.

The shares of washermen, barbers and scavengers were also offered. All the remains in the banana leaf from eating were for the outside attendants. Nothings additional were gone to anybody from the fixed numbers. By closing the door the *utsava* was celebrated, as done by all as usual. By those capable man might have offered perhaps the street feast as thus for the people's welfare service or in worship of Daridranārāyaṇa, otherwise it was unmanageable at all. If something offered to anyone, hence begun, "having offered to him but not to me, why", it was just a battle, a big war if hapless. No banana leaf was used. The dish was made by pinning a kind of leafs coming from the Himalaya. The *donnā*[41] was also made. The water was distributed in a *kulla* (a kind of small pot). According to the items, *kaṭorā* (a kind of small vessel) was also being used.

No formalities were there in the sitting arrangement; just getting a space was enough at all. All the individuals could take part in the celebration if audacious and having resided in Śrī-Kuṇḍa for one year in complete.

Our coming to Braja was not much importantly for having views of the sacred places. It was seemed to be reverenced the services rendered in the temple by grandmother, Khakashi and royal grandfather. Moreover, another thing was that I had been taken there to offer obeisance unto grandmother. Hence, there had never been visited elsewhere well other than Govardhana and Barsānā. Just kept concentrating on works. Buying materials renovation was made by engaging masons whichever were required to have renovation and repairing. The shattered materials of worship were also bought again. Every work was likely completed within one month.

Now started thinking about returns. As no sooner than the Holī was just ended the hot temperature rose quickly, decided to leave for Manipur within two or three days. Having submitted "For you it's up to you but how can the small beloved grandson be taken back unless showing the Yamunā and taking holy bath of the same". After having deliberation, just came to decide that by starting from Śrī-Kuṇḍa overspending the day itself at Madhya Vrindavana, then to approach towards Mathurā, on the next day after having lunch at Yuvarāja Kuñja for which the royal grandpa was to proceed early in advance from Śrī-Kuṇḍa and there to wait for us after having bought the tickets.

Decided the day and sent message to Imphal whereby mentioned *mamoyai* to be in *jillā* to receive as I was herewith.

Departing

Departed with the precious blessing which being the greatest fence in life, "Be capable of rendering kindness service to the elders" in shedding tears in the eyes from the royal grandma and Khakashi who were not being destined to meet in Vrindavana again. The massaging on my head with the adorable hands of the two with several meaningful tears in the eyes is found to feel today when remember.

Reached Madhya Vrindavana and got entranced into Yuvarāja Kuñja. Few women who seemed the wives of royal princes were found staying there; the *eigya* and the grandpa were familiarly received with warm greetings. Besides, something was asked about me also. The resting place was also pleasantly arranged. The pilgrims we were not and didn't consider as thus, behaved like as the family members. In the evening *roṭī-pūrī* was arranged for God to offer while in the morning the rice was being offered by *eigya*.

That was in the morning, the sun had appeared distinctly, just went for taking holy bath to Keśighāṭ. The covering of the widen and lengthy carpet of dunes with white sand, the dark stream ran over at a distance, the waving of water with the sun shine in reddish here and there, on the other side the big ground of green colour in Bhandhirvan and Belvan were found surprisingly charming, the beauties of the landscape and surroundings had satisfactorily been drunk by the duo eyes. Having walked down, not reached the vast sheet, no one ever went there, got prepared to take holy bath at a big wharf, finding a place where no tortoise was there. It was a big glimmer for me as never seen before such big and widen tortoises existed at such a large numbers.

Stepped up from the holy bath. From Kuñja went again for doing obeisance to Lord Gopeśvara. After doing obeisance to Gopeśvara bought some *jaypur*[42] from Gopīnāth bazar. My first journey to witness the Madhya Vrindavana was over with this. As per the short-lived the offering of meal to the God was done very early on that day. Just after taking the *prasāda*[43] left for Mathurā in *ṭoṅgā*. The royal grandfather was waiting there, having already done the tickets. The two grandpas and *eigya* held many conversations. Several things for the family were handed over to grandpa and *eigya*. The bus was almost set for leaving, all the belongings were lifted up and everyone was doing obeisance each other. Hugging me very tightly at this moment of separation by rubbing on my face and belly today also but didn't say *wairagedo* as done as usual during my childhood days. Felt no ludicrous, shedding tears in the eyes when listened to, "go away Choṭe" shedding more tears by leaps and bounds. The infantile heart had never understood the layering manifestations of tears in complete, the long separated dearly loved lap, having seen anew and again when to fall back on separation the heart could not be unmoved, leaning on the bosom of grandpa kept weeping there. Having given the hussle of the cart, grandpa himself uplifted me. The cart started running. The royal grandpa was looking at by standing with tears in longing eyes; watching over we left away, shedding tears profusely in the eyes.

Today the face of the world came to be known. Existed no happiness in life; just lived only the shadows there. Having gone through every turning and loop winnowed by darkness and light of the life, existed no ending for meeting and separating whereby utterly concluded with the last tears and the closing separation. Just remembered:

> Doing many disquieting thou art
> To me,
> To my life
> Several on the happiness
> Many on the weep again.
> Never intervene for a single day,
> Nor stop even for a moment.
> Completing the bundle, crossed the embankment as just
> Coming nearby, running thus away instantly
> Thrilling the heart every moment

The separating inflammation of thy.
Doing several disquieting as thus
To me
To my life.

The world is just like a big tree while the human beings are like the birds. Perching together the birds in the night and as the day broke flying away with their own wills; stepping together for a short while human beings have also thus slipped away depending upon the *karma* of their owns.

The route for "to and fro" was the same. However, since the time retreated with cold and warm and the place was too large apart, the journey was more being harder to happen than the previous one. As the time shifting difference in daylight and darkness was occurred, several hills, rivers, jungles, landscapes, buildings, and different people of hills and valleys which were not seen in the coming trip were also seen. That much had been of many sources to have respite. But one thing, hard to endure but could have not been escaped was that of shouldering the burden to have gone until the final destination of the cart. As the son of the land whereby living neat and clean, even wearing no multiple level of clothes but endeavouring to wear with good smell, opulence with fruit and flower, making and reaping smells from floral scents and fruit aromas for the clothes and being dwelled in a cold place hardly perspired the sweat even for few drops and yet having luxurious with the drops perspired as in such a land to born apparently found extremely hard to endure the bad smells of cloths, bodies, sweat, and mouths. Not only that, unaware of the places to spit and to throw the waste had been thus associated in self to them. In consequence of it the tiredness reached its zenith—intertwining throughout the senses. From this apart, albeit not in every stop but in most of the places a disgusting matter was encountered with. Many facets of having unpleasant on body, whether having suffered still or cured, came bagging in quite disturbing dress, which never been prohibited. That was so sad. Subsequently nothing was preferred to ingest. Completely exhausted the body also as no sunlight was absorbed. Being decided not to go outside as if the cold weather was not there. As travelling very unpleasantly as such meanwhile an interesting event was met—could not but penned it down.

That was in Chandpur, pulling up the *mahjaal*[44] and pilings of white fishes were found. Catfish, Rohu, Bao, Hilsha—multiple categories of fish were being piled as large as hillocks. Boys and girls seated encircling by holding a *loṅg*[45] in each hand and laying the piles of small fish on the front. The eagles were flying high and low in the sky densely. The children rhythmically threw up the fishes with their *loṅg*s and the eagles harvested them in inclines. Never touched and not to be made touching the big fish. On the other side the fishes were put with ice in the box and covered with straws. The boats which used in casting the nets were being washed finding their particular sites, the last end was too far in watching. Having thought, would there have been left fish in the river!

Badarpur was reached in the early morning of the next day and got *jillā* before the lunch time. When the bus stopped *mamoyai* along with a grandpa's disciple of music was found being awaited. "What have you brought for me Choṭe", the uncle asked. I brought the sweet of Govinda for mamo in packet, thus replied loudly "Sweet of Govinda".

Took respite for a while near to the station. I ate some *pūrī*s and went to Lakhipur. On the way about to reach Lakhipur took meal at the residence of a disciple in Tolen *khun*[46] and hence arrived in Lakhipur. In the evening, meal packs for the mountainous journey were prepared, the helpers were also found in search and again the accompanies had also always been there whether acquainted or not. On the next day left for Jiri in the early morning. Crossing the hill range of Phultar and Jiri River, there reached the Jiribam. The meals were taken at the Kālīmāī Temple. Having decided to leave tomorrow and thus stayed over as there would have been inexpedient.

> Today my heart is in peace but the reason cannot be grasped!

There are two facets for the mother of the world which has been seen by all the people with the eyes. Mother and motherland are the she and the face of herself. Once the poet Dwijendralal Rai sang as,

Dhan dhanye pushpa dhara
Aamaderi basundhara
Yar majhe aashe desh ek
Se ye aamar janma bhumi.

(Filled with the natural treasures and fragrant flowers
Beautiful the earth it is.
Living there a land in this run aground
That is my birthplace, my motherland
That is my birthplace, my motherland.)[47]

Just landed on her lap, how the heart could have not been peaceful at all as her pollen grain is my body; her nectar is the blood running in my vein, her air is my soul, and her grains are my strength. As blessed by the God the infantile heart became thus peaceful.

That was on the next day. Eating was done by getting up from the night. One after another we went in cherish. As went thus crossed the Jiribam and hence left it behind, confronting with the large leech ahead. When remember, wish to sing today:

Thou love is powerful, the beloved motherland
Inclining the soul on thy
The beloved motherland
Leaving thou as went aboard
Enduring thus the soul doubted
Gazing back in contrite.
Crossing over a hence
Stepping the path one after another
Getting tired instantly the heart.
When return back by leaving aboard
Running the heart just ahead instantly

Trustily gaze whether thou art seen
Crossing hence instantly
Next by next the stepping
My heart just proud to be at once.
Thou love is powerful, the beloved motherland
Yearning my heart in every thou pelage
My beloved motherland!

Hence, there started climbing up the Tinpha-Iroi and then Motok Pal. By continuous walking throughout the day and again stopped at times in the night, walking day by day through the ranges of mountain, several rivers and jungles were being crossed instantly and five days later reached the adjacent of Laimatol hill, there came to see again my beloved motherland, the Manipur by name after having separated for many days. The land of jewel being amazed distinctly in the enclosure of the mountains. Many images have been painted in mind, given the rhythm to the heart, sung the *lammin, khamin*[48] and the poem of invocation at the different stages of life.

One more thing, it is already 34 years of age if counted by the year yet to complete. It was on 12 January 1949 and in our calendar that was on the eleventh of Hiyangei.[49] On that day the mother extended the blessing afresh with the rhythmic tune as like, "sing as you wish".

My poem, "Nongumlakhoda" was sung in the night of the day itself. Did singing with tears in the eyes on a cloudy day of Hiyangei at a still corner, didn't understand whether it was because of mother's love.

Oh brother poet
Pioneer of the quill
Should thou have been descendible (?)
Please be descended!
Oh! The land of golden hub
The lovely mother's fame
Should it have been portrayable
Please descend to portray!

Shining with the green landscape alluring
Enclosing with the mountain shading
Rippling the seedling of grain in wind's wave
Sporting as widespread
Oh! The land of golden hub
The loving title Maninu
Should it have been recitable (?)
Please descend to recite!

With the affection of heart
Overwhelming the flows of milk,
Streams as Imphal and Nambul,
And nurturing the sons and daughters,
Oh! The land of golden hub
The mother, circling the mountains on the loin
Should it have been invocable
Please descend to invoke!

Perhaps the mother's mercy fell in the heart, kept singing independently, neither the shortage of language was there nor the lack of singing genre was found.

Offering the obeisance today unto the mother as the follower of the sage at once—

Tumi vidya tumi dharma,
Tumi hadi tumi marma,
Twang hi prana: sharire.

NOTES

1. The woman who has devoted to her husband.
2. Lord Viṣṇu or his incarnation.
3. The third age of the world in Hindu cosmology which has been preceded by Tretā Yuga and followed by Kali Yuga.
4. Truth.
5. The quality of passion, activity and movement.
6. The quality of ignorance.
7. Another name of Lord Śiva.
8. One *kosa* is about 1.8 km.

9. A Hindu saint founded the Gauḍīya school of Vaiṣṇavism. He is believed to be the incarnation of Lord Kṛṣṇa.
10. A folk naming especially used in addressing politely to the brāhmaṇas, kings and their family members. The grandmother of the writer belongs to royal family for which he uses the word *eigya* in calling his grandma.
11. Yaiskul Lakpa was a high ranking post in Manipur palace.
12. A kind of curtained canopy.
13. A title to address to the middle uncle (maternal).
14. Something like pudding.
15. Mythical being which is believed to have legs that are opposite to the normal position.
16. This is not the translation of the above Bangali text but a free translation of the Manipuri version of the writer.
17. The fifth *svara* (tune) in Hindustānī music.
18. This is not the translation of the above Bangali text but a free translation of the Manipuri version of the writer.
19. A well-known Meitei British Army official from Cachar.
20. One of the tribal groups of Manipur.
21. Vegetable curry.
22. Small piece of cake made of choroal to kindle tobacco in the bowl of *hookāh.*
23. The river-dolphin.
24. This is not the translation of the above Bangali text but a free translation of the Manipuri version of the writer.
25. The Anglo-Manipuri war fought between the British Force and the Manipuris in 1891 at Khongjom, a place situated in Thoubal District in Manipur.
26. A traditional towel to wear.
27. Wood Apple.
28. A kind of wild varnished fruit.
29. Son of brother when the speaker is female.
30. This is not the translation of the above Bangali text but a free translation of the Manipuri version of the writer.
31. Moving clockwise round a temple or holy place as an expression of reverence.
32. *Daṇḍavata* is a kind of offering greeting which involves bowing down completely in touching with the ground.
33. King of Moirang and a high ranking post in the Manipur palace.
34. Another name of Goddess Rādhārānī.
35. Holī festival is known as Yaoshang in Manipur.
36. Kinds of percussion used in Indian temples and in folk singing.

37. A kind of cymbal.
38. It is the re-enactment of the Holī performed by Rādhā and Kṛṣṇa along with the *gopīs*.
39. One of the most popular temples of Govinda located in Imphal.
40. In Manipur the word *utsava* refers to a sacred grand feast although the literal meaning of this particular word is festival/ceremony.
41. A kind of vessel made of platain leaf.
42. A kind of wrapper worn by the girls in Holī festival.
43. Consecrated foods offered to the God/Goddess.
44. A large cast fishing net.
45. A pointed weapon having a long handle used in fishing.
46. Village.
47. This is not the translation of the above Bangali text but a free translation of the Manipuri version of the writer.
48. In olden days whenever the king of Manipur made an outing or went on a tour a *pena* singer accompanied him, singing song, this tradition of singing song on *pena* music is called Lamin Pena.
49. Usually falls on November and December.

9

Tongjei-Maril Road

The Ancient Route of Manipur for Indic Pilgrimage

Sanasam Amal Singh

Introduction

The first trade route between the state of Manipur and the rest of India is the one which is now known as Old Cachar Road, which runs from Imphal to Lakhipur, a small town on the bank of River Barak. It was initially constructed in 1535 during the reign of Manipur King Kabomba (1524-42) mainly because of establishing a relationship with the king of Tekhao (Assam).[1] It facilitated the cultural contacts between Manipur and Brahmaputra Valley. The local name of the road is referred to as Tongjei-Maril. Literally, it means tube hole, where *tongjei* is the tube or pipe, while *maril* is the hollow part of the pipe. It starts from Imphal and passes through Bishnupur (Lamangdong), Khoupum, Nungba, Jirighāṭ, and then to Lakhipur. It is also said that during the days when the Manipuri kings first encountered Vaiṣṇavite, the Old Cachar Road became a regular Indic pilgrimage route. The then-British government made improvements to the road shortly after the Burmese war and maintained it up until 1865.

After 1865, maintenance was done by the Manipur Kingdom during the time of Mahārājā Candrakīrti. The Old Cachar (Tongjei-Maril) Road was the main trade route between the State of Manipur and the rest of India until the construction of the Imphal-Dimapur Road in 1881 and the Imphal-Jiribam (which is known as the New Cachar) road in 1961.[2] Since then, it has been abandoned for many years. However, in due course of time, with various civil groups imposing frequent economic blockades on the existing highways, the state experienced a severe crisis of commodities. This situation led the Manipur government to revive the economically viable Tongjei-Maril as an alternative supply route. Consequently, different ethnic communities also wanted to open the road again. Thus, in this light, the paper attempts to highlight the historical and economic importance of Tongjei-Maril Road.

Ancient Routes of Manipur

The hill routes of Manipur have been known to the civilized world since pre-historic periods. These routes provided the main links between India and China through Burma. The traders and merchants from both countries used to pass through this state in the early periods. It is also said that the hill-girded valley of Manipur was well decorated by winding hill routes, especially for trade and commerce, and frequently traversed by the invaders. These hill routes were among the most ancient and famous hill routes in the world.[3] Thus, it reveals that Manipur had a good relationship with Southeast Asia and also with the West. These routes were interconnected through the mainland, and the subsequent migration and immigration of people can be traced. Even long-distance and short-distance trades were carried through these routes.

Generally, the most important old roads that are often mentioned today are Imphal to Burma, Imphal to Silchar, and Imphal to Kohima. However, when we research further, various literature has identified trade routes more than the identified routes. For example, in the *Gazetteer of Manipur*,

Captain EW Dun briefly described 32 trade routes in 1886[4]. According to *Meitrabak*[5] (an early research work by Nandalal Sharma in 1960), there were some routes through the hills of Manipur connecting the Surma Valley and the Brahmaputra Valley with the Kabaw Valley. The following table shows the different routes/hill routes connecting different countries since pre-historic times.

Table 9.1: Ancient Routes of Manipur

Sl. Group of Hill Routes	Name of the Routes	Important Countries & Places Connected
First	1. Heirock Route via Machee 2. Aimol Route 3. Ngara Chingjin Route (Ngarian Route) 4. Maring Route	Kabaw, Ava (Burma), China & Southern-eastern Countries of Asia
Second	1. Tongjei-Maril Route (Old Cachar) 2. Ngaprum Chingjin Route (New Cachar Road) 3. Khongjai Route 4. Acqui Route	Cachar, Tripurā, Sylhet, and other Western countries, including Assam
Third	1. North-Eastern Route (Tekhao Route)	Assam, Nagaland, and other north-western areas, including Jorhat)

Source: Nandalal Sharma, *Meitrabak*, OK Store, Imphal, 1960, p. 28.

People from different parts of India could quickly enter the Manipur Valley through one of the routes of the second order, and they could easily reach the Kabaw Valley through one of the routes of the first group. Traders, colonisers and invaders used these routes before the beginning of the Christian era. In the ancient past, Manipur was one of the gates through which there was cultural flow between India on the one hand and Burma and Southeast Asia on the other. The hill routes converged at Imphal and again diverged in different directions to connect various places in Burma in the east and south, as well as Cachar and Assam in the west. These routes generally had a west-east orientation despite the high parallel hill ranges running north to south with deep river valleys between the ranges. Despite the difficult terrain, the people used these hill routes throughout the ancient and medieval periods.

Sir James Johnstone, the then Political Agent of the British government to Manipur, had foreseen the utility of connecting Imphal, the capital of Manipur, with the Assam Valley. The road from Golaghāṭ to Kohima has already been constructed. The Manipur king, Mahārājā Chandrakīrti, also took an active interest in the project of connecting Imphal with the Kohima section road. The road construction between Imphal and Mao was completed in 1881 under the supervision of Lt. Raban of the Royal Engineers.[6] In subsequent years, the road was improved and extended up to Dimapur. When the rail-head was opened at Dimapur, the Imphal-Dimapur Road became the main artery of communication and trade between Manipur and the rest of India. Since then, it has been considered the first lifeline of the people of Manipur. The second lifeline is the Imphal-Jiribam road, which is known as the New Cachar Road, constructed in 1961. This Imphal-Dimapur Road was earlier known as national highway (NH) 39 and the Imphal-Jiribam as NH 53B. Later, in 2011, according to a notification issued by the Ministry of Road Transport and Highways, all the national highways were given new numbers. The new highway numbering system indicates the direction and location of the highways.

The Imphal-Dimapur highway (NH-39) has been renamed NH-2, and the Imphal-Jiribam (NH-53B) NH-37. However, the 100 km-long Tongjei-Maril (Old Cachar road) highway, which is also known as NH-53A, is much shorter than the Imphal-Jiribam and Imphal-Dimapur highways. The Imphal-Dimapur Road covers 207 km, while the Imphal-Jiribam route covers 265 km. It was abandoned after the British constructed the two highways. Since then, for many decades, it has remained neglected.[7]

Historical Importance Associated with Tongjei-Maril Road

Looking deeper into history, we cannot avoid the historical importance associated with this route as many Manipuri kings and queens, princes and princesses, noblemen, and traders alike have trodden along this route. There are also legends and folk tales narrated by the residents of Lamangdong or Bishnupur, which is 27 km south of Imphal. They gave us every bit of information, fact, and fiction associated with the route. For instance, any octogenarian who frequented the route during the 1940s is familiar with the tale of the aged white tiger that refuses to attack travellers along the Tongjei-Maril. Legend says that while a powerful Meitei king was on his way to Cachar, the old tiger attacked his royal convoy and escorts. The king was infuriated by the tiger's swift assault. Instead of giving the order to hunt and capture, the king cursed the tiger so that he would never again possess the sharp, slicer teeth to tear apart his prey. The tiger survived swallowing wild fowls and fruits only.[8]

It is also said that during the days when the Manipuri kings first encountered Vaiṣṇavite, the Old Cachar Road became a regular pilgrimage route. The route is also associated with the history of fraternal feuds and treachery between the royal family members and political exiles. It was the same route that many kings took to escape possible assassinations. During British paramountcy, many political agents had come to Manipur via this route. In 1804, the ousted King Madhucandra, who was taking shelter in Cachar, formed an alliance with King Kṛṣṇacandra of Cachar and invaded Manipur, which was ruled by his brother King Chourjit.[9] The invading forces marched through the Old Cachar Road (Tongjei-Maril) via Jiri and Lamangdong (now Bishnupur). At the time of Chahi Taret Khuntakpa, 1819-25, popularly known as the seven years of devastation during the reign of Mahārājā Gambhīr Singh, many Manipuris, unable to bear the torture and turmoil in the hands of the Burmese, fled to neighbouring places near Barak and Jiri, Cachar, Sylhet (Bangladesh) and Assam by trekking along the Old Cachar Road. The boundary of Manipur State was then extended up to Jiri on the West (1821-27).[10]

Manipuri settlement in Cachar Valley and neighbouring places can be dated back to 1800. The trade and commerce between Cachar and Manipur gradually improved after Princess Induprabhā, daughter of King Madhucandra, married King Kṛṣṇacandra of Cachar in 1800 CE. Jiri and Barak rivers demarcated the boundaries of Assam and Manipur since the British days. It was on the bank of the Barak River; after halting at Jiri and crossing over the Jiri River, the then Mahārājā of Manipur, Śrī Candrakīrti (1850-86), held Zillā Durbār with the then British Viceroy in India, Boortlord and Political Agent of Manipur, Robert Brown in 1874, signed Treaties and exchanged royal gifts with Britishers. Mrs. Ethel St. Clair Grimwood, wife of St. Clair Grimwood, the then political agent in Manipur, escaped with other companions in the wake of the Royal Revolt or Political Revolt of 1891 by trekking along the Old Cachar Road and passing through the border of Jiribam or Jiri, which is still the exit point to mainland India. She reached there in the last part of March 1891 and halted one night in a makeshift bungalow near the Jiri River on her way to Lakhipur and then to Silchar.[11]

Regarding trade, the neigbhouring Indian states with which Manipur exchanged goods are Assam, Cachar, the Naga Hills, the Lushai Hills, Tripurā and Bengal. However, the traders of Manipur had closer contact with Cachar because the Manipuris used to exchange goods for the products of other states mostly through Cachar. The important commodities exported by Manipur before the British occupation were cotton, chillies, tea seeds, buffalo, silk, clothes, wax, etc. The main import goods were betel nuts, coconuts, iron, brass goods, bell metal, etc.[12] The people of the villages inhabiting the western border of Manipur took advantage of exchanging their products for salt with Cacharis. Thus, after reviewing the past history, one can say that Tongjei-Maril Road played an important role in shaping the history of Manipur. So, it surely deserves preservation through regular maintenance.

The Present Situation and Future Prospects of Tongjei-Maril

Apart from its historical significance, Tongjei-Maril, or the Old Cachar Road, continues to be the lifeline of the valley dwellers in the Bishnupur district and the tribes in the surrounding hills. This historic route passes through more than ten villages inhabited by different ethnic communities, such as the Zelianrong, Kukis, and Meiteis. The villages are Ngarian, Zoujantek, Nongmeiband, Luwanglon Khunou, Khoupum Valley, Gaidinjang, Irang, Rengpan, and Nungba. Initially, the Tongjei-Maril Road was very narrow. It was not used for heavy transportation for a long time except for light heavy vehicles that carried passengers and forest produce, mainly fruits, bamboo shoots, and young chalk (botanical name: *Parkia javanica*). Every day, a stream of Naga and Kuki hill-dwellers came down the valley to dispose of their agro-products on their shams (cane baskets) slung on their backs. These products included ripe oranges, local apples (*heitup*), and other varieties of fruits from wild orchards and jungles.

The villagers said the government had neglected the Old Cachar Road since it was blacktopped in 1968. Since then, only potholes have been repaired. Till the mid-1990s, the road was in pathetic conditions. The situation becomes all the more difficult during monsoon when the streets are muddy and slippery. Villagers face a lot of difficulties in communication and transportation. One has to take a long route if one wants to travel to Cachar or Assam. Due to these difficulties, villagers wanted to reopen the Old Cachar Road. Many civil society organizations have also submitted memorandum from time to time to repair and revived this historic routes. For instance, the Old Cachar Road Development Committee Chingmi-Tamme, which is a conglomeration of people from the hill and the valley, submitted a memorandum to the then prime minister in 2004.[13] There are two main reasons why the common people and civil society organizations want to reopen this historic route.

First, the Tamenglong district borders Assam towards Barak Valley. Of course, Guwahati is the nearest north-eastern commercial centre; however, the road from Imphal to Guwahati via Tamenglong is also the best alternative means of road communication, which may solve the bottleneck of road communication in Manipur, particularly in the Tamenglong district. The people of Tamenglong district, especially the villagers of Ngarian, Zoujangtek, Nongmeiband, Khoupum Valley, Gaidinjang, Irang, and Rengpan, have been suffering transport and communication problems due to rough terrain and bad road conditions. They want easy accessibility to the Imphal Valley and the neighbouring state Assam so they can conduct certain activities such as trade and commerce. Thus, reopening the Old Cachar Road can be viewed as boosting economic growth and reducing poverty, which will bring substantial social and economic development to the region. The social benefits arising due to the reconstruction of this road will be triggered due to improved accessibility to various services such as easy access to markets, health facilities, schools, workplaces, etc., which in turn increases the income of the locals and ultimately elevates their standard of living.

The second reason is the frequent economic blockade imposed by various civil society groups on the existing two highways, i.e., Imphal-Dimapur (NH-2) and Imphal-Jiribam (NH-37) road. Economic blockades are often used as an effective pressure tactic in north-east India and Manipur, mainly because of its geography and demography. Most states of the north-east are located in hilly regions, are too diverse on ethnical lines, and are landlocked. Only a few rivers, such as Brahmaputra and Barak, provide some means of water transport, but that is very limited. Manipur depends on rail and road transportation for goods and passengers. Thus, any effort of the blockade in the region can cripple the ordinary life of the people. The economic blockades have been used in the state as a means of agitation since the 1990s for various reasons. Thus, by imposing frequent economic blockades, the state experienced a severe crisis of commodities. The common man across all communities is the only one who suffers, as the elite can afford these blockades, and the powerful do not have a problem with supplies. Even the trade between the valley & hill people has suffered, affecting all communities adversely.

The total loss suffered by the Manipur economy due to the economic blockade in 2011 was estimated to be Rs. 245.64 crore as calculated by the Department of Economics and Statistics, which this time is being pegged at double the amount. The loss due to the destruction of property by the volunteers and supporters is in addition. The prices of essential commodities skyrocketed due to shortage, thus leading to hoarding and black marketing, destabilizing the state's tottering and fragile economy. Even life saving drugs were not available to either of the communities in the state. While the economic losses can be made up, the loss of trust and faith will take a long time to heal. Due to this frequent hardship faced by the ordinary people, many civil society organizations from the valley lobbied hard to revive the economically viable Tongjei-Maril as an alternative supply route. Apart from being an alternative route, experts from different sections express the profitability for the tribal villages in the interior hills by increasing the scope of marketability of their agricultural products. It can also bring social and cultural cohesion and national integration, which are less important than economic development. In this regard, different civil society organizations have submitted memorandums from time to time.

Gradually, the upgradation of Old Cachar Road from Bishnupur to Rengpang via Khoupum as NH-53 (A) assumes great significance given the frequent disturbance by the various organizations on both NH-2 and 37. The total length is 93 km. Notably, while addressing a public gathering at Imphal on 3 December 2011, the then prime minister declared that the centre had agreed in principle to take up the Old Cachar Road project. It was a re-assertion of his statement on 2 December 2006. Given the economic importance of the road and under public pressure, the state government submitted a proposal with an estimated cost of Rs. 43 crore to the Ministry of Surface Transport for funding on a sharing basis of 50:50 between the central government and state government. In addition, a proposal costing Rs. 86 crore has also been submitted to the North Eastern Council (NEC) for inclusion in the 11th Plan proposal for NEC. Thus, after a milestone, the reconstruction of Old Cachar Road was finally initiated in 2014. The concerned minister promises to reclaim its original name as "Tongjei-e-Maril" and will help shorten the Imphal-Jiribam distance by 30 km. The concerned department also pointed out that the construction is expected to be complete by the end of 2018 and ready for the movement of all kinds of vehicles. It may be mentioned that two companies reconstructing the said road are from Bishnupur to Zoujangtek via Tupul, stretching around 51 km, and are being taken up by ABCI Infrastructure Pvt. Limited, funded by Asian Development Bank (ADB) costing Rs. 114 crore; and from Zoujangtek to Rengpang stretching 69.52 km is reconstructed by Keystone Company funded by NEC costing Rs. 92.25 crore.[14]

The people of Bishnupur, Tamenglong, and Churachandpur districts are eagerly waiting for the dream to come true as the road will give a much shorter distance to visit Assam. Many traders and transporters are happy to think that Tongjei-Maril, so called for its narrowness, would no longer suit its name once the construction is over, for the road would be much broader.

NOTES

1. R.K. Jhalajit Singh (1999). *Manipur From 1508 to 1709*, Yaiskul Hiruhanba Leikai, Imphal, pp. 14-15.
2. Hawaibam Biren Singh (2010). *Social Geography of Manipur: A Comparative Study of Tribal and Non-Tribal People,* Rajesh Publications, New Delhi, pp. 172-74.

3. McCosh (1860-61). *On the Overland Communication between India and China*, Proceedings of the Royal Geographical Society, Vol. V, London, pp. 47-57.
4. Captain E.W. Dun (1992). *Gazetteer of Manipur*, Manas Publications, New Delhi, p. 235.
5. Nandalal Sharma (1960). *Meitrabak*, O.K. Store, Imphal, p. 28.
6. Interview with Dr N. Devendra Singh, owner of Uripok Archival Library, Imphal West District, Manipur, 17 February 2016.
7. The Govenment of India, Ministry of Road Transport and Highways (P&M Section) letter No. NH-14019/9/2007-P&M dt. 28 April 2010, addressed to the secretary, PWD, all states & union territories.
8. Interview with L. Pholmani, an 81-year-old resident of Bishnupur district, Manipur, 25 January 2016.
9. Gangmumei Kamei (2015). *A History of Modern Manipur 1826-2000: A Study of Feudalism, Colonialism & Democracy*, Indian Institute of Advance Study, Shimla & Akansha Publishing House, New Delhi, p. 8.
10. *Ibid.*, pp. 11-13.
11. Ethel, S.T. Clair Grimwood (1891). *My Three Years in Manipur*, Richard Bentley & Son, London, pp. 11-15.
12. Usham Dhananjoy Singh (22 November 2007). "Trade and Commerce of Manipur under the Political Agency 1835-1891", in *The Sangai Express,* Imphal.
13. Interview with T. Manihar Singh, a 75-year old resident of Bishnupur district, Manipur (25 January 2016).
14. Tongjei-Maril Road is likely to be ready by 2018 end, in *The Sangai Express,* Imphal, on 31 August 2017.

10

Rādhā-Kuṇḍa–Govardhana Parikramā

Chongtham Jamini Devi
(Translated from Manipuri by Sonia Wahengbam)

This transformative journey bore immense significance for me as it unfolded as a sacred pilgrimage from Delhi to the hallowed grounds of Vrindavana and Mathurā. Given the close proximity of these revered sites to Delhi, I harboured uncertainty about the prospect of undertaking such a spiritually enriching trip in the future. In the company of Rajkumar Dusari, who happened to be in Delhi, we seized the opportunity and extended an invitation for him to join us.

Upon Dusari's arrival, he inquired, "Sister is there anything I can do for you?" Expressing our fervent desire to explore Rādhā-Kuṇḍa and Vrindavana, we sought his guidance for the impending journey. Without hesitation, Dusari generously offered to be our chauffeur, expressing sincere pleasure in rendering his service.

As we ventured into Haryana, the landscape unfolded, revealing lush green fields, and roadside stalls adorned with enticing fresh guavas, berries, and grapes, captivating the attention of passers-by. Enthralled by this vibrant scene, we succumbed to the temptation of acquiring some of these freshly picked fruits for ourselves.

Our arrival in Mathurā exposed us to a harmonious fusion of development and devotion. The signboards of schools, hospitals, and dairy farms were embellished with names evoking divine associations—Rādhā, Kṛṣṇa, Brajabihārī, Govardhana, and more. The local markets presented vegetables at reasonable prices—potatoes at Rs. 2 per kg, tomatoes, carrots, brinjals at Rs. 3 per kg, cabbage for Rs. 5, and gourd for Rs. 3.

Our accommodation in Rādhā-Kuṇḍa was graciously provided by Dusari at his guest house, where we paid our respects to the Rādhā-Govinda idols in the temple. The temple's services were overseen by the then-king of Manipur, Mahārājā Suracandra.

Rādhā-Kuṇḍa, positioned 4 km north of Govardhana and 22 km west of Vrindavana, holds sacred significance for Vaiṣṇavas. In the Vedas, Rādhā-Kuṇḍa and Śyāma-Kuṇḍa are extolled with the utmost reverence. The perspective of witnessing Rādhā-Kuṇḍa, Śyāma-Kuṇḍa, and Vrindavana together is purportedly beyond human reach. Legendary tales recount Rādhā-Kuṇḍa's genesis from the tears shed by Rādhikā upon parting with Śrī Kṛṣṇa, while Śyāma-Kuṇḍa emerged from Śrī Kṛṣṇa's tears when separated from Rādhikā.

Another tale recounts the defeat of the demon Ariṣṭāsura, disguised as a bull, by Śrī Kṛṣṇa. After the battle, when Kṛṣṇa sought to meet Rādhā, her consorts advised him to purify himself by bathing in various holy places. Instead, Śrī Kṛṣṇa created Śyāma-Kuṇḍa by summoning waters from sacred rivers and bathing in them, purifying himself in a unique way.

Śrīmatī Rādhikā, with great pride, and alongside her consorts, undertook the admirable task of excavating a splendid pond near Śyāma-Kuṇḍa. When Kṛṣṇa suggested filling the pond with water from Śyāma-Kuṇḍa, Rādhikā, displaying her independence, declined the offer. She asserted her intention to fill the pond with water drawn from Mānasī

Gaṅgā, utilizing earthen pots with the assistance of her consorts. The deities from various holy sites graciously acceded to Rādhikā's request, causing all the sacred waters to converge at the enchanting Rādhā-Kuṇḍa.

In response, Śrī Kṛṣṇa bestowed his blessing, declaring that Rādhikā's pond be more potent and sanctified than his own. He promised to visit and partake in occasional baths at Rādhā-Kuṇḍa. This sacred site, where Śrī Kṛṣṇa and Rādhikā shared moments of romantic playfulness, has become synonymous with divine devotion. Rāsa-Līlā, a divine dance, is performed near the pond's banks, accompanied by the traditional water sport of *jalakeli.* Devotees of Śrī Kṛṣṇa hold Rādhā-Kuṇḍa and Śyāma-Kuṇḍa in profound reverence, recognizing them as the divine abodes of Śrī Kṛṣṇa and Rādhā.

After the Dvāpara Yuga concluded, and the epoch of Kṛṣṇa's reign came to an end, his grandson Brajanābha ascended the throne approximately 5,000 years ago. Legends unfold that in Braja, the very place where the demon Ariṣṭāsura met his demise, the sacred Śyāma-Kuṇḍa was established. It is a testament to the rich tapestry of stories and spirituality that has been woven through the historical landscape, marking the significance of events and places within the Kṛṣṇa tradition.

Temples embrace Rādhā-Kuṇḍa, surrounded by numerous *kuṇḍa*s (ponds), *ghāṭa*s (banks), and *āśrama*s. The sheer abundance of these sacred sites makes it impractical to explore them all within the constraints of limited time. Opting for a focused approach, the next morning, we visited the most significant ones to offer our prayers. Śrīmatī Gambhinī Devī, from Dusari's guest house, graciously guided my exploration.

Within some *āśrama*s, I encountered several elderly women from Manipur. True to the resilient spirit of Manipuris, they seldom spoke about the trials and tribulations they faced. Amidst this community, I had the chance to engage with an elderly lady. Curiosity led me to inquire, "Aunty, do you stay here due to a lack of someone to care for you at home?" She revealed that she had a nephew who used to provide financial support, but unfortunately, that assistance had ceased. Wondering about her survival, I questioned further, and she replied with a touch of resignation, "What can I do? I sit near the temple alongside other beggars and beg for sustenance."

Not everyone is fortunate enough to experience a life filled with happiness and contentment, especially where familial support in old age is concerned. In places like Vrindavana, Mathurā, and Purī, the presence of numerous beggars may serve as a poignant testament to the ways in which divine providence sustains them. While witnessing this reality, I sought solace by telling myself that this might be the kārmic result of actions in a past life.

In the soothing embrace of this perspective, I consoled and fortified myself with the notion that one reaps what they sow from the seeds of their past existence. According to Hinduism, the consequences of one's actions in a previous life manifest in the form of joys or trials in the current one. This philosophy served as the only means to find comfort and resilience amidst the stark realities.

My guide led me to Rādhā-Govinda, the site where Mahārājā Churachand, the then king of Manipur, rendered his service. Today, this sacred place is maintained by ISKCON followers. At the Jīvaha Temple, the idol was unearthed from beneath the ground, but during the British era, the idol's tongue was cut-off—an unsettling historical event whose accuracy remains uncertain.

During the *parikramā* around the Śrī Govinda Temple, a short distance to the left stands the Śrī Jīvaha Temple. Here, a red-coloured stone, symbolizing the tongue of Girirāja, rests on a white stone. Legend has it that Girirāja's tongue was severed and discovered during the excavation.

Stories tell of Raghunāth Dās, who, to avoid using Rādhā-Kuṇḍa water for cleaning purposes, dug a well on the eastern side. During excavation, labourers witnessed blood oozing from the pebbles, prompting Raghunātha to halt the drilling. In a dream, Girirāja revealed that his tongue had been cut-off.

Raghunātha was instructed to rescue Girirāja from the well and worship him, establishing the location of the Jīvaha Temple. Even a sincere offering of a handful of water at this sacred site pleases Girirāja.

Śyāma-Kuṇḍa serves as the bathing spot for the five Pāṇḍava brothers, and alongside its banks stands a treasure tree that has existed since the time of the five brothers. Devotion, in its true essence, entails complete submission without any reservations or arguments. However, as an individual, achieving such a profound level of devotion is a challenging endeavour. This struggle has led to numerous questions within me, particularly concerning the treasure tree and its age.

In the current era, scientific advancements allow for the determination of the age of objects, including trees. Despite this, I find myself grappling with the moral dilemma of whether it is appropriate to harbour doubts and raise questions about the authenticity of the treasure tree's age.

On the eleventh day of the lunar calendar, women gather at the Āsthā Sakhī Temple to perform kīrtana. Barkuṇḍa, developed by Mahārājā Candrakīrti, hosted the then-Mahārājā Kulacandra at the Bhajan Kuṭīna. The site yielded numerous artefacts related to Manipur's history. For rebelling against the British, Mahārājā Kulacandra was exiled to the Andaman and Nicobar Islands. Upon his return, he was denied entry to Manipur, spending his remaining days at Rādhā-Kuṇḍa. His crematorium lies in Barkuṇḍa, where memorial stones honour figures like Rājkumār Śītalajīt's father Rāmlāl Pāl, Mahārājā Candrakīrti's daughter Thadoisana, Thangal Major, Sougaijamba General, Paona Brajabashi, and Brajabihari Sharma, the most recent (inscribed 3 April 1993).

The place where the memorials were installed was unkempt. There, I met Rājkumār Sanahal, the headmaster of Bengali High School in Manipur. Rādhā-Kuṇḍa has numerous connections to Manipur, drawing many visitors. Prayers and offerings are made to departed souls at Rādhā-Kuṇḍa and Śyāma-Kuṇḍa, where historical memorials are situated. The idol at Barkuṇḍa was served by Gambhīr Singh. Rādhā *maṇḍapa*, with marble stone flooring, is spacious and beautiful. The temple's idol, originally installed by Jaideva and transferred to his students, is currently cared for by the Viṣṇupriyas.

The *sevāyata* informed me that the *maṇḍapa* was constructed through Rs. 10 lakh in donations, with significant contributions from Khangabok residents. Over 1,000 people attended the inauguration. Viṣṇupriyas, claiming Manipuri identity, sang *bhajanas* and provided lunch. Contributions of Rs. 5,000 monthly and daily offerings from 50-60 people fund free lunch for visitors. During my visit, women in Manipuri traditional attire were seen shifting rice grains using bamboo frame plates. Communication was limited due to their twisted tongues, and they spoke sparingly.

Monkeys abound near the Jagatbandhu and Sītārāma Temple. Lalitā-Kuṇḍa appears unsanitary; would taking a dip there not risk infection from germs? Contemplating environmental pollution, observing the filth prompts concerns.

Six enchanting seasons unfold, adorned with resplendent flowers, the melodious hum of bees, the harmonious chirping of cuckoos, and the captivating dance of peacocks. Playful birds frolic along the stream cascading down from Girirāja. At the heart of Govardhana lies the sacred abode of Gopāladeva. On the southern side, one encounters Govinda-Kuṇḍa, Survi-Kuṇḍa, Apsarā-Kuṇḍa, Harji-Kuṇḍa, Irabat-Kuṇḍa, and Śaṅkara-Kuṇḍa. On the hillock's side, Rādhā-Kuṇḍa, Śyāma-Kuṇḍa, and Lalitā-Kuṇḍa enhance the sanctity of the surroundings.

Mānasī Gaṅgā gracefully meanders through Govardhana, fulfilling Śrī Kṛṣṇa's divine desire to provide water for cows and calves. Surrounding Mānasī Gaṅgā are *ghāṭas* on all four sides, where resplendent lotus and lilies bloom amidst the playful activities of bees. In the middle, three pullins are adorned with surrounding verdant creepers, with ducks and swans gracefully adding to the serene ambiance. At the pullin, *maṇḍapa*s provide a celestial setting for Kṛṣṇa, Rādhā, and her consorts to revel in their moments of joy, followed by refreshing baths, delectable feasts, and rest.

The sublime beauty of Govardhana and the enchanting tales of Śrī Kṛṣṇa's divine drama evokes a profound appreciation. After immersing oneself in such tales, an innate desire awakens in the hearts of people of this generation to embark on the sacred journey of Govardhana Parikramā or to pay homage to this celestial abode.

During our journey from Kusum Sarovara to Dāna Ghāṭa, we marvelled at the conscientious development of the Govardhana environment in the name of religion. Though the hillocks were petite, a verdant expanse of trees and fruit-bearing trees contributed to creating an emerald haven. Our knowledgeable guide, Shiela, expertly pointed out the intricacies of the temples and *ghāṭa*s during our auto ride, prompting us to pay our respects from a respectful distance. At Govinda-Kuṇḍa, where Indradeva ceremoniously poured milk over Śrī Kṛṣṇa, we were captivated by the sacred rituals. Along the roadside, a picturesque array of shops offered delectable sweets, fresh milk, and fragrant flowers, tempting us to make delightful purchases as we journeyed toward the hallowed spot where Girirāja lay. Despite the patient wait for our turn, our time in the enchanting realms of Vrindavana was regrettably limited, allowing for only a fleeting visit to Gopeśvara Mandira, the resplendent Glass Temple, the golden pillar of Raṅganātha, and the revered Bāṅke Bihārī. Dusari chauffeured us back on that memorable day.

Returning to Rādhā-Kuṇḍa during the 2005 festival alongside 34/35 cherished friends and fellow pilgrims, we encountered the unique charm of communal travel on a pilgrimage. Sharing anecdotes, dining together, and revelling in joyous moments within the confines of a train compartment for two days forged an unparalleled camaraderie. Despite my inherent love for traversing new horizons, an unexpected sense of loss pervaded this journey. The once fervent desire to meticulously document my travel escapades in my diary seemed to have dissipated. Though there was a bustling presence of a crowd, an unmistakable sense of solitude prevailed within, epitomizing the poignant reality of separation. In 2003, I had visited Rādhā-Kuṇḍa with my husband, and in 2005, I returned to ceremoniously scatter his ashes in this consecrated sanctuary.

11

The Land of Vrindavana

Akoijam Sanaton
(Translated from Manipuri by Pebam Nganthoiba Mangang)

The land of Vrindavana is considered a unique place, enthralled by its natural divine ecstasy by Kṛṣṇa devotees. The landscape covering the Vrindavana extending from Rādhā-Kuṇḍa to Śyāma-Kuṇḍa, including religious places like Mathurā, is known as Caurāsī Kosa.

Caurāsī Kosa

It is calculated that 1 *kosa* is equal to 2 miles. Thus, Vrindavana is surrounded by 84 *kosa*. This means that the place is surrounded by 168 miles. The important places in the surrounding area include Śrī Braja-Vrindavana, Mathurā, Rādhā-Kuṇḍa-Śyāma- Kuṇḍa, and Govardhana.

A bird's-eye view using a telescope-like device from the airplane shows Vrindavana as a lotus with 108 petals. The distance between Mathurā and Vrindavana is 4 km, and from Mathurā to Rādhā-Kuṇḍa to Śyāma-Kuṇḍa is 10 km. As per the beliefs of the Hindu saints, pilgrims, and devotees of Lord Kṛṣṇa of Hindu religion followers, the most sacred place of Hindu is the region of Vrindavana, which is the birthplace of

Śrī Kṛṣṇa, where he was brought up and used to do merry-making. The Lord Kṛṣṇa never wants to leave this beautiful place and always tries to stay forever.

The pilgrims of Vrindavana of Manipur used to participate in and witness the occasion of *jugala parikramā*, which happens once a year and is considered very significant and should not be missed. This pilgrimage journey during the month of Mera intends to eyewitness the celebration of San Senba (herding of cattle) celebrating on *hiyangei nipani paanba* during *jugala parikramā* at Vrindavana and Rādhā-Kuṇḍa. This journey also aims to participate in the event of *jugala parikramā*, which will be performed at midnight the next day, i.e., *hiyangei mapan-ni paanba*. This event is auspicious as it is believed that Lord Kṛṣṇa hails from Vrindavana and conquered Modhupur (currently Mathurā), killing the devil Kaṁsa. The whole event is known as *jugala parikramā*. Since the earlier days, devotees of Lord Kṛṣṇa of Manipur have been eagerly waiting for this event. However, in today's busy schedule lifestyle, as one needs to spare 14 to 16 days to visit the place and participate, hardly people can attend such festivals, and people have started forgetting such festivals.

There is a place called Viśrāma Ghāṭa where it is believed that Lord Kṛṣṇa killed Kaṁsa and took a rest here for a while. The second day of *hiyangei* is considered an auspicious day because on this day, Jamunā, the daughter of Jhom, was invited to a feast by her brother, and she was pretty satisfied by her brother's hospitality. People assume that taking a dip in the water on this day makes them free from sin and curse, free from devil gods such as Citragupta.

Some of the religious places visiting for worship by tourist in Vrindavana:

- *Kusum Sherbo*: It is believed that the devotee of Lord Kṛṣṇa Udhava breathed his last breath, turning into wood rope (URI), and settled in this place. There is also one pond where it is considered that Rādhā cleaned her flowers.

- *Mānasī Gaṅgā:* It is the lighting place on the day of Yomgita, i.e., the previous evening of the first day of Holī. It is also believed that a space was given for Ayon.
- *Cakreśvara Mahādeva:* This is also a place of visit for worshipping.
- *Dhannāghāṭī:* The place where the Lord Kṛṣṇa disguise as a rower.
- *Govinda-Kuṇḍa:* It is believed that the name of this place was given by Soraren (Heaven of God). There is a saying that Lord Govindajī was found in this place.
- *Rāma-Kṛṣṇa Mandira:* The temple is located on the borderline of UP and Rajasthan, where the temples of Balarāma and Kṛṣṇa exist. One road in this location divides the state of UP and Rajasthan. On the other side of the border of Rajasthan, Apsarī-Apsarā Kuṇḍa is located.

Mathurā Kṛṣṇa Mandira

On 6 January, we all left Vrindavana for Rādhā-Kuṇḍa, and we took a break on the way and had a *darśana* at the birthplace of Mathurā. The distance between Vrindavana and Mathurā is about 4 km. Next to the temple of Śrī Kṛṣṇa, we visited the prison, which is the birth site of Śrī Kṛṣṇa.

In 1997, we, the five journalists, went to Gujarat to attend the 58th Indian Federation of Working Journalists. On the way back, at around 9 p.m., we got the opportunity to see the temple of Śrī Kṛṣṇa at Mathurā, but we didn't get the chance to see the prison. However, on this second visit, we felt gratitude this time as we could visit the prison. The prison looked antique, with a small room with no windows or ventilation. The inside prison was very small and looked gloomy, and I almost felt suffocated. There is one entry in the front and an exit in the backdoor. There were never-ending pilgrims who worshipped the historic place. A small prototypical hill of Govardhana was placed nearby the gate of the temple.

On the way back after leaving Mathurā, we stopped at a place called Gopī Talou. This place is believed to be Braja *gopī*s' last appearance and is also considered a spot for a beauty parlour for them. There exists a pond where the pilgrims collect *candana*, and it is also believed that the bodies of *gopī*s turned into *candana*. Thus, the visitors intend to buy *candana* from this place. Eager to know where they collected the *gopī candana*, some of us went down from the bus and searched for the place. Finally, we found it and learned that they dig some colourful earth from the field next to the pond. Some of our fellow travellers bought *candana*, paying Rs. 50 per cement bag and Rs. 20/30 per 3/4 kg. I was thinking of collecting a piece of *gopī candana* as a symbol of memory of the journey, though I had no intention of using it. Then, on the continuity journey, a statue of Lord Śiva Mahādeva having, 30/40 ft tall, was noticed. The industrialist Gulshan Kumar sponsored it. Many of the fellow travellers also went to worship. Some thoughts came to my mind: in this *tīrtha yātrā*, as tourists, we have come across many religious places and innumerable deities. If we visited all these places of worship, it will take many years. At the same time, our fellow travellers are always ready to rush to the spot if it is a temple. The moment our bus stopped, they got down, rushing to pray to the temple, and again came out hurriedly. There is also a saying that it is impossible to count the number of existing Hindu temples, and there might be around 63 crore of temples. Our two buses reached the parking spot of Rādhā-Kuṇḍa-Śyāma-Kuṇḍa at around 7 p.m.

Rādhā-Kuṇḍa-Śyāma-Kuṇḍa

The Kṛṣṇa devotees believed from the oral history that Lord Kṛṣṇa killed a giant named Ariṣṭāsura while he was disguised as a cow roaming among the herd of cattle. From that incident, the *gopī*s blamed Śrī Kṛṣṇa, saying he had become a sinner of Govardhana, Nārī-Dhop, and killer of Giant lady Pūtanā. The *gopī*s suggested he visit all the religious places of the world and dip into the water to do away from the sin. Then, Kṛṣṇa responded,

> "If I travel to all the religious places to dip in the water, my whole life will be gone before I complete the mission. Moreover, I don't want to leave Vrindavana and my *gopī*s. So, I will make all the *tīrtha*s to be here."

Having said that, his flute dug the earth to build Śyāma-Kuṇḍa. Then, Rādhikā dug the earth to make Rādhā-Kuṇḍa. As this religious place was built from her bangle, it was given the name Kaṅgana-Kuṇḍa, Rādhā-Kuṇḍa.

The most important day for worshipping Rādhā-Kuṇḍa, Śyāma-Kuṇḍa, falls after the full moon of Meragi *nipan-ni konba* and *kunhundoi-ni paanba*. On the day of this midnight, the devotees kept on waiting for the moment to dip in water once the moon appeared in the sky. This day is known as Ahoī Aṣṭamī. The process of worshipping Rādhā-Kuṇḍa, dipping in the water, is by offering a torbot with gold ornament. Some couples who wanted to have a baby did the same, offering dipping in water at Rādhā-Kuṇḍa first, followed by dipping at Śyāma-Kuṇḍa, tiding a knot of pieces of clothes worn by the couple. Then, they had to remove the clothes worn by them leaving in the water. This is how couples used to worship to conceive a baby.

There are around 22 Meitei *mandira*s located at Śrī Dhāma-Kuṇḍa. The Meitei pilgrims used to stay at Meitei *mandira* and headed to Caurāsī *kosa* to attend *parikramā*.

Temples of the Meiteis

1. **Śrī Girirāja Mandira:** The temple is located on the front side of the entry of Rādhā-Kuṇḍa-Śyāma-Kuṇḍa. The temple is known as Irengbam Mandira. In 1943, it was founded by Irengbam Anganghal, a resident of Singjamei Kṣetri Leikai. After he was deceased, Irengbam Anganghal Charitable Trust was formed.

His youngest son, Irengbam Iboton, joins the trust as a secretary.

2. **Śrī Brajabinoda Mandira:** It is located on the western side of Pūraṇa-Kuṇḍa before reaching Rādhā-Kuṇḍa. This *mandira* was founded by Shri Koijam Akhiljit Singh (Esinglakpa), a resident of Thangmeiband, on 26 February 1945, on the day of Holī. After the founder expired in 1979, his son Norton took care of the temple. Currently, the fourth son, Rājagopāla, and the sixth son, Rādhābinoda, are taking responsibility for serving the temple.
3. **Pūraṇa Kuñja:** This temple belongs to the family of R.K. Doosri, a resident of Keishamthong Top Leirak. Rādhā, daughter of Gauragopāla, served the temple since the beginning of the Second World War. After Rādhā passed away, her daughter Jamini took charge of looking after the temple. R.K. Doosri did the renovation of the temple during Jamini's tenure, and he also served the temple.
4. There is a temple that was taken care of by Kangbam Iboton from Khongman in Thongju Kendra. He was the adopted son of Brajagopala Sharma. A non-Manipuri named Ramanlala was hired by paying money to look after the temple after Brajagopala passed away. Later, the Non-Manipuri, a local resident, took the temple, saying the owner discontinued sending money from Manipur.
5. **Gokulanda Mandira:** Gopinath Sharma continued to serve the temple after his father expired, then his daughter continued the service. She was married to Mahavira, a Brajavāśī, and Mahavira continued the service after her death.
6. **Kamala Kuñja:** Manihar Kuṇḍa Parikramā is located on the way. Gurumayum Madhav Sharma and Bidhumukhi Devi were looking after the temple in 1932. They were from Beni Leirak of Naorem Leikai.

Later, their daughter Jamini continued the service of the temple. She got married to a Rajasthani postman and settled there.

7. **Jubaraz Kuñja:** "Nawal Govinda" was built by Narasingh Mahārāja in 1871. It was scripted in the door: "Shri Jood Narasingh Mahārājā Tasat Siyadob Singh Mandira *nimaatang ajar sucra ditiya suklabar* 1871". Members of the Narasingh Trust served the temple, and Brajavāsī continued safeguarding the temple by paying an honorarium.
8. **Gopālajī Mandira:** It was founded by Shri Churachand Mahārāja. His grandson Okendra sold out to the International Society for Krishna Consciousness (ISKCON), and it became an ISKCON centre.
9. **Aheibam Nimai Sharma Mandira:** It is located at opposite to Rādhā Dāmodara Mandira.
10. **Achar Prabhu Mandira:** It was founded by Shri Babu Chaoba Sharma. His daughter, Thourani Bidhumukhi, served the temple. ISKCON took over the temple after they expired.
11. **Navin Kishore Mandira:** R.K. Tombisana, a resident of Chingamakhong bought from Kulabidhu and founded the temple. His son-in-law, Sapam Krishna Mohan, did the renovation and took care of the temple after R.K. Tombisana expired.
12. There is a *mandira* that belongs to Yumnam Khoimacha, a resident of Elang Leikai, but no longer worships any deity.
13. **Gopīnātha Mandira:** Bane Singh, a resident of Khaga Bali of (Noutun Ghera) Rajasthan, handed it over to R.K. Khajing Sana, and then, it was handed over to Vanisana to look after. Two daughters of Vanisana, R.K. Jamuna Devi and R.K. Gita Devi, run the temple, bearing the expenses of day-to-day activities. R.K. Sanatombi from Thokchom Leikai looks after the temple as a caretaker.

14. **Giridhārī Mandira:** After caretaker Guru Aribam Tolchou Sharma expired, her daughter Amubi served the temple. After she passed away, Gurumayum Memma Devi, who lives at Noutun Gera, continued serving the temple.
15. **Mahāprabhu Mandira:** This temple is located in the Noutun Gera locality. After caretaker Ibomcha Sharma expired, Hidangmayum Ibetombi Devi did the service for the temple, and her grandson, given birth by her daughter, continued the service after she passed away.
16. **Gopīnātha Mandira:** This temple was founded by Chirom Gopal and Leihao Devi from Singjamei Keithel. Pujārī Kaluwa Sharma (Brajavāsī) took charge of giving service to God after they expired. This temple was supervised by Vaiṣṇava Samāja.
17. **Rādhābinoda Mandira:** This temple belongs to the Sougaijam Clan, and Sougaijam Bhuban, a member of the clan, performed the service of the temple. Currently, it is run by Sougaijam Trust.
18. **Biśambara Mandira:** This temple was taken care of by the late Hijam Iboton from Singjamei Chingamathak. After his demise, his wife Malika continued the service to God. Then, their son-in-law, Dr Yumnam Iboton, continued the service.
19. **Bor Kuñja:** The founder of this temple was Candrakīrti Mahārāja. Currently, Shrimati Aheibi Shija, service provider to the God, was replaced by members of the Kartā clan, such as Geerisana, Gourasana, Sanahal, Sanayaima, Thambalsana, Jaysana, Singhjit, continued the service. Later, it was sold to a non-Manipuri while Manisana left for the service of Govindaji. As it is in a court case, Meitei are not allowed to enter the temple.
20. **Sītānātha Mandira:** The temple was founded by Khoirom Lalji Singh in 1890. Brajagopāla continued the service in 1963 after his father, Khoirom Lalji,

expired. Later, Brajagopāla's son, Shyama Sundera, continued the service.

21. **Rādhā-Mādhava Mandira:** This is run by the Cachar Meitei Trust.
22. **Brajanātha Mandira:** It is located near Mirji Manoranjan on Parikramā Road. It was founded by Moirangthem Chaoren Kaamdor. Parvati, daughter of Moirangthem Chaoren Kaamdor, continued the service after her father's death. Irengbam Brajagopal, Parvati's husband, renovates the temple and serves God. Later, after his demise in 2005, his family generations continued the service.

Temples belonging to the Meiteis are run by a sum of money received from the Meiteis, which was sent by contributing on a monthly basis. Pilgrims from Manipur visited this religious place from time to time but only a particular temple. Though pilgrims were offered to stay inside the premises of the temple complex without taking any charge except offering grand feasts, it is not possible to run the temples with the little amount left after the management of offering grand feasts (*utsava*). Therefore, if the owners of temples discontinued sending money to run the temples, non-Manipuri caretakers or the Meiteis had to take over or sell them. This is the reason the number of Meitei *mandira*s reduced to 22, which was once more than 33.

We arrived at Nataraj Hostel of Rādhābinoda Mandira, which belongs to Koijam. On 7 January, we visited Rādhā-Kuṇḍa. As the colour of the ponds of Rādhā-Kuṇḍa, Śyāma-Kuṇḍa has changed a lot, pilgrims hardly use it for bathing and cleaning purposes. Pilgrims performed *parikramā*, Govardhana *parikramā* walking around the pond at their own choice. Irengbam Nabakumar, from our locality, who is a caretaker of Irengbam Mandira, also came to meet us knowing that we had arrived at Rādhā-Kuṇḍa. He says, "There were 33 Meitei *mandira*s at Rādhā-Kuṇḍa, but due to unable to bear maintenance, it has been reduced to 22".

He continued explaining,

> "Residents of Kuṇḍa agreed upon that pilgrims arriving from Manipur would be allowed to stay in the *mandira* campus without paying fees while there will be taking charge for offering feast to the God as per their understanding. If there are charges for staying on the campus, then pilgrims might look for other places or hotels. If the pilgrims stay in the hotel, the *mandira*s will not get any support, and it would be difficult to manage the maintenance of the *mandira*s. There is an opportunity to manage the functioning of *mandira*s from the little amount received from the offering of the feast to God by the pilgrims. Therefore, pilgrims are allowed to stay for 5 to 10 days free of cost on the campus while they bear expenses for their food, which encourages the pilgrims to visit the *mandira*s. Residents of this place are purely vegetarian even they feel embarrassed taking onion-garlic".

It is observed that Śrī Kṛṣṇa of Vrindavana and Rādhā-Kuṇḍa devotees are purely vegetarian, relying on vegetables and milk as a food habit. This Koijam Mandira is belonged to Rādhābinoda Koijam (former MLA/CM) of Thangmeiband Kendra. A grand feast was being offered from the amount of Rs. 100 which they have contributed at Navadwip. Two/three non-Manipuri residents prepared the food, but it was not the kind of taste we eat at home. Pilgrims were talking; we just ate for survival as it is a prasad. On the other hand, Rs. 50, which was contributed for lodging, was never paid back.

In the north-west corner, towards the left side of Rādhā-Kuṇḍa, there is a *mandira* founded by Churachand Mahārāja and later sold to ISKCON by his grandson Okendra. ISKCON *bhakta* are staying in this campus. Some of us went and saw the environment inside the ISKCON campus. We noticed a monument inside the campus. It is learnt that Kṛṣṇa devotee, late Damudor Swāmījī (Mahārāja) dead body was buried digging the earth in this area. The graveyard is maintained neat and tidy. I felt gratified seeing Kṛṣṇa devotees' humble and simple nature and their way of looking after the graveyard of their late Guru Damudor Swāmījī. It is said that the burial took place by putting the dead body of Swāmījī in a meditative pose by wrapping it with empty sacks, which were used for putting salt.

One surprised incident occurred while roaming around Rādhā-Kuṇḍa was many devotees were performing *parikramā* by doing *daṇḍavata* (crawling) on the periphery of the road that leads to Govardhana hilltop. The length of the road moving around the Govardhana Hill is around 50 km.

They continued the *parikramā* by doing *daṇḍavata* until they got exhausted. They marked the point where they reached in a day so that they could continue the same from that marking point the next day. Though it takes many years, the goal is to reach the destination. Such a kind of performing *parikramā* is possible only by Śrī Kṛṣṇa devotees who are dedicated and deeply involved in religious practices and rituals and have a single-minded attitude towards Kṛṣṇa consciousness. This is performed throughout the whole seasons in a year. In the same manner that happens in Vrindavana, no glasses (tea mugs) are seen to be kept on the table in a hotel for tea or water. There is a system of cleaning the glass after using it by the person himself. Such culture intends to show that they are the true sons of God and belong to a high caste. But this is not a good practice. Such practices, which were seen from small hotels, reveal the prevailing old practice of caste system, untouchable, etc., still in this region. But such things were not introduced by Śrī Rādhā-Kṛṣṇa. Even Śrī Caitanya was against the practice of class and caste system, a pure and polluted concept. This kind of practice demotivates the pilgrims and devalue the Hindu devotees of Śrī Kṛṣṇa. It also gives the depraved image of the Hindu religion. This also could be a factor in reducing the number of pilgrims who visit the *tīrtha-yātrā*.

Many of our fellow travellers have suffered ill health due to improper accommodation, drinking cold water during freezing winter weather, etc. Many suffer from fever and flu, but they maintain their health by taking medicines. Like the residents of Vrindavana chanting Hare Rādhe, Rādhe-Śyāma, and Rādhe-Śyāma while going on the way, we also did the same, moving to our destination. Foreigners who stay at ISKCON located abroad or who are devotees of Kṛṣṇa also walk, murmuring/chanting with their *mālā* bag Hare-Kṛṣṇa, Hare-Kṛṣṇa. Among them are children of 7/8 years of age walking on the road of Rādhā-Kuṇḍa and Śyāma-Kuṇḍa without any shoes/chappal for performing *parikramā*. They are mostly Kṛṣṇa *bhakta* and Vaiṣṇava.

Rādhā-Kuṇḍa is a small town with neighbouring small villages. There are a few small shops spreading randomly. The roads and drains of Rādhā-Kuṇḍa look neat and clean as they maintained cleaning frequently. This is the thing we, as Manipuris, should learn from them. We left Rādhā-Kuṇḍa on 8 January at 2 p.m. for our next destination, the Taj Mahal and Gayā.

The time has come to leave Rādhā-Kuṇḍa, but a thought strikes my mind about establishing so many temples and serving God, which is not seen in any other part of Bhārata. But the sad part is that these temples are managed by hiring non-Manipuri, and in the end, many of the temples are sold or taken over by them, reducing the number of temples to a large extent. The other thing that came to my mind before leaving Rādhā-Kuṇḍa was the stinking smell due to the bad condition of the room allotted upon our arrival. Buffaloes stayed before our arrival; it was cleaned to accommodate us. So, the room was smelly and the surrounding was dirty with the cow dung and urine remains. It was not a good experience.

12

Pilgrimage to Rādhā-Kuṇḍa

Shukhdeba Sharma Hanjabam

Rādhā-Kuṇḍa, from the beginning of the nineteenth century, has become a prominent pilgrimage site of Manipuri Vaiṣṇava of India (mainly from Manipur, Assam, and Tripurā), Bangladesh, and Myanmar, apart from Navadwip in Bengal. However, the opportunity to go on a pilgrimage to Rādhā-Kuṇḍa was mainly confined to the members of the royal families and people under state patronage. The common people used to seek blessings from those who had visited Rādhā-Kuṇḍa, assuming that it was like offering prayer or visiting Rādhā-Kuṇḍa. However, it was only at the beginning of the twentieth century that the commoners, who were close to the royal families, started visiting Rādhā-Kuṇḍa and dedicating the *mandira* in Rādhā-Kuṇḍa. For instance, the *mandira* dedicated by Gurumayum Madhav Sharma and his wife Bidhumukhi Devi (1932), Irengbam Anganghal (1943), and Koijam Akhiljit Singh (1945) were some of the pioneer *mandira*s. beyond the royal families. The commoners, on a limited scale, have since been going on pilgrimage to Rādhā-Kuṇḍa.

Besides the pilgrimage to Rādhā-Kuṇḍa, the pious Vaiṣṇavites of Manipur, used to dedicate themselves to Śrī Śrī Govindajī and spend the rest of their lives and usually breathe their last at Rādhā-Kuṇḍa. The daughter of Rājarṣi Bhāgyacandra, Princess Bimbabatī/Vimvavatī committed herself to Śrī Śrī Annuprabhujī, who was an inspiration among the people of Manipur. Princess Bimbabatī was also popularly known as Shija Lairoibi/Laioibee because of dedicating her life to Śrī Śrī Annuprabhujī Mandira at Navadwip. Princess Bimbabatī has been worshipping Śrī Śrī Annuprabhujī since 1798 at the *mandira* of Śrī Śrī Navadwipchandra Mahāprabhu, Navadwip. The *mandira* of Śrī Śrī Anuprabhujī was built in 1815 by Mahārājā Chourjit (disposed at that time) with the help of Mahārājā Girīścandra Rai of Krishanagar. Mahārājā Girīścandra Rai granted an area of 10 acres along the right bank of the Gaṅgā River, which is presently known as Pūraṇa Rajbhari. Besides, Rādhā-Kuṇḍa, Anuprabhu Mandira at Navadwip is one of the most important pilgrimage sites of Manipur. Even today, the tradition continues and is mostly combined with the pilgrimage along with Rādhā-Kuṇḍa and Purī.

The tradition of Princess Bimbabatī of giving up everything and dedicating the rest of their life to Śrī Śrī Govindajī inspires the pious Manipuris. Thus, the tradition continues by dedicating themselves at Rādhā-Kuṇḍa and Navadwip. Those who declare such a decision will be given a community farewell, assuming that it will be the last opportunity to meet them and, in some cases, Shraddha will be performed for them. Such a person will spend the life of a *saṁnyāsī* at the Manipuri *mandira* and breathe their last at Rādhā-Kuṇḍa. The families will hardly know about their demise. With the advancement of communication and transport systems in the last few decades, the family members at least got to know the news of the demise and performed their last rituals at Rādhā-Kuṇḍa. There are cases when these kinds of persons also return home after staying in Rādhā-Kuṇḍa. In such a situation, these persons will return by shaving their hair, with the indication that they dedicated everything to Śrī Śrī Govindajī and will continue the *saṁnyāsī* life.

The Manipuri Vaiṣṇava goes to Rādhā-Kuṇḍa mostly on four occasions that fall on the four seasons of Manipur. The pilgrimage is to coincide with the religious occasion (Prabaddin) of the Śrī Śrī Govindajī. They are (i) Wakching (December/January)—Mahā Snān; (ii) Meera (October/November)—Jugol Parikramā/Rādhā Aṣṭamī; (iii) Lamta (February/March)—Holī; and (iv) Thawan (August/September)—Badra Parikramā. Every villager mobilized themselves to go on pilgrimage on any of these occasions. However, people from rural areas or who depend on agriculture mostly go on pilgrimage to Rādhā-Kuṇḍa after their harvest session.

Route to Rādhā-Kuṇḍa

The pilgrimage route taken by the Manipuris to Rādhā-Kuṇḍa was mostly the route that was navigated by Rājarṣi Bhāgyacandra.

Chinthangkhomba Maharaja (Rājarṣi Bhāgyacandra) Ganga Chatpa (tr., A pilgrimage account of Chingthangkhomba Maharaja going to Gaṅgā), Rājarṣi Bhāgyacandra have already navigated the waterways route to Vrindavana, particularly Rādhā-Kuṇḍa, when he plans to go for pilgrimages to Rādhā-Kuṇḍa in 1798. The accounts of Chinthangkhomba Maharaja (Rājarṣi Bhāgyacandra) Ganga Chatpa (tr., A pilgrimage account of Chingthangkhomba Mahārāja going to Gaṅgā), highlighted the waterways route in greater detail by eminent Historian of Manipur, R.K. Jhalajit Singh. While describing about the Bhāgyacandra's pilgrimage to Vrindavana, he writes:

> "On 5 February 1798 (20 Phairen 1719 Śakābda), the king with a large retinue started for pilgrimage to Vrindavana. He was accompanied by his queens, four sons, three daughters, and a large number of nobles and attendants. His porter numbered 300,

and the pilgrims about 400. He took arms and ammunition and royal insignia with him. In his absence, Yuvarāja Labanya Chandra carried on the administration.

Passing through Kāñcīpur and Ningthou Khong, he reached the Leimatag. Crossing it he reached the Irang and then the bank of the Barak. Following the course of the latter he reached Cachar. The king of Cachar presented him with a big amount of silver coins and cloths. Proceeding by boat on the Barak the king reached Bhaṅga where the Barak breaks up into two streams—the Surma and the Kushiara. Proceeding by boat on the Surma, he reached Sylhet where he had a formal meeting with the English Commissioner administering a number of districts. Presents were exchanged. Jai Singh's presents were artistic silk goods and a horse. The English Commissioner presented him with a telescope and two tents and provided him with an elephant, to carry his luggage to Tripurā, and two armed sepoys for escort.

While in Sylhet, the king visited Dhaka Dakshin the ancestral home of Caitanya's father, and performed a *kīrtana* (devotional music) there. Then he reached Agartala and gave his daughter Harisheshwari in marriage to Rajdhar Manik, the Rājā of Tripurā.

The king proceeded with his retinue in a fleet of 67 boats out of which 15 were contributions from the Rājā of Tripurā. The pilgrims proceeded on the Meghanā and the Padmā. He received a present of Rs. 700 in British Indian coins sent by the Rājā of Tripurā. Now the king sent back the boats contributed by the Rājā of Tripurā and proceeded by land with his party till they reached an old channel of Gaṅgā.

> After proceeding on the old channel in the fleet of 52 boats for one day, the king sent all his boats to Navadwip with some of his men, and he and his party reached Krishnanagar by land.
>
> The Rājā of Krishnanagar offered to accommodate him at a place called Gaṅgā Bās which he politely declined, and reached Navadwip, a destination of his long cherished dreams· From Navadwip, he went to Ambikā, where the Vaiṣṇavas of the place warmly received him and presented him with rice, salt, milk, *ghee*, and sugar, He held a *kīrtana,* with the team of singers from Manipur. The *kīrtana* was widely appreciated by the local people. From Ambikā the king returned to Navadwip, From Navadwip, he proceeded on the Gaṅgā by boat towards Vrindavana, but he died at Śrīpat Kṣetra on the bank of the Gaṅgā near Murshidabad on 12 October 1798.
>
> In tradition, he was cremated at the spot where Narottam, a great saint of the Caitanya school of Vaiṣṇavism, was cremated before. His *śrāddha* was held at Śrīpat Kṣetra. Five teams of singers (*pala*) —three from Navadwip, one from Śrīpat Kṣetra, and one from Manipur sang."

The route taken by Rājarṣi Bhāgyacandra was mostly the waterways. However, the pilgrims including the commoners initially used to travel to Rādhā-Kuṇḍa by the combination of road, railways and waterways. It was initially travel by foot from Manipur to Silchar or Sylhet towards Bishnupur and then to the most important route, "Tongjei-Maril" of Imphal Jiribam-Silchar, or through bullock cart, horse, and horse cart and travelled by boat through the waterways after reaching Sylhet (now in Bangladesh) and Calcutta towards Vrindavana Dhāma.

Waterways of Manipur

Manipur is blessed with three river systems:

(a) *The Barak River system,* which consists of rivers like Irang, Makru, Tuivai, and Jiri that flow through the northern and western hills of the state. This river system has a total catchment area of 9,042 sq. km and forms approximately 40.5 per cent of the state.

(b) *The Manipur River system*, which constitutes of central valley's water resources includes rivers like Imphal, Iril, Thoubal, Nambul, Nambol, Khuga, Sekmai, and Chakpikarong, along with Loktak and its associated lakes. These have a total catchment area of 6332 sq. km and cover 28 per cent of the state's total area.

(c) *The Chindwin River system* consists of small streams like Akonglok and its tributaries, Chamu and Chingai, and Yu and its tributaries, Maklong, Tuyangai, Taret Lok, Lokchao, Lilimlok, and Tuiyang. The Chindwin system that drains the eastern slopes of Manipur's eastern hills has a total catchments area of 6,953 sq. km and forms approximately 31.1 per cent of the state's total area.

Besides the river system, the National Wetland Atlas 2010, developed by the Space Application Centre, has identified 167 wetlands (>2.25 ha) and 541 wetlands (< 2.25 ha), covering 63.616 of the total geographical areas under different types of wetlands.

The water bodies in the form of rivers, wetlands, and lakes have been part of the national building process of the erstwhile Manipur Kingdom since time immemorial. Ancient manuscripts such as *Tutenglon*, and *Toreiron Lambuba* document the rich tradition of Manipur's advancement in developing and naming of rivers ports, managing rivers for inland water transport, irrigation, and water resources. The war campaigns and the sociocultural relations, including matrimonial ties with Myanmar, were mainly through the

Manipur River system that joins the Chindwin River of Myanmar, locally known as the Ningthi River. There were regular routes between Burma and India which the traders, colonizers, and Buddhist Missionaries used. D.G.E. Hall also mentions routes linking Lower Burma and India via the bank of the Irrawaddy, the bank of the Chindwin, and the Manipur. On the western side, the relationship with the erstwhile Kingdom of Cachar, Tripurā, was also through the Barak River system.

The development of waterways connecting Manipur to Myanmar in the east and Tripurā, Cachar, Sylhet, and Navadwip in the west indicated the advancement of the navigation system and boating technology. It was reported that there were various types of boats, such as boats for gods, kings, and commoners. The boat for the war campaign was also different from these boats. Having achieved advancement in waterways, successive kings expanded the uses and technology for many other activities, including trade and commerce. The jackfruit tree, which carved the idol of Śrī Śrī Govindajī and six idols, including Śrī Śrī Anuprabhu in Navadwip, was transported from kaina to the Palace through the waterways. Many ports locally called *Hithangfam* were developed in a different part of Imphal Valley and extend up to the Palace of Manipur. However, the waterways, except in and around Loktal Lake, have not been effective for many reasons, including road development, deterioration, and encroachment in the riverine system and its connecting canals or Khong (locally).

Pilgrimage Route from Manipur to Lakhipur (Assam)

Shri Ashangbam Mineketan, the celebrated poet and renounced literary figure of Manipur, shared the pilgrimage route to Rādhā-Kuṇḍa, which he undertook along with his grandfather and grandmother. They were accompanied till the Silchar train station by his uncle and two helpers. He stated that, the pilgrims to Vrindavana are popularly known as *vranam chatpa.*

Shri Ashangbam Mineketan and his family travel by the combination of a bullock cart and by foot for six days from Imphal (Manipur) through the riverine route (Leimatak, Irang, and Barak River) and hilly terrain along the Tongjei-Maril (Bishnupur-Tamenglong-Lakhipur-Silchar Route). Yumnam Rajeshwar Singh stated that the Tongjei-Maril was one of the routes that connects Manipur with other princely states and was also used for commercial activities with other kingdoms or nations. The Tongjei-Maril route moves through,

> "Imphal to Bishenpur (18 miles), Bishenpur to Leimatak River (13.25 miles), Leimatak River to Irang River through the Khopum Valley (20 miles), Irang River to Barak Ahu River (24 miles), Barak Ahu River to Makru River (12 miles), Makru River to main Barak River (15 miles). After that, there were no rivers to cross, and the path goes right to Lakhipur and Silchar."

Pemberton, R. Boileau also mentioned about this route that,

> "The Kala Naga route, from Banskandee via Kowpoom to Lumlangtong, is 824 miles, of which not more than 17 miles, or two easy marches, pass through the forest before mentioned, and in a part infinitely less intersected by streams and swamps, than that traversed by the more northern route of Aquee: this route has also the great advantage of crossing the Jeeree at a point not more than 8 miles distant item its mouth, up to which the Barak is navigable for boats of 500 maunds burthen, until the beginning of February…."

It was also in this route that the Gambhīr Singh Mahārāja liberated Manipur through the 500 dedicated soldiers of Manipur Levy from the infamous seven-year (1819-26) Occupation by the Burmese. Ganagumei Kamei stated that,

> "The Levy left Sylhet on 17 May, 1825, reached Baskandi on 23 May. The force proceeded through the western hills of Manipur, perhaps through the Akhui route, which was described by R.B. Pemberton in his Report of 1835."

Lakhipur to Rādhā-Kuṇḍa

Lakhipur has been an important place in the history of Manipur. In 1835, Manipur opened a Political Agent in the British Territory at Lakhipur (Cachar) and Calcutta, while the British retained a Political Agent in Manipur. The Anglo-Manipur Friendship can be traced back to the Anglo-Manipur Friendship Treaty in 1762 and the Anglo-Manipur Defense Protocol of 1763. The British and Manipur continued their friendship by mutually opening political Agents. The relationship broke down in 1891, which resulted in the Anglo-Manipur War, in which Manipur was subsequently defeated.

From Lakhipur (Assam), they further travel for another day to reach Silchar town. From Silchar town, they took the train and travel further for one day to reach Chandrapur junction (Assam). From Chandrapur junction (Assam), they changed the mode of their travel and continued their pilgrimage by ship/ferry for about eight hours till they reached Goyalpur Port (West Bengal). From Goyalpur Port, they travel further by train for about eight hours till they reach Kolkata, which is the most developed city in eastern India. It was also the place for British Residency. From Kolkata, they took another train to Kanpur (UP). From Kanpur, they catch the bus for Mathurā (UP) and then to Vrindavana and Rādhā-Kuṇḍa.

The route from Imphal through the hilly terrain is supposed to be hectic and dangerous, but the Mangai or Ngai system (friendship) among the hill and valley people of Manipur plays a key role for the pilgrims to travel the hilly terrain without much fear or without the fear of shortage of food and any other items. Gangmumei Kamei stated that

> "At the people-to-people level, the Meitei relation with the tribes was maintained through the barter trade. Commercial relationship was institutionalized into social relation system of 'Mangai' meaning 'friendship/ relative'. A prominent tribal family always had a 'Maagai' among the Meiteis families living in the foothills or even with some families of the nobility in the capital. The Mangai relationship continued for generations."

The pilgrimage takes about 10/15 days, depending on the nature of travel. As a pious Vaiṣṇavi, the pilgrims do not eat anything and without taking bath and offering prayer. So, the pilgrims break their journey so they can clean themselves, offer prayer, and have food. The food habit for the pilgrimage was that they would cook their own vegetarian food. Most Vaiṣṇavite Meiteis eat fish, but during the pilgrimage they will drop their most favourite food-fish and cook or eat only vegetarian by their own utensils. So, utensils, cooking materials (rice, *dal*, salt, chilly, vegetables, oil, etc.), and firewood were carried on the pilgrimage. There are pilgrims who sustain their travel by eating *chempak* (flattened rice), *chini agangba* (guṛ), and water. They also prepare *fola/phola*—a traditional sweet dessert, by mixing the ingredients with some banana, milk, honey, etc.

This route was also one of the important routes of Manipur till the late nineteenth century when the British Empire actively moved into the region and opened up new routes for their political and business interest. Besides, pilgrimage, it was an international route connecting Manipur with the kingdoms of Tripurā, Cachar, and Kolkata (Calcutta). As modern higher education was limited in Manipur, people travelled to Sylhet and Calcutta for higher education. Higher education institutes of Manipur were affiliated with Calcutta University. The creation of East Pakistan has almost blocked the route as many segments of the routes fall within the jurisdiction of East Pakistan (now Bangladesh). The coming of the Second World War in early 1940 (1944) and Imphal (Battle of Imphal) was declared as the Britain's greatest battle being the turning point of the Second World War has opened up new motorable routes, which we are now using as National Highways (Manipur–Nagaland–Assam) and Asian Highway connecting India to Southeast Asia through Manipur and Myanmar.

Vrindavana Marup

Every Vaiṣṇava Manipuri wishes that any member of their family, particularly the elderly member or their extended family, visit on a pilgrimage to Rādhā-Kuṇḍa at least once in a lifetime. The pilgrimage tours were usually organized by the villagers (in groups), and individual spiritual tour guides. Even today, the individual(s) spiritual tour guides take pilgrims to Rādhā-Kuṇḍa. The spiritual tour guides to Rādhā-Kuṇḍa are popularly called "Vrindavana Karbar Touba" (literally meaning Vrindavana Business). From the economic point of view, most people of Manipur who wish to go on pilgrimage are mostly not from well-to-do families. They could not support the expenditure of the pilgrimage at one time. So, the traditional institution of the Meities, "Marup" was utilized to fulfil the wish. Marup system (literally means friendship association in Manipuri), is a type of cooperative saving and credit institution. It is also an institution that provides socio-economic security. The idea of Vrindavana Marup was conceptualized to fulfill the wishes of the common people to go on pilgrimage to Rādhā-Kuṇḍa. The families/individuals, through the Vrindavana Marup, contribute a certain amount regularly to accumulate the required expenditure for the pilgrimage. The Vrindavana Marup can be for a year or two, depending on the contribution capacity of the pilgrims. Some pilgrims contribute on a monthly basis, and some pilgrims contribute bimonthly or quarterly to meet the expenditures of the pilgrimage. However, the Vrindavana Marup is mainly within one to two years. The Vrindavana Marup helps them to mobilize their expenditures for the pilgrimage to Rādhā-Kuṇḍa and is exclusively for pilgrimage to Rādhā-Kuṇḍa. It is one of the most popular marup related to spiritual tours.

The pilgrimage was usually organise for an average of 100 pilgrims, which can fit in three to four buses of 56 capacities each. Initially, the pilgrims pay only the fare of the bus and they have to take care of their food. So, all pilgrims carry their cooking materials, cooking utensils, and mud *cūlhā* (clay stove with rice husk). In the early 1980s, Shri Gopal Sharma, visiting Guri of Jawaharlal Nehru Manipur Dance Academy, who has been to Rādhā-Kuṇḍa since early 1980, shared with us that the charge of the bus used to be only Rs. 300 in 1986/87 for the trip to Rādhā-Kuṇḍa and Vrindavana. The pilgrimage was later clubbed in groups (usually around 10) to arrange their own food. It was then the kerosene stoves (double) and firewood's were mostly used during the pilgrimage. It was subsequently upgraded by the domestic gas cylinders and commercials gas cylinders. However, considering the inconveniences of the pilgrims, the expenditure of the food was included into the contribution and the tour guides started providing cook food to the pilgrims. Items such as cooking materials, utensils, firewood/gas, and *pujārī*s will accompany the pilgrimage so that the pilgrims do not eat from unknown places/eateries. The pilgrims cooked their food with the help of the *pujārī*s at a convenient location, usually near the waterbodies.

In 2023, the cost of the pilgrimage to Rādhā-Kuṇḍa ranges from Rs. 18,000 to Rs. 25,000. However, the pilgrimage was not only confined to Rādhā-Kuṇḍa and Vrindavana but was expanded to various pilgrimage sites on the way to Rādhā-Kuṇḍa and also during the return journey from Rādhā-Kuṇḍa to Manipur. However, the maximum time will be spent in Vrindavana and Rādhā-Kuṇḍa (usually 2 days). The pilgrimage also took the smaller super deluxe bus of 36 capacities for the tour. With the development of the road, the road trip takes two days to Navadwip and four days to Rādhā-Kuṇḍa, which

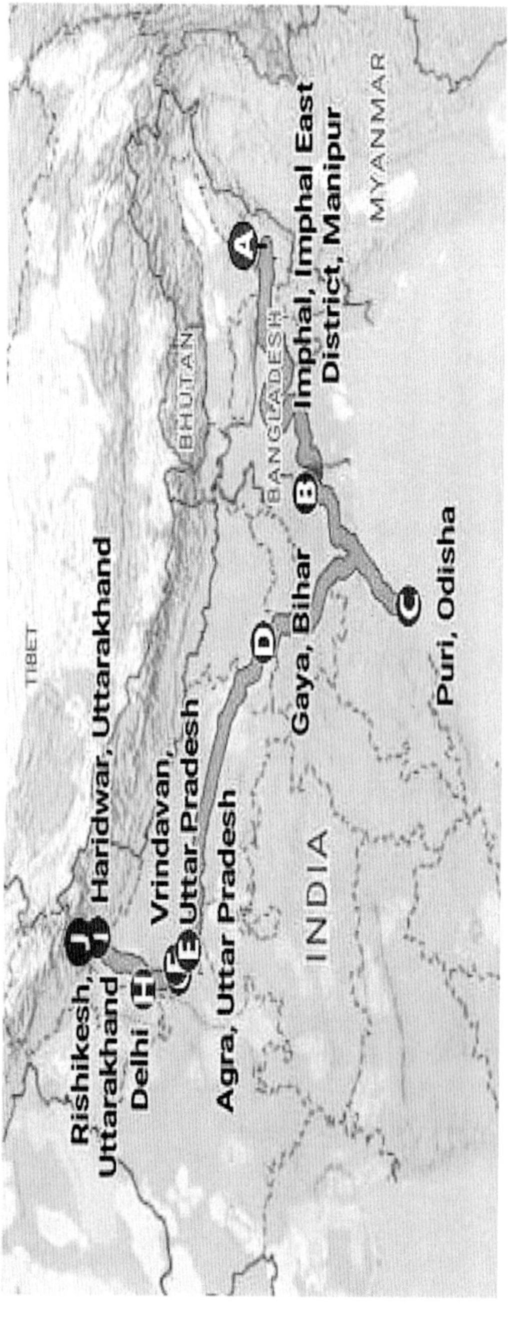
Rishikesh, Uttarakhand
Haridwar, Uttarakhand
Delhi
Vrindavan, Uttar Pradesh
Agra, Uttar Pradesh
Gaya, Bihar
Puri, Odisha
Imphal, Imphal East District, Manipur
TIBET
BHUTAN
BANGLADESH
INDIA
MYANMAR

has been reduced to over half the days, as earlier. The pilgrims start their tour by offering prayer at Śrī Śrī Govindajī Temple. The route of the pilgrimage is as follows:

- Imphal
- Guwahati
- Darjeeling
- Navadwip (Pilgrimage Site)
- Baleshwar (Pilgrimage Site)
- Bhubaneshwar (Pilgrimage Site)
- Purī (Pilgrimage Site)
- Gayā (Pilgrimage Site)
- Triveṇī Saṅgam (Pilgrimage Site)
- Agra (Pilgrimage Site)
- Vrindavana (Pilgrimage Site/2 days)
- Rādhā-Kuṇḍa (Pilgrimage Site/2 days)
- Delhi (Sight Seen)
- Rishikesh (Pilgrimage Site)
- Haridwar (Pilgrimage Site)
- Manipur (Haridwar-Imphal Direct)

Nowadays, the pilgrimage tour also includes south India and the extent of Kanyakumari, which takes 45 to 60 days. The bus pilgrimage system has been reduced to a great extent, but it continues even today. The Manipur violence of 2023 (starting from 3 May) has greatly impacted the pilgrimage tour by bus as crossing the Kuki dominated districts of Kangpokpi became unsafe. Many drop their plan and some who can support choose to travel by flight. Śrī Takhellambam Irabot recently took a group of pilgrimages to Rādhā-Kuṇḍa by flight to Delhi and continued by taxi to Rādhā-Kuṇḍa. But the cost of the trip ranges from 40,000-50,000. Some pilgrims travel by flight to Guwahati and continue their journey from Guwahati to Mathurā by train. Despite the Manipur violence, the pilgrims hoped that they would be able to travel during the Holī season (March) by bus, which did not happen.

Index